BOOKS
AND
THE TEENAGE
READER

A Guide for Teachers, Librarians and Parents

G. ROBERT CARLSEN

BOOKS AND THE TEENAGE READER
Second Revised Edition
A Bantam Book / published April 1967

2nd printing ...... July 1967	*5th printing .. December 1968*
3rd printing .... January 1968	*6th printing .... October 1969*
4th printing .... July 1968	*7th printing .... August 1970*

Revised and updated Bantam edition published December 1971

*Second revised and updated Bantam edition published
March 1980*

*Simultaneous hardcover publication by
Harper & Row, Publishers, Inc.*

Designed by Kathleen Ferguson

Library of Congress Catalog Card Number: 67-16066

ISBN 0-553-13332-2

Published simultaneously in the United States and Canada

*Bantam Books are published by Bantam Books, Inc. Its trade-
mark, consisting of the words "Bantam Books" and the portrayal of a bantam, is Registered in U.S. Patent and Trademark
Office and in other countries. Marca Registrada. Bantam
Books, Inc., 666 Fifth Avenue, New York, New York 10019.*

PRINTED IN THE UNITED STATES OF AMERICA

ACKNOWLEDGMENTS

I'd like to thank those people without whom this revised edition of *BOOKS AND THE TEENAGE READER* would not have been possible.

The bibliographies at the end of each chapter were put together by a team of highly respected librarians:

Wendy Bloom currently directs the Reference and Young Adult Services at the Harrison Public Library in Westchester. A graduate of Rutgers University Graduate School of Library Services, she is a member of Beta Phi Mu, the International Library Honor Society.

Regina Minudri is the Director of Library Services at the Berkeley Library in Berkeley, California. She was project coordinator for the Federal Young Adult Project in Mountainview, California, and from 1967–1975 was editor of the "Adult Books for Young Adults" column in *School Library Journal*.

Ryna H. Rothberg is Coordinator of Children's Services for the Newport Beach Public Library system. A former English teacher, Ms. Rothberg writes for *California Librarian* and the *West Coast Jewish News*. She is a member of several honor societies, including Beta Phi Mu and Kappa Delta Phi.

Special thanks, too, to those contributors whose knowledge of special areas allowed us to expand the scope of the book:

Elizabeth Belden is entirely responsible for the text and bibliographies of Chapter 14, "Literature by and About Women. Ms. Belden is a research assistant with the Books for Young Adults program at the University of Iowa, where she participates in the graduate program in Education. She is an experienced teacher of grades 9 through college, and a secondary language arts consultant with an area agency.

Dr. Dorothy Broderick and Karen Haas collaborated on Chapter 15, "Science Fiction and Fantasy." Dr. Broderick is currently the editor of Voice of Youth Advocates. The author of LIBRARY WORK WITH CHILDREN, she has taught library science for twenty years. Ms. Haas works in the Science Fiction and Fantasy department at Bantam Books. A former English teacher on the secondary school level, she holds an M.A. in English and Secondary Education from Queens College.

CONTENTS

1. The Reading Experience   1
2. The Teenager's World   12
3. The Stages of Reading Development   33
4. Subliterature   44
5. The Adolescent Novel   56
6. The Popular Adult Book   100
7. Reading Rights   121
8. Significant Modern Literature   133
9. The Classics   147
10. Poetry   164
11. Biography   178
12. Drama   191
13. Nonfiction: Something for Everyone   203
14. Literature by and About Women   233
15. Science Fiction and Fantasy   253
    Appendix   279
    Index   285

BOOKS
AND
THE TEENAGE
READER

1

The Reading Experience

In the highest civilization, the book is still the highest delight. He who has once known its satisfactions is provided with a resource against calamity.
—*Ralph Waldo Emerson*

What is adolescent literature? The best definition is simple: it is that literature which adolescents read. Adolescent literature can mean literature written especially for the teenager, with a young person's interests and concerns in mind. Or it can comprise of books that adults read, which teenagers turn to and enjoy.

These young people are in the teenage years, roughly from 12–20. At the lower end, many are still closely aligned to childhood; at the upper end, most 18- and 19-year-olds consider themselves fully adult. In between there is what has been called for centuries a "nowhere" period, a troubled, unformed time of being no longer a child and yet not fully mature.

Teenagers' reading also seems amorphous and idiosyncratic. Some professionals have thrown up their hands and declared that there is no predictability about what teenagers will read. Recently, five teens named the best book each had encountered in the last year. A 13-year-old male said it was *The Mad Scientist Club*. Another cited *The Last Testament of Lucky Luciano*. A 14-year-old female chose *A Star Is Born*. A 15-year-old male chose *The Boston Strangler,* and the same age female picked *Aku-Aku.* With such diversity, what generalizations can one make? One conclusion appears to be that these are all contemporary books. *Aku-Aku,* the oldest, was published in the second half of the 20th century. But when larger numbers of opinions are tabulated, you can see many useful generalities. We will discuss them in later chapters.

Teenagers choose a wide range of titles most of which fall into two big *reservoirs* of literary books, those written especially for them and those written for the adult reader.

TEENAGE BOOKS

The first category, often called junior or adolescent books by serious writers, are published by the juvenile department of a publishing house rather than by the "trade" or adult division. Publishers often label them "12 and up," or sometimes "YA," meaning "young adult." Many such books are read by children as young as 9 or 10, although they are not designed for them, but almost no adult reads this literature—just as there are few teenagers who will read books for children. Apparently readers enjoy books written for people older than themselves, but not younger.

A book has a writer and a reader within. Most writers in telling a story are telling it to someone; usually, they have an exact image of the audience they hope to reach and will tell you frankly that they write for children, for teenagers, or for adults; some stubbornly maintain that they have no idea, when they write, who their readers will be. Yet, almost intuitively, you can pick up a book, read a page or two, and categorize it as a children's, adolescent, or adult book. For clues you use style, diction, images, and tone, as well as subject matter and characters. Editors and publishers, using the same kind of intuition, sometimes transfer a manuscript from the trade to the juvenile division or vice versa.

There are young adult books in most major literary genres: novel, short story, biography, expository nonfiction, poetry, and so on. Note, however, that there are not many good plays written for teenagers. The most popular genre, the adolescent novel, is read most by the 12-to-15-year-olds; about 25 percent of the titles read by seniors in high school are still in this category. There is some evidence that if the adolescent novel were more readily available to the late teenager, if teachers and librarians were more knowledgeable about the development of reading tastes, it would be more widely read by this older group.

ADULT BOOKS READ BY TEENAGERS

Teens read many books written for adults; even 12- and 13-year-olds read them, and the percentage rises with age. Sometimes it may seem as if teen reading is indistinguishable from adult reading, but this is not so; 85 to 90 percent of adult books are never read by teens. On a best-seller list, not more than two or three of the books are popular with teenage readers. The challenge is to learn to recognize the qualities in adult books that will make them popular with teenagers.

Some adult books find their eventual readership among successive generations of teenage readers, for example, *Gone with the Wind, The Yearling,* and *The Catcher in the Rye.* These books seem almost to have become adolescent novels, although they are not originally written with this audience in mind. The adult book the teenager takes to heart is usually ensured a continuing readership for a long time, whereas the great body of adult work quickly fades from public view. However, some books that are initially popular with teens are quickly dropped, such as *Jonathan Livingston Seagull, Love Story,* and *Jaws.*

Teenagers may read adult books from every genre, just as they do with books written for adolescents. Much of their drama reading comes from the adult reservoir, but mature biography and autobiography tends to be too detailed and objective to appeal to teenagers. Expository books on science, the social sciences, and the humanities will generally be read by only the unusually mature and dedicated adolescent. However, teen readers have an enthusiasm for accounts of personal experiences which border on the bizarre or unusual, such as being stranded in the Andes by a plane wreck (*Alive*) or living among wolves (*Never Cry Wolf*). In general, fiction is the principal form of adult literature that adolescents read, and they are highly selective in their choice (see chapters 6, 8, and 9).

In adolescent, as in adult writing, there is an enormous body of what we will call subliterature (chapter 4). One step up is what can be described as pop literature; above this, a relatively small number of books that are significant and enduring in quality. Like adults, teens read mostly in sub- or pop literature. Only occasionally do they dip into the higher level—usually, at the discretion of a teacher.

Adolescent subliterature consists of comic books, some cheap magazines, and juvenile series books. The comic book was born as a commercial venture in the 1930s, grew phenomenally, and peaked in the early 1950s. Television caused it to decline during the 1960s, but during the 1970s it has made a comeback. Some old favorites (*Batman*) have been rediscovered by a younger generation and a series of somewhat different characters have been developed.

Most of the juvenile series books have had an amazingly enduring life. The records show that most teens are hooked on the reading experience through juvenile series books, which are thus a normal stage in one's reading growth. The sad thing is that some people get bogged down in such books, and when they are ready for more advanced books simply move into their adult counterparts: the sentimental romance and the adventure story. Both teenage and adult subliterature are produced en masse. Some prolific writers turn out a book a week following a set formula. In large paperback stores there are subsections devoted to romances, westerns, and mysteries, so that the avid reader of a particular type can indulge his whim without being misled by, say, fiction organized alphabetically by author's name. Though some older teens read adult subliterature, the average reader, judging from the titles on bookstore shelves, is an adult female.

Pop books, unlike subliterature, are honestly written and fairly accurate in their recording of human experience. They are often exciting reading the first time through, but they lack enduring qualities and usually disappear from publishers' lists within a few years. Most adolescent novels are pop novels. Often they deal with a momentary problem of the teen scene: for example, books about the draft were popular during the Vietnam War but no longer hold interest for the teenage reader. Stories about drugs, flower children, communes, and unexpected pregnancy are almost passé. Even the ongoing problems of alienation don't seem as germane as they did a few years ago. At the moment, subjects with high appeal include alcoholism, child abuse, homosexuality, and rape. Probably within a few years these themes will be old hat. Not all pop teenage books are problem centered; many are pleasant little tales, honest enough, but lacking in depth of insight and literary quality.

The adult pop books make up the best-seller list. They are good stories, usually with vividly drawn characters but without a significant theme. As is true of adolescent junior books, they have an impressive sale for a year or two and are completely forgotten.

Above the pop book, in adolescent and adult reading, is the handful of books that we think of as true literature: the classics. The adolescent book is of fairly recent origin, and not enough time has elapsed for anyone to classify the classics categorically. But there are a few that have lived beyond their period— one thinks of *The Adventures of Tom Sawyer*, *Little Women*, perhaps *Treasure Island* and *The Swiss Family Robinson*. Among today's titles for the adolescent, there are a handful of books that rise above the pop level. They are not tied to a current teen problem, and they are more than a bland, pleasant record of teenage experiences. The storyline is a metaphor of human strivings, frustrations, and triumphs. Often the books

are built around old, archetypal patterns; examples are
Cages, in which the two protagonists are alter egos
that must be fused in order to create a whole personality; *Slake's Limbo,* which uses the cycle of nature
bringing about death and rebirth; *The Chocolate War,*
in which evil emerges in a boy's school; and *The Pigman,* which explores the problems of attempting to
trespass on stages of life not one's own. Often the most
literate teenage books are not widely popular—which
is true at the adult level too. We will arbitrarily divide
the adult literate material into the classics and the
modern classics. The classics have endured through
time because of the excellence of their theme and their
style; they are studied and read today. The works of
Sophocles, Shakespeare, Dickens, and Melville fall in
this category. Modern classics are 20th-century books
of unusual merit. Faulkner, Hemingway, and Heller
would be included in this group. The question that
needs to be asked about these books is which ones
teenagers are ready to read. Teenagers find Greek
tragedy in a good modern translation far more comprehensible and moving than Shakespearean plays.
Jane Austen leaves most adolescents baffled and bored,
while the works of the Brontes get an enthusiastic
response, especially from girls. *Tom Jones* is seldom
read by teens, but *Great Expectations* is a frequent
favorite.

The peak of interest in reading often comes between
12 and 14 years of age. One woman reported in her
reading autobiography that she still had a list of the
books she had read in her early teens. It ran to over
300 books a year—almost a book a day. If reading
programs have been successful in elementary school,
most junior high schoolers have internalized their reading skills so that they can concentrate on the unfolding
story (at least on a simple level), rather than on the
process of reading. Most early teenagers are not yet
greatly involved in other activities, so they turn to
reading or television as a time filler.

Reading declines sharply during the middle adolescent years. At least part of the downward slide comes

about because schools thrust overly mature literature (the classics) on senior-high-school students and succeed only in building antagonism toward all books. Another part comes from the young people's expanding involvement in the world around them.

Young adults who have a modicum of reading skill will continue to find books a vital part of their lives if the following conditions hold true:

1. *They are surrounded with reading materials within their spectrum of reading interests.* In America we cling to a puritanical belief that what is distasteful is good for us. How often the well-meaning teacher says, "If they don't read it now, how will they know it exists? They'll come back to it later and really get something out of it." But force feeding kills the individual's love of reading. Reading can be guided without being forced.

2. *They read within a supportive, nonthreatening situation.* Students too often read with the threat of tests and fear of failure before them. Another deterrent to enjoyment is the oral or written book report, a traumatic experience for many. Being assigned to read books within narrow, prescribed parameters, say, English novels from the 19th century, is another shackle on enjoyment. The freer teens are to range widely in their reading with a supportive adult as a guide, the more apt they are to become and remain readers.

3. *They are given time to read.* One of the biggest deterrents to a teen's reading is today's life pattern, in which there is little time put aside for reading either in or out of school. Reading does take time. Television competes for the young person's free time and usually wins out. The schools that are most successful in fostering reading as a pleasant experience set aside time during the school day (for example, blocks of time in English classes) when students can just sit and read. The excitement discovered in a book often induces students to read outside class as well.

4. *They can share their reading experiences.* It sometimes comes as a surprise to people to learn that reading is a social activity, not just a private one.

Readers tend to live their lives in a group of readers. For some this may be the family, for there is abundant evidence that reading families induct their young into the enjoyment of reading. Readers often form clubs in order to have a forum where they can discuss what they read. Evidently there is a need to find people with whom we can share our reactions to books. In free reading classes, comparing impressions and reactions should be spontaneous. The teacher's attitude is of prime importance. Discussion of a just-read book with a student needs to be a conversation, not a quiz about details and facts. Teacher and student need to share reactions, insights, and questions about the book.

5. *They have readily available reading matter.* Books lying around the house on a table, in the bathroom, or on a kitchen counter induce the young to read. Many can recall discovering forgotten books of another generation tucked away in boxes or trunks in attics and spending hours reading them. Some are stimulated to read when they browse through racks of paperbacks and come across a title that sounds vaguely familiar or are attracted to the illustration on the cover. Others have their interest whetted when adults hide books because they are deemed unsuitable. In the empty moments when there is no friend handy to "mess around with" and nothing of interest on TV, the young adult may be snared.

Book talks by classroom teachers, librarians, occasionally by a bookstore person or author who is invited to the school also may open up the possibilities of reading. In some schools book fairs are held, with speakers and displays of books, or classes may be taken to a bookstore. These events give students a chance to share the experience of browsing among books.

What does the teenager want from his reading? The records indicate that young people read almost completely for experience. They want to experience adventure and excitement, or to feel tenderness and caring, to enjoy imaginative wanderings, to know the feeling of self-sufficiency without adult domination, to experience life in various historical periods and cultural patterns, to feel the frustrations and despairs of the psychological deviate. Reading makes possible the living of thousands of lives instead of only one.

Though adolescent readers often want books that take them out of themselves and their lives, they also want books that speak to them of problems they are undergoing. In mid-adolescence, teens read mainly the latter. They want to identify and empathize with characters like themselves and work through them to find a way out of their own problems. Holden Caulfield and Anne Frank have encapsulated in their stories the confusions, doubts, and uncertainty of several generations of young readers. Mid-teenagers often describe the ideal book as one that presents people like themselves living their kind of lives.

Older adolescents of 16 years and up tend to move slightly away from this intense interest in self. Their reading begins to center on the great ongoing human dilemmas: problems of justice, of relationships between the sexes, of the operation of fate, of wealth and poverty, of a minority's status. They immerse themselves in books that stimulate their thinking about philosophy, religion, sociology, morality, and ethics.

Usually only the mature reader is interested in aesthetic satisfaction. Subconsciously, teenage readers may experience it, but it is not the main reason for their reading—in spite of generations of teachers who have emphasized the forms and techniques of literature in high-school classrooms. Adolescents want to discuss literature from an experiential standpoint. They want to find out what the writer is saying and what it means in today's world. They do not want to discuss the author's expertise or the selection's imagery, symbols, plot structure, and diction. To be sure, from the mature reader's point of view, these *are* literature's experiences, but most teenagers are not ready to pursue them.

How do adolescents find the books they read? In *A Tree Grows in Brooklyn* Francie Nolan, a young teen, desperately wants help in finding books. She is afraid to ask the librarian and there are no readers in her immediate environment. So she decides to read all of the books in the branch library near her tenement, alphabetically. Hers is a common plight among young readers. How do you find books that will satisfy you?

Records show that the most satisfying reading often comes from accidental, offhand suggestions of friends and older siblings. Now and then a perceptive teacher or librarian will lead you to interesting reading experiences, or book lists organized by type (mystery, adventure, sports, romance) can be helpful in a teen's finding the "just right" book—but only if the books listed are available in the community. The public library, unless it has a young adult room, can be as baffling to the teen reader as to Francie Nolan. The school library can be a primary source of reading materials if the collection is geared to the interests and tastes of the students rather than to books teachers and parents feel are "good for them." Lack of funds for continuing purchases can drastically affect the ability of a school library to maintain current appeal to new generations of teen readers. One good source of books for the young reader is the commercial book clubs which operate throughout the country, often through the schools, and which offer each month a group of titles printed inexpensively as paperbacks. Most of these titles can be classified as adolescent pop books.

How much will a teenager read? Age and book availability are important determiners. A 13-year-old may consume books like popcorn, reading a hundred or more a year, while 16- and 17-year-olds may average 25 books a year because what they read is longer and more complex, and because they spend less time reading.

Where and when will the teenager read? During the early teens some people may read at any time and any place, but many prefer a private, quiet location. Reading records list as favorite spots a corner of the attic, under a particular tree, a nook in the garage, a window seat in the bedroom, and lying in the bathtub. As teenagers grow older, place becomes less important, but if the reading habit is deeply ingrained, the adolescent may grow to regard reading as part of life.

2

The Teenager's World

> The imagination of a boy is healthy, and the mature
> imagination of a man is healthy, but there is a space
> of life between, in which the soul is in a ferment, the
> character undecided, the way of life uncertain . . .
> —*John Keats*

Teenagers' book choices indicate that they use reading
in a personal if not therapeutic way. Some of the
greatest favorites of the young have been written by
the young: *Seventeenth Summer, The Diary of Anne
Frank, The Outsiders.* Even *The Catcher in the Rye*
and *A Separate Peace* had their origins in stories written when the authors were barely out of their teens.
A young writer brings to his materials an immediacy
of adolescent concerns that a more mature writer usually cannot quite achieve.

Perhaps the central concern of adolescents is the
search for identity. A teen's physical self and emotional reactions are no longer the familiar, comfortable
fit they were in childhood. Relationships with parents
and friends have undergone sudden changes. The state
of aloneness may be faced for the first time. Some
teenagers have the uncomfortable feeling that others
are watching and judging them. Others recognize for
the first time that they have an inner life, and their
thoughts seem unique and troubling. They may experiment with roles and attitudes, as expressed in clothing, hair styles, and deliberately selected behavior
patterns. In attempting to come to terms with self, the

teen talks endlessly to friends or siblings. It has been said that teen love is intensely conversational, not so much for communication as to discover self.

In the search for identity the young use books, particularly fiction and biography, as a main source of information. Through them they try on different roles, and sometimes discover people like themselves whom they can observe handling their lives. This may not be a proper use of literature, but it is a phase that teenagers must go through if they are to keep reading. Unless the books they read offer them experiential encounters, most will be turned off reading.

The developmental tasks facing the adolescent represent experiences in dealing with human relations, dealing with the inner self, and dealing with vocation.

TASKS OF HUMAN RELATIONS

Progressive Independence and Separation from Parents

Teenagers as they mature want to take over control of their own lives. But the relationship between them and their parents for 12 years has been one of dependence: basically, that of superior to inferior. The roles have been deeply imprinted on parent and child, and now teens have a great need to break these ties so that they can emerge as independent beings into adulthood. Unfortunately, it is all too common for the parent to try to impede the child's move toward independence. As a result, homes with teenagers are frequently homes of strife, which is as disturbing to the young person as to the parent. In primitive tribes, the maturation rites usually begin with a literal separation of the children from the parents, placing them in the care of the elders of the tribe and eventually in a living situation with their peers. The modern equivalent in today's society is going away to college, moving into one's own apartment, or running away. Increasingly the teenager treats his home as a place to eat, sleep, and get fresh clothing, while his real life is in the school and on the streets with his peers.

Changed Relationships with Peers

During the teen years, the peer relationship becomes the dominant one, supplanting or at least surpassing the influence of the family. In childhood, friendships are generally based on convenience and propinquity. Who lives next door, who sits next to one in school, who are the children of one's parent's friends—these are the determiners of friendships. During adolescence the individual moves onto a wider stage and becomes more aware of the personalities of others. The "best friends" of childhood are like old soldiers . . . they just fade away. For a while some teens experience intense loneliness as they seek to establish new relationships with members of their own sex. Accomplishing this is difficult for those who don't fit into the cultural patterns of adolescent society; this often includes young people interested in the arts or the world of ideas. Often they do not find a group until well after high school.

Teenagers' relationships with the opposite sex change as they mature. Because girls mature faster than boys, they often seek a heterosexual society before the males their age are quite ready. Teenage love is a fragile thing fraught with insecurity and tensions. The mature writer looking back on this period is inclined to see it nostalgically, with undertones of laughter. But to the teens going through this stage, the romance is grimly serious. The mass media constantly present pictures of teenagers as carefree, wisecracking, coping, and in control, but more often than not this picture distorts reality. One psychologist has said that the teenage romance is a search for identity in which each individual is using the other as a mirror image. It is important even for individuals who appear uninterested in a sexual relationship with a member of the opposite sex to learn how to relate and work with both sexes. It is not a task that can be skipped.

Finding a Significant Role Model

In primitive society an adult member of the tribe, often an aunt or uncle, acts as a guide for the young person in the puberty rites. In our unritualized society, this individual is sometimes referred to as "the significant adult" in the teenager's life. Parents seldom achieve this kind of relationship; aunts, uncles, older siblings often do. A teacher, a counselor, a librarian, a friend of the family may sometimes take on this role with or without being aware of it.

The tremendous mobility of people in America has caused the extended family to disintegrate and more and more teenagers are growing up in situations where it is almost impossible for them to find a "significant adult." This may explain the growth of gangs and the power gang leaders exert over the members. Less active teens may turn to rock stars, TV personalities, sports stars, and actors as their models.

TASKS INVOLVING SELF

Coming to Terms with the Body

We doubt if young children are particularly conscious of their bodies. Since they are constantly told that they are growing and changing, they are satisfied to believe that they will eventually be tall, beautiful, or rugged. With adolescence comes the first awareness that they are prisoners of their genes and can physically become only what is genetically dictated. Most reach their maximum height and body configurations at this time and almost all are dissatisfied with what they have been allotted. They wish they were taller or shorter; thinner or fatter; straighter-haired or curlier-haired: this is why products aimed at curling hair, coloring hair, curing acne, and developing a physique do a landslide business with the young. What is more important is for the young adolescent to develop a realistic concept of appearance, to accept it and live comfortably with it. Acceptance of one's physical appearance is an important component of knowing who one is.

Coming to Terms with One's Sexuality

Though children are conscious of sex from a very early age, it becomes an acute problem during puberty. Girls experience extraordinary bodily changes which are anticipated with both apprehension and delight. Both sexes fantasize and worry about possible inadequacy in sexual encounters. As Holden Caulfield exclaims in *The Catcher in the Rye:* "Sex is one thing I don't understand. I swear to God, I don't!" His cry is seconded by thousands of adolescents. Adding to teens' confusion about sex is the fact that society in America no longer has a unified set of values about sexuality. We are leaving behind our old concepts, but are not ready to accept the new ones of a country like Sweden. This means that teenagers are not only trying to handle internal changes and pressures, but external ones from society and family.

Another element confusing teenagers' image of their sexuality is changing attitudes toward male and female roles in our society. Throughout human history, cultures have set out definite, prescribed roles for each sex. Adolescents' developmental tasks of the past included discovering their sex's role in the social milieu and coming to terms with it. But today the roles are changing, although some of the older expectancies linger and may continue to do so in spite of the new wave of women's liberation. Most young males and females still crave a long-term relationship with someone of the opposite sex. Most still believe it is important to live where the male's vocation takes him. Most place responsibility for family planning on the female. Most experience sexual jealousy if the partner engages in extramarital relationships with others. And a large majority believes that babies get a better start in life if they are nursed rather than bottle-fed (obviously this places severe restrictions on the mother for a number of months). Perhaps because our society is undergoing radical changes in its concept of the family and the roles of each sex, our teenagers are more confused about their sexuality today than they were in a more prescribed culture.

Achieving a Sense of Status

Teenagers need a sense of self-worth, which ordinarily is achieved through finding something at which they excel. A few excel in academic areas, a few in athletics, some in the arts or crafts, others as leaders in school activities. Many, however, drift through school with little or no recognition of their existence. It is not surprising that some of these "anonymous" people turn to antisocial activities to establish their self-importance. They may form gangs to gain a self-image, or lie or shoplift to demonstrate their importance. They may become proficient at stealing cars, selling drugs, or obtaining liquor. In *Johnny Tremain* the hero, an apprentice in Paul Revere's silversmithy, lords it over the others until an accident irremediably injures his hand, the tool of his trade. The author graphically details the frustration of the lad as he finds he has no corner of his life in which he can feel superior. The teenage reader can empathize wholeheartedly with his plight.

Achieving an Integrated System of Values

In late childhood young people may believe in contradictory values. They may attend a Boy Scout meeting and wholeheartedly recite the pledge to help others, then leave the meeting and join a friend in tearing up a neighbor's garden. An integrated value system is achieved when one's beliefs and behavior are consistent.

Consistency is also important within a person's value system to give associates some grasp on the kind of attitudes and actions that can be expected. Thus if you know a friend's stand on the legalization of drugs, you are apt to be able to predict her or his stand on other social issues.

During the teenage years individuals move from inconsistency to consistency in their values. They move from dependence on external restraints by parents, police, and religious advisers to self-imposed control over their actions. Where an integrated value system is not achieved by an individual, that person may be designated as a sociopath. Often these individuals are intelligent and charming, but their behavior is unpredictable.

VOCATIONAL TASKS

Work Experience

At some time during adolescence individuals hold a first job and are paid for work they have performed. If, also, the job has been obtained without family or friends' help, a teenager can discover his or her potential of independent living. Most adults recall their feeling of maturity and exhilaration on receiving their first paycheck. Work is concomitant with gaining independence from parents and developing a sense of status.

Making a Vocational Choice

Individuals cannot be expected to attain maturity without a foreseeable means of support. Even in this day of enlightened education and mass media information, most Americans fall into a vocation rather than making a real choice. Happy are the few who are sure from early childhood what they want to do as adults. Frequently, the brighter the individual, the longer the delay of vocational choice is made and the greater the inner malaise. Very intelligent people drift through a liberal arts program in college, bum around for a year or two, begin and sometimes reject several professional graduate programs before at last finding a vocational direction. The less mentally endowed or the economically disadvantaged teenager may be forced to come to terms much earlier with the task, although sometimes vocationally oriented community colleges give students some options. A significant number of people in today's society never come to terms with a vocation. Like Mr. Micawber in Dickens's *David Copperfield,* they are always expecting something "to turn up." They drift from job to job, always disgruntled with what they are doing, always enthusiastic about the new—but only briefly—and probably never knowing a moment's inner satisfaction with any job.

THE TEACHER'S AND LIBRARIAN'S RESPONSIBILITY TOWARD READING

Knowing something about the psychology of the teenager is important for teachers and librarians in their guidance role of developing the avid reader. Such knowledge will help professionals, not to serve as therapists, but rather to find the right books for a reader . . . books that will give him an experience that will keep him reading. The 20th-century works that have been most enduringly successful with adolescents are those that have one or more of the developmental tasks as their themes. Good writers probably do not consciously set out to clothe a psychological task in fiction, but evoke the teenage world. Their intuitive perceptions lead them to show their fictional characters succeeding or failing in dealing with the psychological tasks necessary for maturation. The relationship between a book's popularity and the needs of the readers is after the fact; knowing it is a tool for the teacher and librarian in analyzing books, not a tool for writers.

Teenagers derive great satisfaction from meeting themselves in books, as do most others. Even recognizing unpleasant personal experiences or emotions in a book is somehow gratifying. We are reassured that we are not alone in feeling guilt, despair, or fear, or grateful that our experience is not *that* bad. Someone else, the writer himself or the character, has been there too. Thus the evocation of teenagers' problems in imaginative fiction can serve as a definition of the junior novel.

Books can play an important role in helping adolescents reach maturity. They can become a part of the adolescent's rebellion against the adult world. Often teenagers dislike the reading adults like and praise, and scorn their selections. The teenager's own favorite authors, the writers for his generation, are usually experimenters, both with literary forms and with basic human concepts. Yet literature has always held a mirror up for the reader in which to see himself sharply and clearly. Literature, by its very nature, is selective and suggests integrations, connections, insights into experience, and values which the individual might not find by himself. At its best, literature confronts the reader with the basic, eternal problems of human beings, helping the individual to see himself as a part of an ongoing history.

Some nonfiction books frontally attack specific problems the adolescent faces. They deal with problems such as sex, dating, grooming, and vocational choices. They are frank and objective in their presentation and are eagerly sought by great numbers of young readers. The bibliography for this chapter is composed of such self-help books.

Bibliography

HOBBIES

Barkin, Carol, and Elizabeth James: *Slapdash Sewing*. Lothrop, Lee & Shepard, 1975. Simplified and personalized patterns and the techniques needed for creating your own clothes.

Berndt, Fredrick: *The Domino Book*. Thomas Nelson, 1974. A comprehensive guide, including game variations, puzzles, etc.

Brady, Maxine: *The Monopoly Book*. David McKay, 1974. Strategy and tactics to improve your play of the world's most popular game.

Braverman, Robert, and Bill Neumann: *Here Is Your Hobby: Slot Car Racing*. G. P. Putnam's Sons, 1969. Detailed information on buying and building model cars, establishing a track, and conducting races.

Bridge, Raymond: *America's Backpacking Book*. Charles Scribner's Sons, 1976. Covers every facet of backpacking for the novice or expert.

Carter, Ernestine R.: *Gymnastics for Girls and Women*. Prentice-Hall, 1968. Complete instructions for mastering the techniques of the sport.

Chisholm, K. Lomneth: *The Candle Maker's Primer*. E. P. Dutton, 1973. All aspects of candlemaking, including how to set up your own shop.

Clow, Barbara and Gerry: *Stained Glass: A Basic Manual*. Little, Brown, 1976. Brief and concise history and presentation of the technique of stained-glass craft for the beginner.

Collier, James L.: *Making Music for Money*. Franklin Watts, 1976. Helpful handbook for amateur musicians interested in forming a money-making group.

Cummings, Richard.: *Make Your Own Comics for Fun and Profit*. Henry A. Walck, 1975. An oustanding practical guide that tells how to develop ideas, stories, and style.

Cyporan, Dennis: *The Bluegrass Songbook*. Macmillan, 1972. Attractive collection of good, easy folk songs for guitar or piano.

Daniels, Alfred: *Drawing for Fun*. Doubleday, 1975. Comprehensive introduction to drawing techniques for still life, figure, portrait, or landscape drawing.

Dickson, Paul: *Mature Person's Guide to Kites, Yo-yo's, Frisbees, and Other Childlike Diversions*. New American Library, 1977. A compendium of folklore, history, equipment, and rules for frivolous amusement.

Dolan, Edward F., ed.: *The Complete Beginner's Guide to Ice Skating*. Doubleday, 1974. Clear, simple instructions with good illustrations to help you with the first strokes.

Drake, Russell, et al.: *How to Make Electronic Music*. Harmony Books, 1977. A survey of electronic music including how to create with synthesizer and tape recorder.

Explorer's Limited Source Book. Harper & Row, rev. ed.,

1977. A potpourri of information on every conceivable outdoor activity.

Fairfield, Del: *Jewelry Making*. David McKay, 1976. An outstanding introduction to the art of creating jewelry.

Fantel, Hans: *Durable Pleasures*. E. P. Dutton, 1976. A practical guide for getting professional results from your tape recordings.

Feinman, Jeffrey: *The Catalog of Kits*. William Morrow, rev. ed., 1975. A marvelous assortment of kits for do-it-yourself projects.

Feldman, Mark: *Archeology for Everyone*. Quadrangle Books, 1977. How to become an amateur archaeologist.

Felsen, Henry G.: *Living with Your First Motorcycle*. Berkley, 1977. The basics of riding, care, selection, and all-important safety tips.

Fichter, George S., and Phil Frances: *Guide to Fresh and Saltwater Fishing*. Golden Press, 1965. Copious illustrations give reader practical know-how.

Fischer, Bobby, et al.: *Bobby Fischer Teaches Chess*. Bantam Books, 1972. A champion presents the game to both novices and initiates.

Fox, Michael W.: *Understanding Your Cat*. Coward, McCann & Geohegan, 1974. Bantam Books. Information on what makes the cat tick for the pet owner, breeder, potential buyer, and student of animal behavior.

————: *Understanding Your Dog*. Coward, McCann & Geohegan, 1972. Bantam Books. A clear, comprehensive, and thoroughly contemporary guide to the mental development and behavior of dogs.

Gaines, Charles, and George Butler. *Pumping Iron*. Simon and Schuster, 1974. The art and the skill of bodybuilding. Profusely illustrated, this book captures the world and the discipline of big-time body-building.

Gerani, Gary: *Fantastic Television*. Harmony Books, 1977. A look at all the popular TV series.

Herkimer, L. R., and Phyllis Hollander, eds.: *The Complete Book of Cheerleading*. Doubleday, 1975. Absolutely everything about the art of eliciting a resounding "Yah team!"

Hilton, Suzanne: *Who Do You Think You Are? Digging for Your Family Roots*. Westminster Press, 1976. New

American Library. The basics on tracing your ancestors.

Horenstein, Henry: *Black and White Photography: A Basic Manual.* Little, Brown, 1974. Comprehensive coverage includes the use of camera and film, technical processing.

Jacoby, James and Mary Z.: *The New York Times Book of Backgammon.* Times Books, 1973. New American Library. Step-by-step instructions for learning the intriguing game of backgammon.

Johnson, Jann: *Jann Johnson's Discovery Book of Crafts.* Reader's Digest Press, 1975. Sixty-five outstanding craft projects. Beautifully illustrated and well conceived.

Kaplan, Arthur: *Basketball: How to Improve Your Technique.* Franklin Watts, 1974. Guide to conditioning the body and perfecting its moves for those who know and love the game.

Keith, Harold: *Sports and Games.* Thomas Y. Crowell, 6th ed., 1976. Rules, playing tips, history, and highlights of 16 popular games.

Kiss, Michaeline: *Yoga for Young People.* Bobbs-Merrill, 1971. Archway Paperbacks. Fully descriptive book on elementary yoga postures and meditation techniques.

Koelzer, William: *Scuba Diving: How to Get Started.* Chilton Book, 1976. Discusses the selection and correct use of scuba equipment, with emphasis on safety.

Liebers, Arthur: *Liebers' Guide: How to Organize and Run a Club.* William Morrow, 1977. Complete practical information for getting it together with your friends.

Lightbody, Donna: *Let's Knot: A Macrame Book.* Lothrop, Lee & Shepard, 1972. Beginning macrame book with project ideas to help you learn by doing.

Liman, Ellen, and Carol Panter: *Decorating Your Room: A Do-It-Yourself Guide.* Franklin Watts, 1974. Projects for redoing your personal living space to reflect *you.*

Linder, Carl: *Filmmaking.* Prentice-Hall, 1976. Best practical guide to film production for the novice. Put together by a UCLA faculty member and filmmaker.

Linsley, Leslie: *Wildcrafts.* Doubleday, 1977. Contemporary designs for over 100 craft projects made from natural materials.

MacFall, Russell P.: *Gem Hunter's Guide*. Thomas Y. Crowell, 5th ed., 1975. Semiprecious stones: where to find them and how to identify them.

McIntyre, Bibs: *The Bike Book*. Pyramid, 1974. Everything you need to know about owning and riding a bike.

McWhirter, Norris: *Guinness Book of World Records*. Sterling, 17th ed., 1976. Bantam Books. The all-new, up-to-date edition of the only complete book of world records in every field.

Malo, John W.: *All Terrain Adventure Vehicles*. Macmillan, 1972. A description of kinds of vehicles, uses for which they are suited, suggestions for the novice, lists of competitions and rallies.

Meilach, Donna Z.: *Contemporary Batik and Tie-Dye*. Crown, 1972. How-to book for batik and tie-dye including methods, materials, and inspiration.

————: *Creative Carving*. Galahad Books, 1969. Excellent instructions for working in soap, wax, wood, and stone.

Milinaire, Caterine, and Carol Troy: *Cheap Chic Update*. Harmony Books, 1978. Very high fashion for those not able to afford the designers. Information on how to make the various "looks" work. Interviews with fashion authorities.

Okun, Milton, ed.: *The New York Times Great Songs of the Seventies*. Times Books, 1977. Sheet music arrangements for voice, piano, and guitar.

Olney, Ross R.: *Hang Gliding*. G. P. Putnam's Sons, 1976. An introductory book describing equipment and technique, with emphasis on safety and the need for professional instruction.

Page, Patrick: *The Big Book of Magic*. Dial Press, 1976. Simple, detailed instructions for hundreds of classic tricks.

Parker, Robert B., and John R. Marsh: *Sports Illustrated Training with Weights*. J. B. Lippincott, 1974. Exercises for developing muscles by weight lifting, for both sexes.

Phillips, Mary W.: *Knitting*. Franklin Watts, 1977. Equipment, stitches, and projects for the beginner.

Poynter, Dan: *Hang Gliding: The Basic Handbook of Sky-surfing*. Parachuting, 8th ed., 1977. Illustrations show how it is done, what equipment is needed. Some advice to beginners.

Price, Steven D., et al., eds.: *The Whole Horse Catalog*. Simon and Schuster, 1977. Detailed information on keeping a horse, from selection to health, stabling, wearing apparel, and equestrian activities.

Pucci, Cora: *Pottery: A Basic Manual*. Little, Brown, 1974. Creative exploration of the potter's art.

Reinfeld, Fred: *The Coin Collector's Handbook*. Doubleday, rev. ed., 1976. Catalogs all United States and Canadian coins and offers guidance in buying and selling.

Roth, Bernhard A.: *The Complete Beginner's Guide to Archery*. Doubleday, 1976. History, techniques, target practice, hunting, and Olympic competition.

Sakoian, Frances, and Louis S. Acker: *The Astrologer's Handbook*. Harper & Row, 1973. How to cast and interpret a horoscope and where to send for computerized version.

Saunders, Rubie: *Baby Sitting: A Concise Guide*. Archway Paperbacks, 1974. Brief and to the point for the young entrepreneur.

Scarne, John: *Scarne on Cards*. New American Library, 1973. How to win at poker, gin, pinochle, blackjack, cribbage, bridge, and other card games.

Ski Magazine Editors and Robert Scharff, eds.: *Ski Magazine's Encyclopedia of Skiing*. Harper & Row, rev. ed., 1975. Everything a skier needs to know, from equipment to Olympic competition rules.

Snyder, Jerry, ed.: *Big Golden Encyclopedia for Guitar*. Crown, 1975. Excellent sheet music for beginning and advanced players.

Sommer, Elyse: *Rock and Stone Craft*. Crown, 1973. Projects involving rocks, including jewelry and mosaics.

Sports Illustrated Editors: *Sports Illustrated Swimming and Diving*. J. B. Lippincott, 1973. Swimming and diving techniques for students or beginning coaches.

Teller, Raphael: *Woodwork: A Basic Manual*. Little, Brown, 1974. How-to-do-it of woodworking techniques, tools, projects, and designs.

Temko, Florence: *Paper: Folded, Cut, Sculptured*. Macmillan, 1974. Well-structured, clearly illustrated guide to origami, kirigami, and sculptured paper.

Torbet, Laura: *The T-Shirt Book*. Bobbs-Merrill, 1976. How to decorate your T-shirt in every imaginable way.

Truscott, Lucian K.: *The Complete Van Book*. Harmony Books, 1976. A dream book of incredible interiors and paint jobs, with a buyer's guide to van shops, parts, and customizers.

Villiard, Paul: *Collecting Stamps*. Doubleday, 1974. New American Library. Guide to philately, emphasizing proper care and display of your collection.

Wallechinsky, David, and Irving Wallace: *The People's Almanac*. Doubleday, 1975. *The People's Almanac 2*. William Morrow, 1978. Bantam Books. Compendiums of entertaining, useful information covering a wide variety of topics.

Wallechinsky, David, Irving Wallace, and Amy Wallace: *The Book of Lists*. William Morrow, 1977. Bantam Books. The first comprehensive book of lists. Includes every fascinating list possible involving persons, places, happenings, and things from "The Five Most Hated Persons in History" to "The Ten Best Movies of All Time."

Weiss, Harvey: *Ship Models and How to Build Them*. Thomas Y. Crowell, 1973. A clear guide with good plans.

Wheeler, Tom: *The Guitar Book*. Harper & Row, rev. ed., 1978. An inclusive and informative guide to acoustic and electric guitars.

Wheelus, Doris: *Baton Twirling*. Lion Books, 1975. Warner Books. A complete illustrated guide for beginners and would-be pros.

Wilson, Jean: *Weaving is For Anyone*. Van Nostrand Reinhold, 1975. A guide for beginning weavers about yarns, baskets, cloth, and tapestry.

PERSONAL ADVICE

Boston Women's Health Collective: *Our Bodies, Ourselves: A Book by and for Women*. Simon and Schuster, rev. ed., 1976. Feminist-oriented, somewhat controversial, covers information on health and needs of all ages and all classes of women.

Eagen, Andrea Boroff: *Why Am I So Miserable If These Are the Best Years of My Life? A Survival Guide for the Young Woman*. J. B. Lippincott, 1976. Straightforward information and advice on all aspects of sex, relationships, planning for independence, and legal rights.

Ewen, Robert B.: *Getting It Together*. Franklin Watts, 1976. Causes and cures of neurotic behavior.

Fromm, Erich: *The Art of Loving*. Harper & Row, 1956. Learn how to love others, love yourself, and become a better, whole person.

Gilbert, Sara: *You Are What You Eat*. Macmillan, 1977. A guide to fad diets, health foods, nutrition, additives, and other facets of food.

Hyde, Margaret O.: *Hotline*. McGraw-Hill, rev. ed., 1975. For teenagers in crisis.

————: *Mind Drugs*. McGraw-Hill, 3d ed., 1974. Various experts discuss the use and abuse of some of the popular psychedelic and other drugs currently in legal and illegal use.

Johnson, Eric W.: *Sex: Telling It Straight*. J. B. Lippincott, 1970. Simple, straightforward explanations of sex for the young teenager.

————: *V.D.: Venereal Disease and What You Should Do About It*. J. B. Lippincott, rev. ed., 1978. Clear and concise explanation of syphilis and gonorrhea, their prevention and cure.

Landau, Elaine: *Yoga for You*. Julian Messner, 1977. Comes complete with instructions and advice on postures, breathing, and diet.

Larrick, Nancy, and Eve Merriam, eds.: *Male and Female Under 18*. Avon Books, 1973. Contains writings of young people from 8 to 18.

LeShan, Lawrence: *How to Meditate*. Bantam Books, 1975. An introduction to Zen, Sufi, Yoga, and other methods of meditation.

Lieberman, E. James, and Ellen Peck: *Sex and Birth Control: A Guide for the Young*. Schocken Books, 1975. Contains complete information on birth control and VD. Discusses the need for sex education, the future of the family, and the population explosion.

Lubowe, Irwin, and Barbara Huss: *A Teen-Age Guide to Healthy Skin and Hair*. E. P. Dutton, rev. ed., 1972. Expert advice, presented clearly, with an eye to the intended audience.

Mann, Marty: *Marty Mann Answers Your Questions About Drinking and Alcoholism*. Holt, Rinehart and Winston, 1970. A former alcoholic discusses alcoholism, its prevention and cure.

Medea, Andra, and Kathleen Thompson: *Against Rape*. Farrar, Straus and Giroux, 1974. Practical guide to understanding the motivations of rapists, and avoiding situations where rape is a danger. Supportive of women, strongly feminist.

Milgram, Gail Gleason: *The Teenager and Smoking*. Richards Rosen Press, 1972. Depicts realistically the effects of smoking on the human body, and the teenage body in particular.

Mitchell, Joyce Slaton: *Free to Choose*. Delacorte Press, 1976. Deals with decision making for young men.

Prudden, Bonnie: *Teenage Fitness*. Harper & Row, 1965. A day-by-day course of exercises that will make any follower more fit and healthy.

Richards, Arlene, and Irene Willis: *How to Get It Together When Your Parents Are Coming Apart*. Bantam Books, 1977. Helps teenagers get through the pain and fear of a divorce in as good shape as is possible. Coping with the split; maintaining integrity.

Rinzler, Carol Ann: *What the Ads Don't Tell You About Cosmetics*. Thomas Y. Crowell, 1977. Inside information about the industry, the preparations we all use and some of their effects.

Shedd, Charlie W., ed.: *You Are Somebody Special*. McGraw-Hill, 1978. Bantam Books. Ten authors write about the concerns and problems of teenagers and their world.

Sims, Naomi: *All About Health and Beauty for the Black Woman*. Doubleday, 1976. Beauty advice for black women by a topflight fashion model.

Sussman, Alan N.: *The Rights of Young People*. Avon Books, 1977. The American Civil Liberties Union handbook for young people. It gives sound, accurate advice on basic rights of those not yet adults.

Webster, Jonathan, and Harriet Webster. *Eighteen: The Teen-age Catalog*. Quick Fox, 1976. A listing of over 1000 subjects of interest to teenagers.

Winship, Elizabeth: *Ask Beth: You Can't Ask Your Mother*. Houghton Mifflin, 1972. The columnist's responses to questions about sex, depression, VD, drugs, and other matters of concern to young adults.

CAREER AND COLLEGE INFORMATION

Arnold, Arnold: *Career Choices for the Seventies*. Macmillan, 1971. Practical advice to guide career choices, with special information for minorities and girls, and extensive source lists for further information.

Barron's Handbook of American College Financial Aid. Barron's Educational Series, rev. ed., 1977. *Barron's Handbook of College Transfer Information*. Rev. ed., 1975. *Barron's Handbook of Junior College and Community College Financial Aid*. 1977. Three sources of specialized information about the American college community.

Barron's How to Prepare for College Entrance Exams. Barron's Educational Series, 8th ed., 1976. The standard guide to success with the College Boards.

Barth, George F.: *Your Aptitudes: You Do Best What You Are Best Fitted To Do*. Lothrop, Lee & Shepard, 1974. How to use your special aptitudes as a criterion for choosing a satisfying career.

Bird, Caroline: *Everything a Woman Needs to Know to Get Paid What She's Worth*. David McKay, 1973. A question-and-answer format offers women suggestions on selecting and successfully pursuing careers in spite of the special problems that face the ambitious workingwoman.

Brechner, Irv: *The College Survival Kit*. Bantam Books, 1979. Fifty-one proven strategies for success in today's competitive college world. For the incoming freshman.

Cass, James, and Max Birnbaum: *Comparative Guide to American Colleges*. Harper & Row, 9th ed., 1979. *Comparative Guide to Two-Year Colleges and Career Programs*. Harper & Row, 1976. National listing of colleges including locations, fields of study, admission policies, costs, and a summary of campus life and the academic environment.

The Encyclopedia of Careers and Vocational Guidance. Doubleday, 3d ed., 1975, 2 vols. A guide to planning your career and available career choices, written by specialists in each field.

Ewen, Robert: *Choosing the College For You.* Franklin Watts, 1976. A brief look at economic and personal factors influencing the choice of a college.

Freede, Robert: *Cash for College.* Prentice-Hall, 1975. An excellent source book for the college-bound student interested in cutting costs and alternate funding.

Garraty, John, et al.: *The New Guide to Study Abroad.* Harper & Row, 6th ed., 1978. A valuable reference source covering scholarships, credit transfer, dates, and costs for high-school and college courses abroad.

Gleazer, Edmund J., Jr., ed.: *American Junior Colleges.* American Council on Education, 8th ed., 1971. A thorough guide to junior colleges throughout the U.S.

Halacy, D. S., Jr.: *Survival in the World of Work.* Charles Scribner's Sons, 1975. How to prepare for entry into the working world, starting with the selection of a career that will provide intrinsic satisfaction.

Hebert, Tom, and John Coyne: *Getting Skilled.* E. P. Dutton, 1976. An outstanding guide to private trade and technical schools.

Hecht, Miriam, and Lillian Traub: *Alternatives to College.* Macmillan Information, 1974. Presenting some fairly conventional alternatives such as apprenticeships and work-study programs.

Keefe, John: *The Teenager and the Interview.* Rosen Richards Press, rev. ed., 1978. A concise, clear, pragmatic handbook for the teenage job seeker.

Kesselman, Judi R.: *Stopping Out: A Guide to Leaving College and Getting Back in.* M. Evans, 1976. A consideration of the option of dropping out of college, with alternative suggestions for education and advice for getting back in at a later date.

Kursh, Harry: *Apprenticeships in America.* W. W. Norton, rev. ed., 1965. With manpower shortages proving the need for skilled workers, apprenticeship becomes a key route to building, printing, mechanical repair, and machining.

Lederer, Muriel: *The Guide to Career Education*. Times Books, 1974. Guide to post high-school education in over 200 occupations.

Liston, Robert A.: *On the Job Training and Where to Get It*. Julian Messner, rev. ed., 1973. A guide for the high-school graduate who cannot go to college, emphasizing the skills most in demand in a technological society.

Lobb, Charlotte: *Exploring Careers Through Part-Time and Summer Employment*. Richards Rosen Press, 1977. *Exploring Careers Through Volunteerism*, 1975. A broad approach to career education. Offers ways to identify career preferences and gain job experience.

Lovejoy, Clarence E.: *Lovejoy's Career and Vocational School Guide*. Simon and Schuster, 5th ed., 1978. A source book, clue book, and directory of job-training opportunities.

Mitchell, Joyce S.: *I Can Be Anything*. Bantam Books, 1978. A concise introduction to careers and colleges for young women.

Resume Service Staff: *Resumes That Get Jobs*. Arco, 1976. How to write the resume that will get the job.

Sandman, Peter, and Dan Goldenson: *Unabashed Career Guide*. Macmillan, 1969. Gets down to the nitty-gritty of many professions, stripping away the romantic veneer.

Splaver, Sarah: *Nontraditional Careers for Women*. Julian Messner, 1973. Brief descriptions of the many nontraditional careers now open to women.

————: *Nontraditional College Routes to Careers*. Julian Messner, 1975. A guide to universities offering different degree programs for the young adult who wants to learn without doing four more years of the same old thing.

————: *Paraprofessions: Careers of the Future and the Present*. Julian Messner, 1972. An overview of the unique role of the paraprofessional and the many career opportunities available to him/her.

————: *Your Career—If You're Not Going to College*.

Julian Messner, rev. ed., 1971. An aid to determining career choice by matching interests and capabilities with the many jobs available without a college degree.

Stevenson, Gloria: *Your Future as a Working Woman*. Richards Rosen Press, 1975. Facts, figures, and advice about the labor market, occupations and occupational trends, skills and expectations, and earnings for the career woman to be.

Summer Employment Directory of the United States. National Directory Service, annual. General information and suggestions for job hunting as well as lists of available jobs.

Todd, Ronald, and Karen R.: *Aim for a Job Working with Your Hands*. Richards Rosen Press, 1975. A description of various jobs, training programs and preparation, and opportunities in the manual crafts, trades, and technical arts.

U.S. Bureau of Labor Statistics: *The Occupational Outlook Handbook*. Government Printing Office, biennial. This panorama of occupations in the United States includes job descriptions, qualifications and training, earning and working conditions, and employment outlook.

3

The Stages
of Reading Development

A man ought to read just as inclination leads him;
for what he reads as a task will do him little good.
—*Samuel Johnson*

Human beings grow up physically in a slow, ordered pattern. Their literary tastes develop in a gradual, predictable way. Most adults accept that youngsters go through stages in their reading: at first, young children favor stories of talking animals and personified machines; a bit later, they turn to fairy stories, books of magic, and fantastic happenings; next, they read tales about pirates and knights and princesses and castles. But oddly enough, adults do not seem to realize that teenagers are still growing, and changing in their literary tastes just as in their physical bodies. They assume that the teenager is ready to move into *great* literature. Nothing is further from the truth.

Recognizing that teenagers are still passing through reading phases is important in nurturing enthusiasm for reading, for this is the period when many potential readers stop reading for pleasure. Paradoxically, it is also the period when the young person, if encouraged, may devote more time to books than at any other period of life, provided interest is not killed by an overzealous adult.

Reading patterns have been carefully mapped through research studies conducted with thousands of adolescent subjects, coming from diverse home back-grounds in all parts of the country. According to these studies, chronological age is more important than mental age in determining what a child will enjoy reading. The average and above-average 13-year-old are interested in reading books with the same subject matter and themes, though titles may vary. A difficult book on a subject that their age group likes can be read aloud to a group of teens with varying mental abilities and they will all enjoy it. Accelerating the intelligent child by giving him or her the adult classics of literature will not increase enjoyment of reading. The great modern French writer Jean-Paul Sartre reports in his autobiography, *The Words,* that he read the classics because his family was extravagant in its praise of his precociousness. When he heard footsteps, he says: "I faked. I would spring to my feet, take down the heavy Corneille. I would hear behind me a dazzled voice whisper: 'But it's because he *likes* Corneille.' I didn't like him." What really appealed to Sartre were trashy adventure stories that his mother bought him by the hundreds. "I owe to those my first encounters with Beauty. When I opened them I forgot about everything."

Reading preferences are determined not only by age but by the physical and emotional differences between male and female, and their acculturation. These differences may continue into adult life, but the more mature the reader, the more the differences are obscured. Many books on the adult best-seller list are not classifiable as appealing to a predominantly masculine or feminine audience.

Boys are generally more pronounced in their likes and dislikes than girls, so it is easier to predict what a boy wants in a story. Overwhelmingly, boys want a male protagonist. They prefer the outdoor settings, and physical action, in other words, an adventure-suspense story. Males generally prefer realistic style to romanticism. They like science fiction (whose imaginary worlds seem to carry the essence of romance), but only when its worlds are evoked through realistic detail.

Girls often like similar narratives, but usually opt for a female protagonist. Girls tend to prefer internal settings (both in the sense of inside the mind, and physically inside) and a neat, tightly organized plot. This means a defined cast of interrelated characters and a defined temporal setting: the story takes place during a summer, or a school year, with a clearly defined beginning, middle and end. Girls often enjoy internal rather than external action. They want to know what a character is thinking and feeling, not just what he or she is doing. Boys are more rigid and limited in their preferences, while girls exhibit an interest in a wider range of reading experience.

Because high-school English during the early 20th century was taught predominantly by women, there was a preponderance of literature alien to boys' tastes: *Silas Marner, Evangeline, A Midsummer Night's Dream, Snowbound,* and *Lady of the Lake,* to mention a few. Following the mapping of sex differences in reading, there has been a swing to predominantly boys' books in the classroom in the last 20 years: *The Catcher in the Rye, A Separate Peace, Light in the Forest, Swiftwater, Johnny Tremain.* Because of the women's movement, selections are being reevaluated to see if they do not cater to masculine interests in the same way that the earlier group did to feminine interests.

A story with feminine protagonists may appeal to teenage males, but only if the book has other predominantly male characteristics such as a high degree of external action and setting. One such book is *Island of the Blue Dolphins.* Girls respond favorably to books with male protagonists when the book has other feminine qualities: internal action, an interior setting, and a tight plot pattern, as in *A Separate Peace* and *The Chosen.*

Also, adolescents generally choose books according to their subject matter. They will read books of great language difficulty if the subject is close to their interests, and they will reject even simple books about subjects that bore them. From age 10 or 11 to 18, three stages of preference can be distinguished.

EARLY ADOLESCENCE

These children are 11 to 14 years old and are in grades five through eight or possibly nine. They usually find the greatest satisfaction in one or more of the following types of stories.

Animal Stories

Children who are passionate readers of animal stories often read 150 to 200 such tales before outgrowing them. The really avid reader may become specialized, reading only stories about horses, dogs, or African beasts. Some children prefer stories about wild animals in nature such as *Snowdog;* others prefer that the animal be dependent upon human beings as in *Lassie Come Home*.

Adventure Stories

Boys in their early teens are the biggest readers of adventure tales. The story often revolves around a group of young men who find themselves cast adrift in a small boat or lost on a mountain or wandering through the wastes of the Arctic. The characters must solve their problems through intelligence and fortitude, attaining success in the last chapter.

Mystery Stories

The adolescent mystery story is somewhat different from the adult whodunit. Teenage characters are involved in a case of mistaken identity or with a mysterious person whose motives are baffling. The story may deal with kidnapping or with a hunt and chase sequence. The teen may be the unwitting observer of murder, robbery, or espionage. There is a tendency for boys to prefer adventure-suspense and for girls to like a more clearly defined mystery, but the categories often overlap.

Tales of the Supernatural

Closely related to mystery stories are tales that send a pleasant chill up the spine of the reader. Young people love to be frightened by mysterious accounts of ghosts, zombies, and misshapen characters. The weirder the setting, the more eerie the sounds, the better they like it. Graveyards filled with flickering, mysterious lights are a favorite setting.

Sports Stories

Baseball, football, basketball, track, and swimming stories usually hit the high point on the interest scale for boys of this age. A boy's inability to excel in sports may make him seek books centering on sports excellence. Many girls, too, read sports stories. In recent years there have been attempts—though not completely successful—to write sports novels with female protagonists. Biographies of female sports figures have been more successful. In the last few years the young teens have shown less interest in sports fiction and more in sports biographies, often ghosted by a professional writer as autobiographies. Only the occasional teenager becomes intrigued enough with sports history to read biographies of oldtime sports heroes like Babe Ruth, Bobby Jones, or Jesse Owens. Contemporary sports heroes have such a short moment of glory that their biographies must be quickly published to take advantage of their popularity. Sports biographies are an important body of reading materials for this age, and a school collection must be kept current.

Growing Up Around the World

Stories of contemporary adolescent life in other countries interest girls especially, who like to compare their experiences with those of young people growing up in other cultures. English stories by Ruth Arthur and German stories by Margot Benary-Isbert provide this satisfaction. Such books may be a mixture of home and family life, mystery, and adventure. Because such books may color the picture of a foreign culture that young readers carry with them for the rest of their lives, they should be accurately and competently written.

Home and Family Life Stories

Ever since Louisa May Alcott wrote *Little Women,* the story of a warm and loving family group has been a prime favorite with girls—but not with boys. Girls love the romanticized picture of family relationships in which a teenage girl by hard work, ingenuity, or self-sacrifice pulls her family through a crisis. Bill and Vera Cleaver have written a number of family life stories with strong heroines living in poverty. *Where the Lilies Bloom* is probably the best known: a teenage girl holds her family together after the parents die, leaving the children destitute. While dealing with other themes as well, the early Judy Blume books such as *Are You There God? It's Me Margaret* are in large part about contemporary family relationships.

Broad, Bold Slapstick

Boys and girls glory in slapstick. Humor is intimately related to age; what is funny to one age level may not be funny to another. As adults, we have left behind the adolescent stage of humor; when we are exposed to samples of it, we find it stupid. But each new generation has to experience the same stock humorous situations for itself. Unfortunately, there is not much material in book form that adolescents find amusing, so they turn to television or such a periodical as *Mad* for humor.

Settings in the Past

In early adolescence, girls are often enamored with books that have a thin veil of history. They are not accurately researched historical novels, but just "books about the olden times," where history is used to lead the reader into a world different from her own where costumes, customs, and human emotions are on a higher, more romantic plane than we experience today.

Fantasy

Girls more often than boys become enthralled with books that create imaginary, almost mythological kingdoms. These frequently are related to old legends that unfold through a three- or four-book series. The forces of good and evil, of darkness and light, of destroyers and maintainers are pitted against each other in books by Ursula K. Le Guin, Susan Cooper, William Mayme, and C. S. Lewis.

MIDDLE ADOLESCENCE

At age 15 or 16 (ninth or tenth grade), reading interests deepen and may change direction.

Nonfiction Accounts of Adventure

Boys and girls who had an enthusiasm for imagined adventure will have matured into wanting a more realistic story—a firsthand account of exploring a cave, climbing a mountain, sailing alone on a raft, or exploring the Arctic.

Historical Novels

Girls' interest in books about the olden times develops into an interest in the longer historical novel. *Gone with the Wind* has found its greatest popularity among girls in middle adolescence.

Mystical Romances

Girls hit the peak of interest in the romantic novel now. They like a story of two intense people who love each other in unusual circumstances, as in *Rebecca* or *Wuthering Heights*.

Stories of Adolescent Life

Both sexes are interested in stories about characters a year or so older, living in the same kind of community and facing the same sort of problems they are facing. Literature becomes a way of seeing themselves and of testing possible solutions to their own problems.

The more the writer gets inside the chief character's mind and feelings, showing the inner struggle taking place, the more popular and enduring the book. This accounts for the continuing popularity of *The Catcher in the Rye* with boys and *Anne Frank: The Diary of a Young Girl* with girls. Holden and Anne, although their circumstances are extreme, are at heart "every teenage boy" and "every teenage girl" during the troubled years of adolescence.

LATE ADOLESCENCE

Young people who are finishing their last two years of high school and entering college or the adult working world tend to take up the books generally read by adults, but they may still read books written for teenagers.

Search for Personal Values

It is time for adolescents to crystallize their value systems. This means searching, questioning, probing, even destroying. They have a driving need to find personal direction for their lives, so it comes as no surprise that books about individuals struggling to find values are immensely popular. The success of the German writer Hermann Hesse (*Demian* and *Siddhartha*) can be attributed to teens' concern with the "seeker," a figure with whom young people easily identify.

Books of Social Significance

Someone has said that the way to ensure the popularity of a book for young adults is to focus the story on deprived or persecuted persons. This has some validity, for young adults are interested not only in finding a set of personal values, but in a code of social values, and respond, therefore, to a book with a plot about economic deprivation, racial inequality, or religious discrimination. These books can be graphic, strong, and shocking in their presentation of human situations. Past generations of young readers favored Victor Hugo's *Les Miserables,* Harriet Beecher Stowe's *Uncle Tom's Cabin,* Upton Sinclair's *The Jungle,* and Richard Wright's *Native Son;* today's young adults seek the same value-testing experiences through George Orwell's *Nineteen Eighty-four,* Claude Brown's *Manchild in the Promised Land,* and Arthur Miller's play, *The Crucible.*

Strange and Unusual Human Experiences

Moving still farther along the path of personal experience that was at first satisfied by adventure stories are books detailing an odd experience, often taking place on the fringes of human life. As the young reader matures, he develops an almost insatiable hunger to find out what a human being is capable of in unusual circumstances. The book may be *I Never Promised You a Rose Garden,* which gives insights into schizophrenia, or it may be *Alive,* in which a group of survivors of a plane crash in the Andes are forced to eat the bodies of dead comrades to survive. Or may center on someone like Dr. Martin Luther King, Jr., who had a life strikingly different from that of most of us.

Transition to Adult Life

Of all the categories, the one with the greatest appeal involves the growth of a character from adolescence into adulthood. At this age, young people are suddenly aware of the uncertainties of the transition period. How do you move from being a schoolchild dependent upon parents to being an independent adult?

Arrowsmith, Of Human Bondage, and *First Blood*

are three titles that combine the appeals discussed above: exploring personal values, social criticism, unusual experience, and transition to adulthood. The first centers on a young man in the last years of medical school and the early years of practice; the second is the story of Philip Carey, whose clubfoot makes his journey toward maturity tortuous; the third begins with the experiences of a returned Green Beret in a southern town who bucks the system. Each book says something important about the problems troubling the young adult.

One reading interest that is not easily classified by age is science fiction (SF); these books may be adventure stories, mysteries, fantasies, or psychological or sociological novels. SF readers may start in early adolescence with one kind of book and shift to others as they mature. One enthusiast said, "Did you ever find a person who liked just one science fiction book?" The junior high schooler reads principally adventures; Buck Rogers comics and "Star Trek" stories represent the category. Bradbury's and Heinlein's titles are popular in the middle bracket. But the greatest interest seems to be among the college-aged, who are fascinated by the scientific projections suggested by plots which often deal with psychological, sociological, and philosophical speculations.

What falls outside the scope of teens' reading interests? Generally, the concerns of the great middle-aged section of the population have little appeal. Teens rarely care to read about characters who are middle-aged unless, as in spy stories, the individuals are highly romanticized and lead lives of incredible adventure. They are not interested in the character who has had to compromise with life or who is bowed down by the humdrum. Clyde Griffith in *An American Tragedy,* though young, is branded despicable by the young reader and not worth reading about. Sinclair Lewis's *Babbitt* and *Main Street* are beyond teenagers' emotional understanding. Books about the wealthy usually have little attraction for the young. Wealth is tolerated only in a historical romance or story of intrigue. Nor do teenage readers care for stories of the industrial or political world or the trials and tribulations of marriages. They cannot understand someone like Isabel Archer in Henry James's *Portrait of a Lady* who is wealthy and caught in an untenable marriage, yet will not attempt to break free. Young readers have little tolerance for a pessimistic world view such as Thomas Hardy's, presented through characters pursued by an uncaring, irrational fate.

It is surprising but logical that teens find more delight in books about the elderly than those about the middle-aged. Many of the tasks of adolescence (chapter 2) are also the tasks of old age. Both groups find changes in their peer groups. Both must make profound adjustments to physical and mental changes; one must adjust to entering the work world and the other, to leaving it. To both groups, the middle-aged are the enemy.

It is constantly asked of those dealing with young people and books whether it isn't wrong to pander to teenagers' interests instead of trying to broaden them. It is easy to say that books should do both. But there is a pitfall here, as with most simple solutions: there is no great number of titles that can do both. For generations adults have tried to force-feed teens literary materials that teens are not ready to experience, fostering the feeling in millions of adults that literature is a strange forbidding territory, too obscure to attempt to penetrate. One side effect is to make great masses of people feel culturally inferior. And in spite of all the promises of those prescribing great literature for the teens, the program has not enlarged the reading public. The adult population in the United States is outread by several other nations. Most of the book reading in the U.S. is done by less than 10 percent of the population. The consistency of reading interest patterns among teenagers from all parts of the world indicates that we are dealing with a matter of nature, not nurture.

4

Subliterature

There's no book so bad but has some good in it.
— *Miguel de Cervantes*

Comic books, juvenile series books, formula romances, westerns, and tales of intrigue are perhaps the material most widely read by teenagers and adults. They are the literature of the masses, just as soap operas on television are the dramas of the masses. The books have almost all the elements of literature: characters, setting, and a plot. But they come into being without the real involvement of their author, being created through a predetermined formula which once discovered is repeated in book after book with only changes in setting and in characters' names. The writer fills in details from an outline without necessarily grappling with his own experiences, perceptions, or concepts about life. Such books are often turned out with incredible speed. They hold the reader's interest as stories, but they do not engage the mind with insight into human motivations, emotions, or relationships. They are like junk food: tasty, fattening, but not very nutritious.

Almost inevitably children will have a period of reading comic books, juvenile series books, and adult potboilers, generally near the end of elementary school or during junior high. No matter how excellent the literary guidance children have had, they suddenly find these books fascinating. Basic needs are satisfied by something in them. It is important to examine subliterature carefully, to understand why it appeals to the child and to see how we can eventually help the young person grow beyond it.

COMIC BOOKS

As every parent knows, few children wait for adolescence to discover comic books: the peak of interest comes late in elementary school. The comic book grew out of the daily comic strips in newspapers, one of the first of which, "The Yellow Kid," appeared in a New York paper in the 1890s and was soon syndicated. Newspaper readers found the strip so appealing that other publishers quickly hired cartoonists to draw comics for their papers. Because the early strips were humorous, the word "comic" has been used to describe all work that has a sequence of pictures showing a stock group of characters talking among themselves to convey the story line.

The first comic books were reprints of newspaper strips; the books were often given away as premiums for products. The first venture into the commercial comic book, a paper-covered book to be sold at newsstands, came in the 1930s. These comic books were only moderately successful at first, but by the end of the thirties had become a standard part of American culture. The first crime comics made their appearance in the late thirties. When the Second World War got under way, the popularity of the comic book zoomed. Comics provided cheap, easily accessible, portable escape for men under severe tensions. The material was simple, usually full of action and centered on dashing heroes and beautiful heroines. Success made comics, now in a uniform size and shape, a major American publishing enterprise.

By the 1950s, comics ran the gamut of subjects, characters, and language. Many carried vulgar stores appealing to the worst in human beings by stressing horror, crime, and perversion. Some communities became horrified at what was available to teenagers on newsstands and brought pressure to bear on retailers to sell only selected comics. As a result, the more vicious and distasteful comics all but vanished. Of late, there has been a feeble attempt to portray life-styles of minority groups in national comic strips.

Although comics tend to reinforce white middle-class values, it is a mistake to assume that all comics are alike. Roughly, comic books can be classified in the following types.

Slapstick Comics

The descendants of the first comic strips, these present ludicrous characters in ridiculous situations. Some of them poke fun at human foibles and society's pretenses, serving a satiric purpose.

Family Life Comics

These usually depict a typical middle-class family group living through daily adventures. Certain standard situations are repeated: the mother outwits the father; the children outwit the parents; the family has a series of crises with pets or accidents or money troubles.

Hero Comics

A central character like Spiderman or Batman always comes out on top after a series of trials and adventures. Sometimes the hero has supernormal powers, but he is always a magnificent physical type, with great intelligence and a keen sense of justice and honesty.

Crime Comics

The popularity of crime comics ebbs and flows. At this writing they are less prevalent. The emphasis is on the criminal, even though he may be caught and punished in the end; in the hero comic, we noted, emphasis is placed on the detective and his successes.

Horror Comics

The picture on the cover shows a grotesque monster, a gargoylelike creature looming over a frightened girl or being attacked by an audacious young man. These stories descend from Edgar Allan Poe's spine-chilling tales and provide for the young reader the delicious fright that almost all of us have enjoyed at some period. Adults may find the events revolting and horrible, but for young readers such feelings seldom arise, for they do not associate these stories with reality. They intuitively enter an imaginary world; the more goose pimples produced, the better they like the story.

Love Comics

The highly romantic, semierotic contents appeal to girls. Usually the cover promises more thrills and titillation than the story delivers. The girls remain virtuous in spite of dastardly companions and compromising situations. Similarity to reality is seldom sought or delivered. It is a foregone conclusion that the heroine will succeed in her romantic adventures.

Pornographic Comics

This type is usually found on college campuses or among intellectual enclaves of young adults. The thrust is satiric through choice of situation and illustration, but the presentation is frankly lewd. They seem to be caricaturing the subject matter of hard-core pornographic magazines and films.

The 1970s have seen a change of emphasis in comics, which have returned to their original satiric and humorous mode. "Pogo," an unusually intellectual comic originating in the 1940s, ridiculed American politicians and human follies. The type has reappeared in such strips as "Doonesbury" and "Peanuts." There is a change in the monsters appearing in today's comics, which tend to be funny and charming rather than terrifying. Even superheros are no longer spoof-proof and may be frustrated by inconsequential annoyances such as a rip in the costume at a crucial moment. *Mad* retains its popularity as it continues to make fun of all the heroes of society.

JUVENILE SERIES

Almost every American reader of the 20th century has cut his reading teeth on juvenile series books. One man and his children have been responsible for a large proportion of these books. Edward Stratemeyer began writing in the 1890s and continued at a fantastic pace, using several pseudonyms, until his death in 1930, just after he had created *Nancy Drew* and *The Hardy Boys*. His daughters (later only one daughter, Harriet Adams) continued their father's business, adding many new series. It is estimated that Stratemeyer had a hand in producing 1200 books. His closest rival is probably Enid Blyton in England, who has written over 400 books in a variety of series.

Stratemeyer sketched a plot in detail, chapter by chapter, and sent it to a ghostwriter to be fleshed out. Bit by bit he honed his formula down to a precise pattern designed to grab and hold a reader's interest. The book must set up danger, mystery, excitement on the first page. The middle of every chapter must have a dramatic high point. Each chapter must end with a cliff-hanging event. Early in each book there is a replay of the exciting stories before it in the series and in the last chapter there is a statement about even more exciting adventures to come in the next book. No one else has done so well with a formula in series after series.

ADULT ROMANCE AND ADVENTURE

Sentimental romances and adventure stories are generally written for adults; they are serialized in women's magazines before book publication or appear as paperback originals on newsstands. The older titles were

written by such writers as Zane Grey, Grace Livingston
Hill, Harold Bell Wright, and Gene Stratton Porter.
Modern books resemble earlier ones: there is usually
a great deal of action; the characters are "superlatives"
. . . the most beautiful or handsome, the most courageous, the most brilliant. The ending is happy and just
what the reader hopes for. It is not surprising that today
these books deal more frankly in eroticism than their
forerunners did.

The books are formulized. One prolific producer,
Barbara Cartland, has spelled it out: "My heroines are
always virgins. I don't approve of going to bed without the ring on the finger. It's so hard to find virgins
nowadays—that's why I set them in historical periods.
Now in the East, they understand virgins. I'm a riot
in India, Hong Kong, and Ceylon.

"My heroines always pray, and they are kind and
sweet to old people and dumb animals. They're very
well educated, or they read and read and so they
educate themselves.

"The heroes are raffish and wicked—just what we
all want. Then they get converted by the little woman.
She points out that he has a duty to other people, a
sort of mission, so he'll have things to do, perhaps a
great estate to administer, and so he won't be bored
by marriage."

MOVIE AND TV TIE-INS

In the past many books were made into movies or
radio and TV scripts. Recently the process has been
reversed: movies and TV scripts are rewritten as
books. The visual form stimulates a desire to repeat the
experiences through reading. The significance of tie-ins
depends on the significance of the original program
and on the skill of the author. Critics have pointed
out for years that the media—books, movies, and TV
—each have their limitations and conventions, and it is
seldom that a performance in one can be successfully
transferred to another. It takes the same perceptiveness

needed by a translator of a literary masterpiece from a foreign language.

Books are produced for the adolescent from TV series popular with teenagers. The programs center on teenage performers as fictionalized characters, moving through stereotyped situations in stereotyped settings to an expected ending. Any series has a limited life expectancy; the books based on them are similarly limited. They are easy to read, with a great deal of dialogue and profuse illustrations—stills from the TV performance. Reading records indicate that these books are the most popular category among teenagers.

Popular adult motion pictures, including some of the finest, are retold in novel form. Usually the cover features the name of the director with the statement "As based on the film by . . ." and only then is the name of the book author, usually a commercial writer, given.

Like other works of subliterature, these books are based on formula: the writer's perceptions of living do not appear in development of character or plot.

Adults may wonder why this subliterature fascinates youngsters, but on taking time to review their own pattern of growing-up-in-reading, they recall that they once had an enthusiasm for similar stories. The universality of the experience indicates that it is not the result of poor cultural background or inferior education, but is a necessary step in the maturation of reading taste. To help guide the child to better kinds of books it is essential to understand what in these materials has such compelling and general appeal.

THE APPEAL OF SUBLITERATURE

The books are cheap and easily accessible. Even adults tend to read what is at hand rather than make the effort to acquire something more interesting and worthwhile. Children do this even more. They browse through magazines their parents subscribe to, or pick up books and magazines sold at the neighborhood drugstore, the newsstand, or even the nearby supermarket. Subliterature generally sells at a reasonable price, which is important to the teenager. Today, paperback editions of good literature can provide youngsters with a better level of reading matter at low cost, and they are becoming more accessible in libraries and bookstores. Paperback book clubs that mail directly to students through the school's services are serving an important need.

Most patterned stories are easy to read. Reading ease does not lie in a simple vocabulary, short sentences, and uncomplicated ideas, but rather in that each story repeats a familiar pattern. Once you recognize who are the good guys and who are the bad guys, you can throw yourself into enjoying the intricate, unfolding action. You know that no matter how impossible the situation may be, the good guys will come out on top. There is an innate need in the young to know that right will triumph, and the reader races through the intricacies of the plot to see how it will happen.

The story pattern is that of all folk literature. Folk ballads and stories passing from generation to generation by word of mouth used the simplest, most appealing elements of storytelling. The tale moved from one peak of action to the next without the sophisticated buildup of information and motive that a more profound writer might use. Folk narrators seldom worried about the how or why of their stories: they were only interested in telling what. Subliterature too moves from climax to climax with little effort expended on description, characterization, motivation, or explanation. It is not surprising that young, half-formed readers respond to the same kind of stories that have always delighted and entertained the unsophisticated common people.

The most important reason for the appeal of subliterature is the high degree of wish fulfillment and escapism. The stories pitch readers into lives they secretly yearn to experience, but never can. They are written as if they were taking place right now, perhaps in a nearby town. And what lives the characters live! Not the humdrum one that most of us face each day, but lives filled with excitement, challenge, delight, and rewards, where everything works out for the best in the end.

Adolescents in real life are hampered by their parents and by the restrictions of society, but in subliterature they can experience the hopes they secretly dream of. If the stories have teenage protagonists, they are shown as ingenious, clever, perceptive, astounding the adults of their world—who are pictured as clumsy, inept, bumbling. The adventure tales present experiences that chill and thrill involving dashing, intelligent strong men and beautiful women. The young girl can feed her yearning for romance in the romantic novels with their unreal plane of emotional intensity, where beauty and right always win. Though the Cinderella story seldom occurs in real life, adults as well as teenagers relish living through the impossible dream with the characters.

Subliterature gives the appearance of literary sophistication and does not demean the self-esteem of the teenage reader. This is often accomplished through manipulation of vocabulary. While the level of the general narration is simple, the book uses a sprinkling of big words where simpler ones would do the job better. Examples are: "The *abode* of the *elect*"; "She had *divulged* the information"; "*engulfed* in the situation." Purple passages lull the reader into feeling he is reading something rich and splendid: "She was answering the call of youth to youth"; "The luxurious horror of the harem world"; "The path that was made by those that go one in front of the other, they found wide enough for two." To the naive reader, such language gives an appearance of sophistication.

The potential harm of subliterature is that it purveys an unrealistic, often false view of life and human relationships masquerading as reality. The point of view changes over time as cultural values change, reflecting rather than creating the popular shibboleths of the time. Through their structure subliterary books imply some questionable or false assumptions:

1. Adolescents are more perceptive than adults and

if left to their own devices can do a better job than older people.

2. Personality and personal appearance can undergo dramatic change in a short time. (During a summer vacation, for example.)

3. Premonitions turn out to be accurate.

4. There is a solution for every problem, often a simple one.

5. One's physical appearance indicates one's character. (The clean-cut, short-haired male is good—the swarthy, heavily bearded one is evil.)

6. Today's teens are a unique generation, the first ever to encounter their particular problems. Parents' experiences as young people have no validity for today's young because they happened long ago in a different world.

7. Sexual relations are the most important, worthwhile interaction possible between a man and a woman. The adolescent who has not achieved sexual intercourse is a failure.

8. It is the woman who pays for unwanted pregnancy. Men and boys escape without emotional scars.

9. Sexual activity is never shadowed by the possibility of venereal disease.

10. Love is the only prerequisite for an enduring relationship.

11. Girls are attracted to the macho male and boys to the feminine female.

12. Teenage life is experienced in a noisy, carefree, fun group. The solitary life is to be avoided at all costs.

13. People are either good or bad. Good always wins over bad and the wrongdoer will be punished materially or physically.

14. It is all right for the good to use duplicity or illegal techniques because they have the right goals.

15. The wealthy tend to be corrupt, evil schemers. Good people come from the lower or middle class.

16. Heroes tend to have Anglo-Saxon names: Nancy Drew, the Hardy Boys, Jack Armstrong. Villains have Italian, German, Russian, or Chinese names: Fu Manchu, Hooch Lazzo.

The same false assumptions about human life are prevalent in other media: television and radio programs, magazine stories, and the advertising that appears in the media. Certain assumptions are deeply embedded in our culture; endless repetition of them makes it probable that they will be passed to the next generation.

While continued reading of subliterature may distort the reader's beliefs about life through myriads of false assumptions, we do owe the material some gratitude for being an important, apparently inevitable step in the development of a reader as he moves toward literary sophistication:

Through reading subliterature, most of us for the first time encountered a story so exciting that we forgot we were reading. Any skill when first learned is conscious and labored. We are continually aware of the mechanics of what we are doing. Can you remember when you were first learning to type and had to think which letter was where and what finger to use to press it down? The skill has to move from the conscious to the subconscious level, so that action is automatic, if it is to be useful. Thus in reading for real enjoyment, we have to forget the process and focus on what the words are saying. For most individuals this transition is made while reading subliterature. Failure to make reading an automatic process may be the greatest cause of ultimate retardation and frustration in reading.

Subliterature embeds in us the literary conventions and patterns, but in skeletal form. Subliterature uses the basic structures of literature: suspense, foreshadowing, protagonists and antagonists, archetypal plot patterns and characterization. Because such elements are so clear in subliterature, they prepare the reader for their use with greater subtlety in real literature.

For most of us the first unconscious delight in reading comes through subliterature. This delight is fundamental to the development of appreciation of literature. Can you remember trying to vacuum the rugs while reading a Nancy Drew book or perhaps baby sitting for a younger brother and paying no attention to the job as you slipped deep into a romantic story by Zane Grey? Such moments can lead to one's becoming a committed reader.

We should not be concerned when children reach this stage, but only if they do not pass through it. Satire is a useful tool to help the teens see some of the glaring flaws of subliterature. You can make a game out of trying to pick out the telltale signs of the good guys and the bad guys, in TV scripts as well as in books. Sometimes you can challenge the teen to a guessing contest, taking turns after reading the first chapter at surmising what the outcome will be. You can become very accurate in figuring out the plot line in advance. When teens are set the task of creating their own comic or juvenile plot, they almost always use satire. *Mad* is a mass magazine that maintains its popularity by satirizing not only today's people, but the media.

What moves readers away from subliterature is the literary ladder. Take some type of book such as mysteries, and set yourself the task of placing the titles on a ladder, rung by rung from the lowest to the most superb. At the bottom we might put *Nancy Drew*. Somewhere in between would be *Deathman, Do Not Follow Me*. And at the top? Perhaps Henry James's *The Turn of the Screw*. In guiding a teen reader we should not attempt great leaps. We would never suggest the James novel to an ardent Nancy Drew enthusiast. Instead we would try to find something one step up, that avoids the gross misconceptions about human relations in Nancy Drew books. A Jay Bennett or Lois Duncan story might be the right prescription. Always consider what the young person wants in a story.

The adolescent or junior novels discussed next are usually the next step upward. They deal with problems, people, and events that hold young readers' attention, and are written with a degree of sensitivity and truth not present in subliterary fare.

5

The Adolescent Novel

For everything there is a season, and a time,
for every matter under heaven.
                                        —*Ecclesiastes* 3:1

In adolescent novels, writers direct their stories to the 12- to 18-year-olds; some children may also read these works, but the general reading adult will not. These are not series books. Characters may be carried through a trilogy or tetralogy as in Margaret Bell's story of a family's move to Alaska (*Watch for a Tall White Sail*) or Henry Felsen's Bertie books, but they are not carried through 30 or 40 books which keep repeating the same plot pattern. Thus most young adult novels present a unique, self-contained experience. A more important difference from series books lies in perceptions about teenage life and relationships as found in adolescent novels. They do not use the formulistic patterns of subliterature: that people are either good or bad, that character is revealed by physical appearance, that teenagers are more perceptive and competent than adults, and so on. They are written by serious writers, who try to evoke the feelings and emotions, the triumphs and failures, the tensions and releases that teens experience. Far from being Sunday-school-paper stories teaching moral truths and exhorting young people to live the moral life, many of the better books do not offer a pat solution to the characters' difficulties. Like good adult literature, the adolescent novel shows the whole spectrum of human life: the good and the bad; people's successes and failures; the indifferent, the vicious, the lost.

This kind of book developed slowly. Some of the earliest ones are literary accidents, which were written for an adult audience but were later claimed by teenage readers hungry for good books at their level of interest and ability. Mark Twain's *The Adventures of Huckleberry Finn,* a subtly crafted novel with many possible levels of interpretation, is one of these accidents; Louisa May Alcott's *Little Women* is another. Robert Louis Stevenson's tales of the sea are highly crafted novels which quickly became the property of the boy of 12 or 13; Jack London's stories of man and nature have a similar appeal.

Several hundred teenage novels are published each year. Some are stereotyped in plot, devoid of characterization, and dull in language; but a substantial number rise above mediocrity, and a handful are books of distinction. The best of each year's crop has accumulated to a respectable number, making a shelf of distinguished books for young people to read. Their success may be measured by how long they are in print: a good young adult book stays in print for years.

Seventeenth Summer, by Maureen Daly, published in 1942, is often credited with being the first junior novel of distinction and quality. Miss Daly was scarcely more than an adolescent herself when she wrote this book, which shows adolescent life, not from the adults' viewpoint as they look back, but rather from the adolescents' viewpoint. (The technique was also used in *Huckleberry Finn* and *Little Women.*) Her book succeeds because it parallels the emotions of many teenage girls. The story centers on Angie in the summer between her graduation from high school and her enrollment in college; it details her first romance. Because Angie has attended a girls' school, not until her 17th summer does she meet Jack, who delivers bakery goods in her small Wisconsin town. The book tells sympathetically of Angie's doubts, her fears, and the unwritten code that governs adolescent behavior. First, she is afraid that her family will disgrace her when Jack comes for the initial date, and after he arrives, she is afraid that Jack will not measure up to her family's standards. She discovers that her admired older sister has a poor reputation among the boys. And she tastes for the first time the experiences of the dating girl who can join the gang at the drugstore, the beer shack at the lake, the Coke spot . . . all off limits to the nondating girl. She is aware of the growing intensity of her feelings for Jack; yet she realizes she still wants to go to college. When Jack and Angie say their passionate goodbyes and vow always to love each other, she instinctively knows that the romance is over and that never again will they be able to recapture the feelings they have at that moment.

When the book was published it represented a whole new approach to the junior novel. Adolescent problems and reactions were taken as seriously as they are taken by the young people experiencing them. Furthermore, the book gave a truthful picture of adolescent life: beer parties and blanket parties; the girl who makes the mistake of dating a boy with a bad reputation; the sister who attempts to attract boys in all the wrong ways. Today the book seems rather innocent, but at the time many parents and teachers were startled and offended by its frank detailing of adolescent mores and actions.

The subtle understandings Maureen Daly imparts about human relationships are one element that lifts *Seventeenth Summer* above the ordinary. One couple has dated long and faithfully, not because of any real attraction, but because of the desperate need of the security of each other's attention. Angie's understanding at the end of the book that her romance is a passing thing, that the love she and Jack feel is not strong enough to survive separation, is a far cry from the easy solutions in patterned stories where love conquers all.

The response to *Seventeenth Summer* was immediate and has continued. Probably no book has captured the imagination of so many adolescent girls so quickly. The English teacher of the 1940s was inclined to bypass it and to continue proclaiming the merits of *Julius Caesar* and *Silas Marner,* but libraries found it impossible to keep copies of *Seventeenth Summer* on the shelves. One high-school library I visited in those days had 70 copies on its shelves and still had to maintain a waiting list for those who wanted to read or perhaps reread the book. The reaction of the readers was almost unanimous. They loved it. They begged the librarians for more . . . "just as good as this one." But it remained the lone specimen for years. The book is still read, but adolescent mores and experiences have changed so that the story now seems a little old-fashioned.

Today's young reader wants what *Seventeenth Summer* gave an earlier generation: an honest view of the adolescent world from the adolescent's point of view; a book that holds a mirror up to society so that readers can see their own world reflected in it. Books that succeed with the young reader are usually told in the subjective first person rather than the objective third person. They detail what it feels like to be ashamed of one's parents, to be afraid in a crowd, to be lonely and on the sidelines, to be pushed to the limits of one's physical endurance in a sports event and fail, to enter a contest and be only second best. The book that is psychologically oriented in plot line outlives the one that just tells what happened.

Today's books keep going deeper into the problems that have faced teenagers through the years, and that have become more confusing in today's world of changing mores. Developing sexuality has always been a major concern of teens. The attitude in *Seventeenth Summer* was one of hands off: "Sex is for adults." Recent books detail the trauma and confusion in almost a step-by-step report from the first stirrings of sexual interest to sexual intercourse. The fact that a sexual relationship is only temporary seems unimportant. Experiencing the act is what matters. Male and female homosexuality are now investigated in teenage books, and several deal with the effects of rape and incest. A common theme in recent books is the broken family and the teen's emotional ambivalence about separated parents.

In the past 30 years the number and merits of teenage novels have steadily increased, in several categories.

STORIES OF CONTEMPORARY TEENAGE LIFE

This largest category can be divided into junior novels with female and those with male protagonists. Only a few books, for example, *The Pigman* by Paul Zindel, have co-protagonists, a male and a female.

Besides the struggle of teenagers to come to terms with developmental tasks, other archetypal themes appear. One of them springs from a pseudo myth recounted by Aristophanes in Plato's *Symposium*. The original human beings are described as having one head, two faces, four legs, and four arms, as if two people were joined back to back. These creatures were of three sexes: male-male, male-female, and female-female. Each half had opposite characteristics from the other and together they formed a perfect whole. Terrible was the might and strength of these creatures; they attacked the gods and failed. As punishment for their audacity, Zeus ordered them cut in two; henceforth each half desires only to find his or her other self. Only when they are reunited can a whole identity be established.

A number of adolescent love stories unconsciously use this theme in describing male-female pairing. The female is of high social status, the male, low; or the female is intellectual, the male, physical; or the female is artistic, the male, athletic; or the female is introverted, the male, extraverted. Most of these stories are told from the girl's point of view, and at root they are not so much love stories as identity stories in which the pairs of opposite characteristics are fused.

Some of the best books built on the identity theme

have male-male protagonists experiencing a tightly knit friendship: *A Separate Peace* by John Knowles, or *The Chosen* by Chaim Potok.

Another theme is that of rites of passage, which are most clearly defined in the puberty ceremonies of primitive tribes. There, children are dragged from the protesting family by an adult. They are placed with others of the same age and initiated into the secrets of the tribe. Initiation involves pain, endurance, and a period of separation. Henceforth they live not with families but with peers. After a while, they are re-admitted to the society of adults, usually at a public ceremony. Thus the phases are separation, initiation, and incorporation.

A number of books like *The Pigman* deal with the period of separation: John and Lorraine are still clinging to childhood in their telephone games, roller skating, and dressing up in grown-ups clothes as if they were costumes. But more adolescent books deal with initiation, often beginning with some sort of alienation and struggling toward reconciliation. More and more such books see initiation in terms of sexual gropings and fulfillment. Only a few books really deal with the last stage, incorporation. Instead, there is a popular belief that teens find nothing desirable in contemporary society with which to be incorporated. Anne Frank comes to an acceptance of her family before tragedy strikes them all down. But Holden Caulfield in *The Catcher in the Rye* is more typical: he is still wandering at the end of the book, with no desire to join the adult world.

The book with a female protagonist has undergone a great change during the 1970s. It used to deal almost exclusively with building a relationship with the opposite sex. *Seventeenth Summer* is the prototype which one can see running through the books of Mary Stolz, Betty Cavanna, and Ann Emery. Today it is hard to find a real love story. There are many stories about sex, but few about love. The plot has become problem-centered, about drugs, unexpected pregnancy, homosexuality, troubles in the first years of married life, abused teenagers, alcoholism, mental crack-ups, and runaways.

Books with male protagonists generally do not treat such problems. They tend rather to deal with a boy's finding identity as he struggles through the adolescent years.

ANIMAL STORIES

The peak interest in animal stories is reached in late childhood, but there are teenage and even adult readers. Animal stories can be roughly divided into four categories.

Talking Animals

This is often the first kind of book the very young child encounters (*The Three Bears, The Three Billy Goats Gruff,* or *Peter Rabbit*). When the convention is used in adult literature, it becomes the animal fable. Swift used talking horses in *Gulliver's Travels* to satirize humanity's obnoxious foibles and George Orwell had rebellious farm animals take over in *Animal Farm* as a vehicle for ridiculing totalitarian societies.

Wild Animals in Nature

The story of the primitive animal in nature interests boys particularly. These books often use the life cycle as the framework, beginning with an animal's birth and ending with its death in old age. There are stories about wolves, bears, eagles, wild horses, foxes, raccoons, dogs, and even cats. Farley Mowat's *Never Cry Wolf,* for example, provides a close look at the ways of Arctic wolves who, Mowat discovers, are skillful providers and devoted protectors of their young.

The animal hero is usually the pick of the litter, sometimes the sole survivor; it grows into a superb physical specimen; it has an innate canniness that helps it survive. The relation of animals to humans and to the wild can take several forms. These books are generally built on the theme of the survival of the fittest. *The Call of the Wild* by Jack London details the adventures of an animal that is dognapped, sold as a sled dog to harsh masters in the Klondike, saved from a deadly beating by a decent man . . . then after serving his master until the master's death, returns to the wolves and the life of the wild.

Animal-Human Relationships

This type of animal story centers on the relationship between a person (usually a teenager) and an animal. In junior high, girls become enamored of horses and read all the stories they can find about them. One wonders why few boys are attracted to horse stories in this way. *Lassie Come Home* presents an almost symbiotic relationship between a teen and a dog. In the finest books of this category, the animal plays a part in a larger problem of human relations as in *Old Yeller, National Velvet,* and *The Yearling.* In some, the themes have such depth and the action is so compelling that you tend to forget they are animal stories.

Nonfiction Accounts

The mature reader is often fascinated by accounts of people detailing experiences with animals. James Herriot has written a series of books laced with delightful humorous touches about his veterinary practice in Yorkshire. (*All Creatures Great and Small; All Things Bright and Beautiful.*) Equally interesting are Farley Mowat's many perceptive and amusing observations about different animals, documented in well over a dozen books.

People have always been attracted to animal stories —but why, one might ask, should this reading interest peak at the end of childhood? It seems to be because these children are developing needs for status and awareness of their own ego. In real life, what is more gratifying than having an animal dependent on one for food, care, and affection? This feeling emanates vicariously in books. The animal tends to be personified (even in nonfictional accounts) that is, human emotions and qualities are attributed to it.

The animal is often a kind of superbeast: strong, courageous, intelligent. It chooses to give its affection to human beings, or if it does not, the reader unconsciously realizes that human beings, as a species superior to animals, have greater potential than even a superbeast.

For young readers the animal is a surrogate hero, a projection of what they would like to be: brave, high-spirited, loyal, wily, or mischievous. So animal heroes, like human heroes and heroines, project teenagers' wishes.

MYSTERY, SUSPENSE AND ADVENTURE

When teens of any age describe their concept of the ideal book, mystery, suspense, and adventure stories top the list. These are not three rigidly distinct categories: suspense is a common denominator of both mystery and adventure. Mysteries may have little adventure, and adventure stories may have little mystery, but both have suspense. Teenage mystery stories tend to have more female protagonists, and adventure stories, more male protagonists. This may be why girls tend to prefer mysteries and boys, adventure stories. These preferences may also be partly due to the settings: mysteries tend to have "neat," enclosed locations; adventures, large open ones. The mystery story appeals to the puzzle-solving instinct; the adventure story provides vicarious satisfaction as we see what people are capable of under great stress.

Lois Duncan's *I Know What You Did Last Summer* is a fine example of the teenage mystery-suspense. Four teens have been in a car involved in a hit-run accident: they pledge one another to secrecy. A year later, each gets a mysterious letter saying, "I know what you did last summer." The book details the psychological effects of the deed and the resulting relationship among the four guilty participants—as well as building up and resolving suspense.

Perhaps the best suspense adventure story is Robb White's *Deathwatch*, a nerve-tingling tale of man hunting man. A teenage guide has seen his client, a middle-aged man, commit murder. His employer strips him, sends him off into the desert, and gives him an hour's start before starting after him to hunt him down.

BOOKS ABOUT FOREIGN CULTURES

The first great flood of books for teenagers was in the United States; but since World War II, writers all over the world have been creating a similar literature for their own young people. This is said to be the golden age of teenage literature in Australia and Sweden, and masses of books published in England for their own teens are crossing the Atlantic to be read by American adolescents. Some German, French, Norwegian, Swedish, Czech, and Russian teen books are reaching our shores via translation. In addition, many books written by American authors who have often lived in other parts of the world and have an intimate knowledge of the culture, people, and locale, have a foreign setting and characters. *The Shadow of a Bull* by Maia Wojciechowska is an American author's evocation of a teenager's problem with traditional expectations in Spain.

Translated books are difficult for the American teenager and are therefore less popular than books written by Americans. A German author does not have to explain to young Germans the customs, institutions, and slang they are already familiar with, but the American teen bogs down in unfamiliar details and loses the story line. Even in British books a term like "estate living" suggests a wealthy person to the American reader when it actually refers to government housing for the poor built on estates.

However, translated books give a better sense of the similarities of teenagers the world around. The American book about a foreign culture provides the needed informational exposition, but it also tends unconsciously to contribute to a sense of cultural distinctiveness. Writing as an outsider, the American tends to fall back on cultural stereotypes, which may unfairly color the characterizations. You will find it easy to see this if you read a British book written by an Englishman about American teenagers in an American setting.

Thus teachers and librarians should encourage the young to read translations as an avenue to intimate understanding of another culture. It is important to recommend up-to-date books, so that the young reader does not build an outmoded picture of a foreign culture.

BOOKS WITH HISTORICAL BACKGROUNDS

Over 50 percent of teenage books have historical settings, although teenagers prefer contemporary settings. Obviously, writers are more interested in history than teenagers are. To succeed, a historical book must have elements of appeal, such as adventure, that transcend the period.

All books become historical after a while, as their setting is outdated. *Little Women* (end of the 19th century) and *Seventeenth Summer* (World War II) were contemporary when published, but no longer are. In the real historical book, the author takes a period other than his own. Dickens's *A Tale of Two Cities* (1859) is historical since Dickens was writing about the 1790s. Raucher's *Summer of '42* was written almost 30 years after *Seventeenth Summer*, so it is the Raucher book that is truly a reconstruction.

The most successful book of this kind is probably *Johnny Tremain* by Esther Forbes. After writing her great biography, *Paul Revere and the World He Lived In,* she apparently had so many tag ends of details left over that she converted them into a fictional account of a teenage silversmith apprentice at the onset of the American Revolution. Using vivid characters, she presents the Tories, the Hessians, and a group of historical figures in a moving account of the times. The characters and events are mainly background for the problems and emotions of a confused teenager.

There is a small group of teens who read historical books for the history in them. Certain periods have a glamour that intrigues teenagers: The kingdoms of ancient Egypt, the golden age in Greece, the era of knights and castles, Victorian England, the antebellum South, the early American West. Recently there have been many nostalgic books about the 20th century since World War I: the twenties, the depression, the forties, the fifties. In books and on TV we see the "good old days" when life was simpler and cozier.

Girls tend to savor the quality of life of a period, while boys read mainly for old-time excitement and adventure. Still, historical novels color the teenager's concepts of social as well as political history; therefore, historical accuracy is important.

SPORTS STORIES

Boys and girls want two things from sports stories: an account of how a person has overcome odds to succeed in a sport; and a description of sports action that makes them feel like participants. As one young man put it: "I want to feel the grass under my golf shoes when I read about golf." Sometimes readers may be teenagers who are unsuccessful at sports. The book provides a wish-fulfilling experience.

Since sportswriters are well aware of these two reader needs, sports books tend to be stereotyped, with one book reading much like another.

The best of sports books deal with a theme bigger than physical activity. The great master of this form was John R. Tunis, who wrote one great story after another until he was over 80. One of his last books, *His Enemy, His Friend,* may be his masterpiece. The story is of a man and his conscience; the sport is soccer. Hans, a star player, is the German officer in charge of a small French village during the occupation in World War II. Having a French mother, he feels very close with the villagers and they with him. He teaches the small boys soccer. But then he is ordered to take hostages and execute them for the assassination of a German officer, and in spite of his attempt to disobey orders, the French are put to death. After the war he meets one of his proteges in a championship match between the French and German teams. Another distinguished sports story is *The Contender,* by Robert Lipsyte. A school dropout decides to train as a boxer and dreams of returning to Harlem as a great success. He learns that one needs to be a contender in life as well as in sports.

In recent years, sportwriters and readers seem to be turning more to the lives of contemporary sports heroes (chapter 11). It is not certain whether readers are influencing the writers toward this change, or if writers are influencing the readers.

The teenage novels described in this chapter are quite different from subliterature like *Tom Swift, Nancy Drew, Hardy Boys,* and *Tarzan.* Since few adults have read the newer variety, they do not realize that the modern teenage novel is as different from the series book as *Gone With the Wind* is different from a simple romance. The best adolescent books are seriously crafted, written by competent, dedicated writers who use subtlety in characterization, logical development of plot lines, and significant themes that are important to the teenager. In countless libraries and classrooms it is this body of literature that bridges the gap between children's literature and subliterature, and serious adult literature. Without the adolescent novel, many potential readers would fall into the chasm of nonreading.

Bibliography

ABOUT YOUNG WOMEN

Banks, L. R.: *My Darling Villian.* Harper & Row, 1977.
　　Class consciousness and parental discord are at the

core of this romantic story set in contemporary England, where a 15-year-old girl's first love sparks her first adult decision.

Bach, Alice: *Mollie Make-Believe*. Harper & Row, 1974. Dell. Her beloved grandmother's death, the family's formal grief, and a new boyfriend give Mollie a new perspective on her status-seeking family.

Baird, Marie-Therese: *A Lesson in Love*. G. K. Hall, 1974. Popular Library. The value of friendship is explored through the relationship of Sally Norton, a precocious but troubled 15-year-old, and Ashley Sinclair, aged portraitist who is anxious to help the girl he knows as Sarah become an adult.

Beckman, Gunnel: *Admission to the Feast*. Holt, Rinehart and Winston, 1972. Dell. A 19-year-old girl searches for life's meaning when she discovers that she is dying from leukemia.

————: *Mia Alone*. Viking Press, 1975. Dell. Despite her lover's wish to marry, Mia considers an abortion rather than the risk of an unhappy marriage like that of her parents.

Bell, Margaret E.: *Watch for a Tall White Sail*. William Morrow, 1948. Morrow Junior Books. The story of a 16-year-old girl's adjustment to pioneer life in Alaska in the 1880s.

Blume, Judy: *Are You There God? It's Me Margaret*. Bradbury Press, 1970. Dell. The joys, fears and uncertainties that surround a young girl's approaching adolescence are humorously and sensitively captured in this novel.

————: *It's Not the End of the World*. Bradbury Press, 1972. Bantam Books. Judy Blume explores the effects of divorce on a family—in particular, on 12-year-old Karen Newman. She delineates Karen's emotions: bewilderment, anxiety, and fear that the dissolution of her parents' marriage will be "the end of the world."

Brancato, Robin: *Something Left to Lose*. Alfred A. Knopf, 1976. Bantam Books. As Jane Ann learns that her friend isn't all that perfect and that underneath Robbie's sarcasm lies a deep hurt and fear, she accepts the fact that her "doormat" qualities have not helped her friends or herself.

Bridgers, Sue Ellen: *All Together Now*. Alfred A. Knopf, 1978. Twelve-year-old Casey Flanagan spends the summer in a rural southern town, where she becomes the catalyst that causes the grown-ups around her to sort out their own emotions.

————: *Home Before Dark*. Alfred A. Knopf, 1976. Bantam Books. When her father takes his migrant family back to his childhood home in Florida, 14-year-old Stella Willis is determined to put down roots and have a home for the first time in her life.

Christman, Elizabeth: *A Nice Italian Girl*. Dodd, Mead, 1976. Bantam Books. A young girl finds herself pregnant, the victim of a group who sire children to order. She refuses to give up her baby despite the battle she will face.

Cleaver, Vera and Bill: *Queen of Hearts*. J. B. Lippincott, 1978. Bantam Books. Two children care for their sick and unpleasant grandmother, and learn to love her despite her crabbiness.

————: *Trial Valley*. J. B. Lippincott, 1977. Bantam Books. An abandoned child found in the woods near Mary Call's southern Appalachian home brings more complications to the life of the 16-year-old who is struggling to raise a younger brother and sister.

————: *Where the Lilies Bloom*. J. B. Lippincott, 1969. New American Library. Fourteen-year-old Mary Call Luther becomes "mother" to her siblings after their father's death.

Coles, Robert: *Riding Free*. Atlantic Monthly Press, 1973. Two runaway 14-year-old girls hitchhike to Chicago, encountering some boring and some frightening people along the way.

Colman, Hila: *After the Wedding*. William Morrow, 1975. After the excitement of the wedding, a young couple slowly discover their very different goals, and eventually divorce.

————: *The Amazing Miss Laura*. William Morrow, 1976. Josie takes a summer job as a maid-companion to a wealthy elderly woman and discovers the indignity of old age.

Conford, Ellen: *The Alfred G. Graebner Memorial High School Handbook of Rules and Regulations*. Little, Brown, 1976. Archway Paperbacks. Humorous episodes of a girl's first year in high school as she copes with the school's unbelievable official handbook of regulations.

Corcoran, Barbara: *A Dance to Still Music.* Atheneum, 1974. Runaway Margaret is befriended by a perceptive widow who helps her come to terms with her deafness.

————: *Hey, That's My Soul You're Stomping On.* Atheneum, 1978. While her parents discuss a possible divorce, 16-year-old Rachel spends a summer with her grandparents and realizes everyone has problems, some much more serious than hers.

Daly, Maureen: *Seventeenth Summer.* Dodd, Mead, 1942. Pocket Books. A major step forward for the adolescent novel; the sensitive story of a young girl's summer between high school and college, her first real love, and its bittersweet end. The first book to treat teenagers' strong emotions seriously.

Danziger, Paul: *The Cat Ate My Gymsuit.* Delacorte Press, 1974. Dell. A teenager with a negative self-image and 100 excuses for not dressing for gym, learns to think positively about herself.

Dizenzo, Patricia: *Phoebe.* McGraw-Hill, 1970. Bantam Books. This is a novel about Phoebe, a 16-year-old girl who must find the maturity and courage to admit her pregnancy to her parents, her boyfriend—and herself.

Elfman, Blossom: *The Girls of Huntington House.* Houghton Mifflin, 1972. Bantam Books. "What can you teach pregnant girls that they do not already know?" ask Blossom's friends when they learn she has accepted a teaching assignment in a home for unwed mothers.

————: *A House for Jonnie O.* Houghton Mifflin, 1977. Bantam Books. Jonnie and her three friends—students at a school for pregnant unmarried teenagers—search for a dream house where they can be independent and support one another and their babies.

Gauch, Patricia L.: *The Green of Me.* G. P. Putnam's Sons, 1978. Traveling to meet her teenage sweetheart, Jennifer thinks back to moments of joy and pain during her growing years.

Go Ask Alice. Avon Books, 1972. The true and painful diary of a young girl who accidentally fell into the contemporary drug trap by way of a teenage acid party.

Greene, Betty: *Morning is a Long Time Coming*. Dial Press, 1978. The sequel to *The Summer of My German Soldier* follows Patty Bergen, who, after her high-school graduation, travels to Europe to find Anton's mother and resolve her problems.

————: *The Summer of My German Soldier*. Dial Press, 1973. Bantam Books. Sheltering an escaped prisoner of war is the beginning of some shattering experiences for a 12-year-old girl in Arkansas.

Guy, Rosa: *The Friends*. Holt, Rinehart and Winston, 1973. Bantam Books. Rejected by her classmates because she "talks funny," Phyllisia Cathy, a young West Indian girl, becomes friends with poor, frazzled Edith, the only one who will accept her.

————: *Ruby*. Viking Press, 1976. Bantam Books. A lonely West Indian girl in Harlem finds solace in a young lesbian relationship with a strong-willed black student she meets at school.

Hamilton, Virginia: *Arilla Sun Down*. Greenwillow Books, 1976. Dell. A seventh-grader from a small Ohio town, Arilla Mooning Running Adams, comes from an interracial background—part black, part Indian. When she saves the life of her beloved older brother, Sun, Arilla emerges with an identity of her own and a new name to match—Arilla Sun Down.

Hautzig, Deborah: *Hey, Dollface*. Greenwillow Books, 1978. Bantam Books. Val and Chloe's friendship develops into more than the usual teenage girl "best friends" phase. It's funny, tender, and perceptive.

Head, Ann: *Mr. and Mrs. Bo Jo Jones*. G. P. Putnam's Sons, 1967. New American Library. July and Bo Jo marry in haste when they discover that she is pregnant. Determined to combat the dismal odds against teenage marriage, they learn to share and grow in their new roles.

Hunter, Mollie: *A Sound of Chariots*. Harper & Row, 1972. Avon Books. In the early decades of this century, a Scottish girl overcomes poverty and family tragedy in her determination to become a writer.

————: *The Third Eye*. Harper & Row, 1979. "Tell me, Jinty, have you ever heard talk about the Ballinford doom?" The question sounds again in Jinty's mind as she waits to give evidence in the earl of Ballinford's death.

Jones, Adrienne: *So Nothing Is Forever.* Houghton-Mifflin, 1974. The children of an interracial marriage struggle to stay together after their parents' sudden death.

Kerr, M. E.: *Is That You, Miss Blue?* Harper & Row, 1975. Dell. The ups and downs in the lives of three teenage girls in a boarding school where the unforgettable Miss Blue was "the best teacher" in spite of her unusual habits.

Klein, Norma: *It's OK If You Don't Love Me.* Dial Press, 1977. Fawcett Books. Jody introduces Lyle to sex, though they realize their relationship is temporary.

———: *Sunshine.* Holt, Rinehart and Winston, 1975. Avon Books. The transcript of tape recordings made by a young dying mother for her infant daughter to play when she grows up.

Koehn, Ilse: *Mischling, Second Degree: My Childhood in Nazi Germany.* Greenwillow Books, 1977. Bantam Books. Unaware of her Jewish heritage, 6-year-old Ilse Koehn spent the war years as a member of the Hitler Youth.

Konecky, Edith: *Allegra Maud Goldman.* Harper & Row, 1976. Dell. A sensitive, funny, and at times sad story of a precocious, strong-willed girl's struggle to find her identity while growing up in Brooklyn during the 1930s.

Konigsburg, E. L.: *Father's Arcane Daughter.* Atheneum, 1976. The overprotected children of wealthy parents get their chance to grow up normally because of the efforts of their mysterious half-sister.

Lowry, Lois: *A Summer to Die.* Houghton Mifflin, 1977. Bantam Books. Thirteen-year-old Meg poignantly relates the story of her older sister's death from leukemia.

Madison, Winifred: *Growing Up in a Hurry.* Little, Brown, 1973. Archway Paperbacks. Lonely and alienated from her family, Karen finds solace in her love for a Japanese boy until she discovers she is pregnant and must face the problem alone.

Mathis, Sharon B.: *Listen for the Fig Tree.* Viking Press, 1974. Avon Books. Blind, 15-year-old Muffin takes care of her mother after her father is murdered.

Mazer, Norma F.: *Dear Bill, Remember Me? And Other Stories*. Delacorte Press, 1976. Dell. Eight short stories range from a sensitive portrayal of an 18-year-old dying from cancer to the tale of a turn-of-the-century immigrant who defied tradition by not getting married.

————: *A Figure of Speech*. Dell, 1975. The special relationship between Jenny and her grandfather leads to tragedy when Jenny's parents want to place him in a home for senior citizens.

Mohr, Nicholas: *Nilda*. Harper & Row, 1973. Bantam Books. Nilda, who lives with her large and affectionate family in Spanish Harlem, begins the painful process of growing up.

Neufeld, John: *Lisa Bright and Dark*. New American Library, 1970. Lisa's dark days increase when her parents refuse to recognize her growing madness and only her teenage friends are there to help her.

Peck, Richard: *Are You in the House Alone?* Viking Press, 1976. Dell. After receiving a series of threatening notes, Gail Osbourne is raped by one of the most popular boys at her school—but no one believes her.

————: *Don't Look and It Won't Hurt*. Holt, Rinehart and Winston, 1962. Avon Books. An adolescent girl grows toward maturity as she confronts the problems of family life.

————: *Representing Super Doll*. Viking Press, 1974. Avon Books. Two Indiana girls, one eagerly and one reluctantly, enter the U.S. Teen Super Doll contest.

————: *Through a Brief Darkness*. Viking Press, 1973. Avon Books. Forced to ask herself if her father was indeed a criminal, Karen comes to rely on her own instincts and judgments.

Pfeffer, Susan B.: *Marly the Kid*. Doubleday, 1975. Dell. Plump and plain Marly stands up for her rights when she runs up against an unreasonable, sexist history teacher.

Reiss, Johanna: *The Upstairs Room*. Thomas Y. Crowell, 1976. Bantam Books. An autobiographical novel depicting the trials of the author's Dutch-Jewish family during World War II. The youngest of three daughters, Annie, tells how she and her sister Sini hid for more than two years in the upstairs room of the peasant Oosterveld family.

Ruby, Lois: *Arriving at a Place You've Never Left*. Dial Press, 1977. Seven moving short stories dealing with such personal crises as coping with a mother's nervous breakdown, being 17, pregnant, and unmarried, and facing anti-Semitism.

Samuels, Gertrude: *Run, Shelley, Run!* Thomas Y. Crowell, 1974. New American Library. Sixteen-year-old Shelley runs from an alcoholic mother, an intolerable training school, and an arrest, searching for a place to live in dignity.

Scoppettone, Sandra: *Happy Endings Are All Alike*. Harper & Row, 1978. Janet and Peggy love each other. When Janet is raped by a disturbed teenage boy who wants to punish her, the nature of the girls' relationship comes out.

————: *The Late, Great Me*. G. P. Putnam's Sons, 1976. Bantam Books. Geri uses alcohol to escape from the loneliness of her junior-high years until the tragic results send her seeking help.

————: *Trying Hard to Hear You*. Harper & Row, 1974. Bantam Books. Camilla Crawford discovers that her longtime friend, the boy next door, is a homosexual.

Wersba, Barbara: *Tunes for a Small Harmonica*. Harper & Row, 1976. J. F. McAllister, a constant source of worry to everyone, masters the harmonica and uses her talents to help a poetry teacher with whom she is in love.

Wilkinson, Brenda: *Ludell and Willie*. Harper & Row, 1977. Bantam Books. Two high-school seniors from a poor black Georgia community fall in love but are separated because of a family tragedy. (Sequel to *Ludell*. Harper & Row, 1975).

Windsor, Patricia: *Diving for Roses*. Harper & Row, 1976. A 17-year-old girl with an alcoholic mother searches for and discovers her own strengths as she faces responsibilities, which include her decision to keep her baby.

————: *The Summer Before*. Harper & Row, 1973. Dell. Alexandra makes her way back to normalcy after the traumatic death of Bradley the summer before.

Wolitzer, Hilma: *Out of Love*. Farrar, Strauss and Giroux, 1976. A young girl tries to cope with her parents' divorce and her father's remarriage, and to understand what love really is.

Yep, Laurence: *Child of the Owl*. Harper & Row, 1977. Dell. When she is sent to live with her grandmother in San Francisco's Chinatown, Casey learns about her Chinese heritage.

Zindel, Paul: *My Darling, My Hamburger*. Harper & Row, 1969. Bantam Books. Four high-school friends love and support each other through the crisis of Liz's pregnancy and abortion.

ABOUT YOUNG MEN

Ames, Mildred: *Without Hats, Who Can Tell the Good Guys?* E. P. Dutton, 1976. Convinced that he will never get used to his new foster family, a young boy dreams of the day his father will come to take him away.

Angier, Bradford, and Barbara Corcoran: *Ask For Love and They Give You Rice Pudding*. Houghton Mifflin, 1977. Bantam Books. A wealthy but unloved teenage boy discovers the journal of his father, who left many years ago, and through it learns a lot about himself and others.

Bethancourt, T. Ernesto: *The Mortal Instruments*. Holiday House, 1977. Bantam Books. A teenage boy from Spanish Harlem develops ESP and other strange powers; he eventually becomes a threat to the entire planet.

————:*New York City, Too Far From Tampa Blues*. Holiday House, 1975. Bantam Books. Newly arrived from Florida with his family, a Spanish-American boy tells of his experiences living in Brooklyn and his friendship with an Italian boy who shares his passion for music.

Blume, Judy: *Then Again, Maybe I Won't*. Bradbury Press, 1971. Dell. Joel's problems of dealing with adolescence are further compounded when his family moves from their old comfortable environment to a strange wealthy area.

Bower, George: *November, December*. E. P. Dutton, 1977. Bantam Books. B.D. experiences the trauma of a broken first love affair, the discovery of his parents' incompatibility, and his father's death in a two-month period during his freshman year in college.

Bradford, Richard: *Red Sky at Morning*. J. B. Lippincott, 1972. Pocket Books. When his father goes off to World War II, Josh and his mother are sent to Sagrado, New

Mexico, where life is very different from their native Mobile, Alabama.

Childress, Alice: *A Hero Ain't Nothing But a Sandwich.* Coward, McCann & Geoghegan, 1973. Avon Books. Benjie, a 13-year-old in Harlem, cannot face the reality of his drug addiction or the realization that someone cares about him.

Cormier, Robert: *The Chocolate War.* Pantheon Books, 1974. Dell. "Sweets" abound at Trinity High while a schoolmaster feasts on his students' fear. A bitter story of one student's resistance and the high price he paid.

————: *I Am the Cheese.* Pantheon Books, 1977. Dell. A victim of amnesia and under the influence of drugs, teenage Adam searches through haunting memories that must not be recalled or revealed if he is to survive.

Covert, Paul: *Cages.* Liveright, 1971. Two very different teenage boys form an intense friendship and run into the cruelty of small-town gossip.

Crawford, Charles P.: *Letter Perfect.* E. P. Dutton, 1977. Three boys plan the perfect crime against their high-school English teacher, but one is plagued by moral doubts.

Cunningham, Julia: *Come to the Edge.* Pantheon Books, 1977. Avon Books. Gravel, a 14-year-old without a single emotional tie to another person, runs away from an orphanage and becomes drawn strangely—even dangerously—into the lives of some "crippled" adults.

Dixon, Paige: *May I Cross Your Golden River?* Atheneum, 1975. The rare terminal disease which killed Lou Gehrig was also killing 18-year-old Jordan, but with his family's support he tried to live a normal life.

Donovan, John: *I'll Get There: It Better Be Worth The Trip.* Harper & Row, 1969. Dell. The death of Davey's beloved grandmother precipitates his move to New York City apartment life, where he must learn to adjust.

————: *Remove Protective Coating a Little at a Time.* Dell, 1975. A lonely, wealthy New York City boy makes friends with a 72-year-old woman who has to scrounge and "con" to survive.

Eyerly, Jeanette: *He's My Baby Too.* J. B. Lippincott, 1977. Pocket Books. Charles discovers unusual feelings about a baby and himself when his casual affair produces a child whose mother intends to put it up for adoption.

————: *See Dave Run.* J. B. Lippincott, 1978. Fifteen-year-old Dave Hendry runs away to Colorado. His story is narrated by the people who have known him.

Felsen, Henry Gregor: *Hot Rod.* E. P. Dutton, 1950. Bantam Books. Bud Crayne's love of cars and his skill with them give him his sole sense of status among his peers.

Hall, Lynn: *Sticks and Stones.* Follett, 1977. Dell. Sixteen and a newcomer to tiny Buck Creek, Iowa, Tom Naylor suddenly realizes that the hostility of his fellow students and teachers is due to his friendship with Ward Alex.

Hentoff, Nat: *Jazz Country.* Harper & Row, 1965. Sixteen-year-old Tom finds that his dream of entering the top ranks of jazz musicians in New York must be deferred until he has learned more about life.

Highwater, Jamake: *Anpao: An American Indian Odyssey.* J. B. Lippincott, 1977. The story of a brave young man who undertakes a quest that takes him across the face of the American Indian's ancient world.

Hinton, S. E.: *The Outsiders.* Viking Press, 1967. Dell. Ponyboy and Johnnym both members of the Greasers, hide from the police after a "soc" from the opposing rich gang is killed.

————: *Rumblefish.* Delacorte Press, 1975. Brothers caught in an environment of violence are as incapable of changing their behavior as are fighting fish who battle to the death.

————: *That Was Then, This is Now.* Viking Press, 1971. Dell. In this sequel to *The Outsiders,* Bryon and Mark are still inseparable at 16, but Bryon is beginning to care about people while Mark continues to hot-wire cars, steal, and do things for kicks.

Holland, Isabelle: *The Man Without a Face.* J. B. Lippincott, 1972. Bantam Books. Chuck learns about love during his 14th summer when he befriends a man whose face is badly disfigured.

Holman, Felice: *Slake's Limbo.* Charles Scribner's Sons, 1974. Aremis Slake at age 13 takes to the New York city subways as a refuge from an abusive home life and an oppressive school system.

Hotchner, A. E.: *Looking for Miracles: A Memoir About Loving.* Harper & Row, 1975. Results are hilarious and poignant when Aaron masquerades as an experienced camp counselor to get himself and his young brother into a summer camp.

Joran, June: *His Own Where*. Thomas Y. Crowell, 1971. Dell. Buddy and Angela gain strength through their love to face the struggle of city life in the ghetto.

Kerr, M. E.: *Dinky Hocker Shoots Smack*. Harper & Row, 1972. Dell. Forced to give up her cat, Tucker bestows it on a 14-year-old overweight girl called Dinky and becomes involved in her problems.

————: *Gentlehands*. Harper & Row, 1978. Bantam Books. Sixteen-year-old Buddy Boyle, son of working-class parents, is in love with Skye Pennington. To impress her, Buddy takes her to visit his grandfather, a cultivated, gentle German emigrant—who turns out to be a wanted Nazi, the infamous SS officer at Auschwitz known ironically as "Gentlehands."

————: *If I Love You, Am I Trapped Forever?* Harper & Row, 1973. Dell. High-school hero Alan Bennett becomes acquainted with the many faces of love.

Krumgold, Joseph: *And Now Miguel*. Thomas Y. Crowell, 1953. A memorable story of a family of New Mexican sheepherders, in which Miguel tells of his great longing to accompany men and sheep to summer pasture and be recognized as an adult.

————: *Onion John*. Thomas Y. Crowell, 1959. A penetrating picture of a boy growing up, told with perception and humor.

Lee, Mildred: *Fog*. Seabury Press, 1972. Dell. An adolescent boy growing up in South Town finds his comfortable life suddenly disrupted when he faces responsibilities and challenges entering the adult world.

Le Guin, Ursula K.: *Very Far Away From Anywhere Else*. Atheneum, 1976. Bantam Books. An intellectually-inclined teenager finds companionship with a music-loving girl.

Levitin, Sonia: *The Mark of Conte*. Atheneum, 1976. Conte Mark wages war against his high-school computer in an effort to make a mark on the school and graduate in two years instead of four.

Lipsyte, Robert: *One Fat Summer*. Harper & Row, 1977. Bantam Books. Overweight Bobby Marks confronts the ridicule of friends and sheds his excess pounds in a comical story of his last fat summer.

Mathis, Sharon B.: *Teacup Full of Roses*. Viking Press, 1972. Avon Books. Three brothers try to rise above their ghetto environment and find meaning in their lives.

Mojtabai, A. G.: *The Four Hundred Eels of Sigmund Freud*. Simon and Schuster, 1976. Summer at a scientific community for gifted teenagers ends in a tragedy for Isaiah, the rebel among them who prefers music to science.

Ney, John: *Ox Goes North*. Harper & Row, 1973. At a Vermont summer camp, Ox learns that his bunkmate's grandparents are attempting to steal his trust fund. Ox plans a rescue mission on behalf of his friend.

Peck, Robert Newton: *A Day No Pigs Would Die*. Alfred A. Knopf, 1972. Dell. Through his relationship with his hard-working father, 12-year-old Rob learns to cope with the harshness of Shaker life and emerges a mature individual.

————: *Millie's Boy*. Alfred A. Knopf, 1973. A boy searches for his real father and encounters many adventures along the way.

Platt, Kin: *The Boy Who Could Make Himself Disappear*. Dell, 1971. A move to New York, his parents' divorce, and his speech impediment are too much for a teenager who retreats from reality.

————: *Headman*. Greenwillow Books, 1975. Dell. Told in swift, sharp, and realistic street language is Owen's desperate fight for survival through the streets of Los Angeles, in a "rehabilitative" youth camp and as headman of a gang.

Powers, John R.: *Do Black Patent Leather Shoes Really Reflect Up?* Contemporary Books, 1975. Popular Library. Doing battle with an army of pimples, being a teenager, and spending four years in a southside Chicago high school far exceed Eddie's worst fears.

Travers, James and A. Davis: *I Can Stop Any Time I Want*. Prentice-Hall, 1974. Dell. Graham turns to alcohol in an attempt to escape the hard-drug scene.

Wersba, Barbara: *Run Softly, Go Fast*. Atheneum, 1970. Bantam Books. David Marks uses his diary to attempt to integrate his love/hate relationship with his father.

Wier, Ester: *Loner*. David McKay, 1963. A nameless abandoned boy suffers the harshness of a migrant worker's life until he finds a stopping place on a Montana sheep ranch.

Zindel, Paul: *Confessions of a Teenage Baboon*. Harper & Row, 1977. Bantam Books. Sixteen-year-old Chris Boyd, dominated by an overbearing mother, gains self-confidence and control over his life after a tragic encounter with a 30-year-old misfit who befriends the lonely teenager.

————: *The Pigman*. Harper & Row, 1968. Bantam Books. John and Lorraine, sophomores in high school, tell the tragic story of their friendship with a lonely old man whom they love and destroy.

ANIMAL STORIES

Aaron, Chester: *An American Ghost*. Harcourt Brace Jovanovich, 1973. Trapped by a flood on the Mississippi River, Albie finds that his sole companion is a mountain lion.

Adamson, Joy: *Born Free: A Lioness of Two Worlds*. Pantheon Books, 1960. Elsa, an orphan lion cub, is reared by the Adamsons for three years and after learning the ways of her own kind is returned to the wild.

Aldridge, James: *The Marvelous Mongolian*. Little, Brown, 1974. Tachi, a spirited wild stallion, makes his way, despite rough terrain and innumerable dangers, from a nature reserve in Wales back to his Mongolian mountains with a Welsh pony mare he adopts.

Armstrong, William: *Sounder*. Harper & Row, 1969. A poverty-stricken black family's dog, Sounder, is severely injured by white men who come to arrest the father for stealing food.

Bagnold, Enid: *National Velvet*. William Morrow, 1949. Pocket Books. A passionate horse fan disguises herself as a male jockey to ride in the National Steeplechase in England.

Beatty, John and Patricia: *Holdfast*. William Morrow, 1972. Catriona Burke, daughter of an Irish rebel, is taken to Elizabethan England accompanied by her faithful Irish wolfhound, Holdfast. They are separated and Holdfast goes on to become London's best-known bear- and bullbaiter before they are reunited.

Beatty, Patricia: *How Many Miles to Sundown*. William Morrow, 1974. The saga of two boys and a girl traveling through the wilds of the Southwest of the 1880s accompanied by a pet steer.

Bethancourt, T. Ernesto: *The Dog Days of Arthur Cane*. Holiday House, 1976. Ridiculing an African exchange student about his beliefs in black magic results in the hero being turned into a dog.

Burnford, Shelia: *Bel Ria*. Atlantic Monthly Press, 1978. Bantam Books. Many people's lives are enriched by their encounters with a performing dog that wanders through France and England during World War II.

————: *The Incredible Journey*. Atlantic Monthly Press, 1961. Bantam Books. Realistically told story of the struggle for survival of two dogs and a cat on their 400-mile journey through the Canadian wilderness to their home.

Canning, Victor: *Flight of the Grey Goose*. William Morrow, 1973. A 16-year-old running from a juvenile home finds a happy refuge caring for injured wildlife on a Scottish estate.

Caras, Roger: *Monarch of Deadman Bay*. Penguin Books, 1977. A novelistic treatment of the life of a bear from conception to death.

Clarkson, Ewan: *In the Shadow of the Falcon*. E. P. Dutton, 1973. A year in the life of two falcons, Frika and Freya, as they struggle to raise offspring and survive.

Crisler, Lois: *Arctic Wild*. Harper & Row, 1973. In the strange, dangerous Alaskan wilderness, Lois and Herb Crisler film wildlife for Walt Disney. Lois writes about the caribou herds and a litter of wolf cubs that she adopts.

Eckert, Allan W.: *The Crossbreed*. Little, Brown, 1968. The offspring of an abused cat who escapes to the wild and mates with a bobcat is caught between two worlds.

Ellis, Mel: *The Wild Horse Killers*. Holt, Rinehart and Winston, 1976. To save a herd of wild mustangs from horse killers, 18-year-old Sandra attempts to lead them several hundred miles across desert and mountains to safety on federal lands.

Gallico, Paul and Suzanne Szasz: *Silent Miaow*. Crown, 1964. A household cat's view of humans is presented as a manual for kittens, strays, and homeless cats, and reveals a great deal about the nature not only of cats, but of their human owners.

George, Jean Craighead: *Julie of the Wolves*. Harper & Row, 1972. Lost in the Alaskan wilderness, 13-year-old Julie is gradually accepted by a pack of Arctic wolves and learns their survival techniques.

Gipson, Fred: *Old Yeller*. Harper & Row, 1964. Classic story of a boy and his dog during the frontier days in the Texas hill country.

Hyde, Dayton O.: *Strange Companion*. E. P. Dutton, 1975. Fawcett Books. Stowaway David survives a plane crash in the Canadian wilderness and searches for civilization, accompanied by a rare whooping crane.

James, Will: *Smoky*. Charles Scribners' Sons, 1926. The training, work, and mistreatment of a cow pony on the range are described in colorful cowboy language and authentic detail.

Kjelgaard, James: *Big Red*. Holiday House, 1956. Bantam Books. The famous wilderness adventure of a boy and a prize-winning red setter who form an unbreakable friendship.

London, Jack: *The Call of the Wild*. Macmillan, 1963. New American Library. Stolen from his wealthy California home and sold as a sled dog, Buck learns to fend for himself against men and beasts.

Mannix, Dan: *Drifter*. Reader's Digest Press, 1974. Fawcett Books. A young boy grows up to love animals in a very special way although his father is a professional hunter.

Meriwether, Louise: *Daddy Was a Numbers Runner*. Pyramid, 1976. Francie, a 12-year-old black girl, faces the daily hazards of life in Harlem during the 1930s.

Montgomery, Rutherford: *Rufus*. Caxton Printers, 1973. A young bobcat struggles against hunters, a flash flood, an avalanche, and the laws of nature in an effort to survive, find a mate, and provide for a family.

Mowat, Farley: *Never Cry Wolf*. Atlantic Monthly Press, 1973. Bantam Books. Eloquent study of wolves in the sub-Arctic barrenlands. Informative and amusing portrait of habits and character of these animals, which have often been unfairly described as vicious and murderous.

North, Sterling: *The Wolfling*. E. P. Dutton, 1969. Bantam

Books. Robbie Trent, living in the Midwest during the 1870s, has a great love of the wild and gathers his courage to crawl into a wolf den to take a cub to raise.

Neville, Emily C.: *It's Like This, Cat*. Harper & Row, 1963. The trauma and joys of adolescence in New York City are depicted in the story of Dave Mitchell and the tomcat he must hide from his parents and landlord.

O'Hara, Mary: *My Friend Flicka*. J. B. Lippincott, 1973. Dell. *Thunderhead*. 1943. *The Green Grass of Wyoming*. 1946. These three books follow Ken from childhood to young manhood on a ranch in Wyoming, as he is torn between his military father and his sensitive mother.

Knight, Eric: *Lassie Come Home*. Dell, 1975. Lassie, a high bred collie, makes the lonely journey from Scotland to Yorkshire to be with the boy who had cared for her as a pup.

Rawlings, Marjorie Kinnan: *The Yearling*. Charles Scribner's Sons, 1962. Jody and his pet fawn grow to maturity together in the Florida Everglades.

Rawls, Wilson: *Where the Red Fern Grows*. Doubleday, 1961. Bantam Books. A young boy growing up in the Ozarks treasures his two redbone hounds as he teaches them to be championship coon hunters before Dan is killed by a mountain lion and Little Ann dies of grief.

Robertson, Keith: *In Search of a Sandhill Crane*. Viking Press, 1973. Link Keller learns to appreciate the northern Michigan wilderness and its wildlife as he spends the summer stalking the sandhill crane as a photography project.

Sherman, D. R.: *The Lion's Paw*. Doubleday, 1975. An obsessed white hunter, a young Bushman, and a crippled lion confront one another in a conflict for survival.

Steinbeck, John: *The Red Pony*. Viking Press, 1959. Bantam Books. A boy's love for his pony leads him into frightening responsibilities as well as joy.

Street, James: *Goodbye, My Lady*. J. B. Lippincott, 1954. Archway Paperbacks. Being reared by an almost illiterate uncle in the southern swamplands, Skeeter finds a valuable runaway dog and learns about himself and others.

Walker, Frank: *Jack*. Coward, McCann & Geohegan, 1976. Bantam Books. The heartwarming story of a Belgian sheepdog and his life on a Yorkshire countryside estate.

Wibberley, Leonard: *Meeting with a Great Beast*. William Morrow, 1971. On an elephant hunt in Africa, a man dying of cancer and the elephant he stalks develop an intriguing bond in their awareness of death.

MYSTERY, SUSPENSE, AND ADVENTURE

Aiken, Joan: *Died on a Rainy Sunday*. Holt, Rinehart and Winston, 1972. Jane's four-year-old daughter, Caroline, is instinctively terrified by the new baby-sitter, Mrs. McGregor—for good reason, as it turns out.

————: *Night Fall*. Holt, Rinehart and Winston, 1971. Nineteen-year-old Meg Frazer returns to Cornwall to rid herself of the terrifying dream memory of a childhood accident, only to find herself at the center of an unsolved murder she witnessed five years before.

Annixter, Paul: *Swiftwater*. Scholastic Book Services. Bucky takes over his injured father's place as a hunter and trapper and shares with him a dream of sanctuary for the wild geese.

Bass, Milton K.: *Mister Jory*. G. P. Putnam's Sons, 1976. Young Jory earns both gratitude and a job from a wealthy rancher by gunning down his kidnappers.

Bennett, Jay. *The Birthday Murder*. Delacorte Press, 1977. Seventeen-year-old Stan O'Rourke doesn't know whether or not he is a murderer and sets out on an adventure of self-discovery.

————: *Deathman, Do Not Follow Me*. Hawthorn Books, 1968. Assigned to write a theme on a Van Gogh painting, a boy begins to question its authenticity, involving him in a difficult situation.

————: *Say Hello to the Hit Man*. Delacorte Press, 1976. Dell. When freshman Fred Morgan gets threatening phone calls, he is forced to accept protection from the father he has rejected because of his "syndicate" affiliation.

Cameron, Ian: *The Mountains at the Bottom of the World*. Avon Books, 1974. An entry in a dead man's diary sends his nephew and a group of scientists to remotest Chile in search of a tribe of primitive man and an active volcano.

Christie, Agatha: *Murder on the Orient Express*. Dodd, Mead, 1968. Pocket Books. Hercule Poirot investigates a variety of motives for murder as the Calais Coach races across Europe. The passengers provide the intriguing clues.

Corcoran, Barbara: *The Clown*. Atheneum, 1975. Sixteen-year-old Liza Parker plots to save a Jewish circus clown from the Russian authorities by smuggling him out of Moscow.

Cormier, Robert: *After the First Death*. Pantheon Books, 1979. Dell. A busload of children is hijacked by armed terrorists, with a tension-filled denouement.

Crawford, Charles: *Bad Fall*. Harper & Row, 1972. Bantam Books. Everyone is charmed by the new boy in school, but he is a demonic instrument of evil.

David, Mildred: *Tell Them What's Her Name Called*. Pocket Books, 1976. A series of possible accidents seems suspicious to the daughter of the first victim, so she and her friends take up an investigation.

Doyle, Arthur Conan: *Complete Sherlock Holmes*. Doubleday, 1933. Master detective Sherlock and his friend Dr. Watson are perennial favorites. The seven Holmes books can be obtained separately in many editions.

Duncan, Lois: *I Know What You Did Last Summer*. Little, Brown, 1973. Archway Paperbacks. Four teenagers desperately trying to conceal their responsibility for a hit-and-run accident are pursued by a mystery figure seeking revenge.

————: *Killing Mr. Griffin*. Little, Brown, 1978. A group of students decides to kidnap their teacher. When he dies of a heart attack during the escapade, they are involved in a cover-up which reveals their insecurities.

Eckert, Allan W.: *Incident at Hawk's Hill*. Little, Brown, 1971. Dell. In a strange, touching tale of survival, a tiny child lives for days and then weeks in a hole with a fierce wild badger.

Esmond, Harriet: *Darsham's Tower*. Dell, 1976. After being hired as a companion to Oliver Darsham's daughter, Kate Quantrill is drawn into the mystery of who the real Oliver Darsham is—or was.

Fenner, Phyllis, ed.: *Full Forty Fathoms*. William Morrow, 1975. Ten suspense stories set in the alluring but deadly underseas world.

Forman, James: *So Ends This Day*. Farrar, Straus and Giroux, 1970. Mystery and terror prevail in Guy Cameron's voyage aboard a whaler in pursuit of whales, a ship, and a murderer.

Garfield, Leon: *The Strange Affair of Adeliade Harris*. Pantheon Books, 1971. Bostoch and Harris, two young schoolmates, leave Harris's baby sister in a lonely place in hopes that a wolf will suckle her so that Harris can write up the experiment for the Royal Society.

Gordon, Mildred, and Gordon: *That Darn Cat*. Scholastic Book Services, 1973. A cat helps catch a pair of bank robbers who are planning a murder.

Hamilton, Virginia: *The House of Dies Drear*. Macmillan, 1968. Dell. A black professor and his family move into a haunted deserted station of the underground railroad, where they become involved in mystery and danger.

Holland, Isabelle: *Grenelle*. Rawson Associates, 1976. Fawcett Books. The disappearance of a religious relic seems a minor event on Grenelle campus until the arrival of menacing anonymous letters, the death of a small boy, and a threat to the life of Susan Grenelle.

Irving, John: *Setting Free the Bears*. Avon Books, 1974. Two young men tour Europe on a motorcycle and plot to free the animals of the Vienna Zoo in a symbolic gesture against the cruelty of the Nazi invaders.

L'Engle, Madeleine: *The Arm of the Starfish*. Farrar, Straus and Giroux, 1965. Adam Eddington becomes entangled in an international intrigue involving scientific work and has to decide which of the opposing forces represents his beliefs.

————: *Dragons in the Water*. Farrar, Straus and Giroux, 1976. On a trip to Venezuela, Poly and Charles O'Keefe help solve a murder.

Mazer, Harry: *Snow Bound*. Delacorte Press, 1973. Two teenagers, each running away from home, must work together to survive when they become snowbound in a desolate area of upstate New York.

Michaels, Barbara: *Witch*. Dodd, Mead, 1973. Fawcett

Books. After buying a house in Virginia that formerly belonged to a witch, Ellen is also labeled a witch; she flees through a secret tunnel that leads to more danger.

Morey, Walt: *Canyon Winter*. E. P. Dutton, 1972. A fifteen-year-old boy manages to survive a plane crash and winter in the northwest wilderness.

Norton, Andre: *The White Jade Fox*. E. P. Dutton, 1975. Fawcett Books. A young governess tries to protect her charge and a mysterious Chinese legacy from an evil guardian.

O'Dell, Scott: *Island of the Blue Dolphins*. Houghton Mifflin, 1960. Dell. An Indian girl left by her tribe survives alone 18 years on a bleak island off the coast of California. Based on an actual happening.

Phleger, Marjorie: *Pilot Down, Presumed Dead*. Harper & Row, 1975. The survivor of a crash landing struggles to stay alive on an uninhibited island off the coast of Baja California with a coyote for his only companion.

Roth, Arthur: *The Iceberg Hermit*. Scholastic Book Services, 1974. The tale of a young man's seven-year ordeal after his whaling ship sinks in the Arctic during the 18th century. Based on a true story.

Shimer, R. H.: *The Cricket Cage*. Harper & Row, 1975. On a visit to Seattle, Kate finds her younger sister dead from mysterious causes.

Townsend, John Rowe: *The Intruder*. J. B. Lippincott, 1970. Sixteen-year-old Arnold Haithwaite suddenly finds his secure, contented existence with an old shopkeeper threatened by a sinister stranger claiming to have the same name and to be a close blood relative of the shopkeeper.

Ullman, James Ramsey: *Banner in the Sky*. J. B. Lippincott, 1954. Archway Paperbacks. Rudi is determined to conquer the Citadel, the treacherous mountain his father died trying to climb. Many descriptions and details are based on an actual ascent of the Matterhorn.

Van Der Loef, A. Rutgers: *Avalanche*. William Morrow, 1958. The dramatic account of an avalanche that swept away a Swiss village.

Viereck, Phillip: *The Summer I Was Lost*. John Day, 1965. When he gets lost on a hike at summer camp,

Paul discovers his survival depends less on brawn and physical coordination than on resourcefulness, persistence and good judgment, and the application of skills learned while camping with his father.

White, Robb: *Deathwatch.* Doubleday, 1972. Dell. When Ben observes an accidental killing, he is stalked by the killer in the wilderness. When he manages to reach civilization and charge his pursuer with murder, no one believes him.

Windsor, Patricia: *Something's Waiting for You, Baker D.* Harper & Row, 1974. Dell. Mary the Hulk wanted to protect Baker D.—but she wasn't sure from what, even when she saw the car pull up and take him away. Only Baker D. knew they were Slynacks, whoever (or whatever) they were . . .

BOOKS ABOUT FOREIGN CULTURES

Anaya, Rudolfo A.: *Bless Me, Ultima.* Quinto Sol, 1972. Antonio's experiences as a Mexican youth growing up in New Mexico include a special relationship with Ultimo, a *curandero* (curer), who comes to live with the family.

Arundel, Honor: *The Blanket Word.* Thomas Nelson, 1973. Dell. Jan Meredith is forced to reexamine her attitudes toward life and love after coming home to Wales from the University of Edinburgh to join her older sisters and brother at her mother's deathbed.

Ballard, Martin: *Dockie.* Harper & Row, 1973. Forced to quit school and go to work on London's docks, Moggy is determined to rise above his poverty.

Banks, Lynne Reid: *One More River.* Simon and Schuster, 1973. Fourteen-year-old Lesley rebels at leaving her comfortable life in Canada to live in Israel, but the Arab Israeli Six-Day War hastens her maturity and she finds her identity as an Israeli.

Baudouy, Michele-Aime: *More Than Courage.* Harcourt Brace Jovanovich, 1968. A French boy whose parents are displeased with his poor grades and his choice of friends is turned on only by the motorcycle that he finds hidden under a straw sack.

Clark, Mavis T.: *Min-Min.* Macmillan, 1969. Beset by overwhelming family problems, Sylvia finds life in the outback of southern Australia hard and joyless, but when she and her brother run away she comes to terms with herself.

Cordell, Alexander: *The Traitor Within*. Thomas Nelson, 1973. Life in modern China is explored through the story of 14-year-old Ling, a member of the Red Guard who lives on a commune near the coast where conflict with Taiwan is constant.

Craven, Margaret: *I Heard the Owl Call My Name*. Doubleday, 1973. Dell. Indian beliefs and nature lore enhance the poignant story of a dying young minister who wins the respect and friendship of the Kwakiutl Indians of British Columbia, with whom he lives while coming to terms with death.

Freedman, Benedict and Nancy: *Mrs. Mike*. Coward, Mc-Cann & Geohegan, 1947. Berkley. A 16-year-old Bostonian marries a Royal Canadian Mounted Police-man and shares with her husband the rugged often heartbreaking life in the north.

Gerenstain, Grigori: *The Fall and Other Stories*. Harper & Row, 1976. A young Russian expatriate depicts all aspects of life in his homeland in these 13 short stories.

Godden, Rumer: *The Peacock Spring*. Viking Press, 1976. Fawcett Books. When two British teenagers journey to India to join their diplomatic father, they are un-prepared for the clash of cultures as modern India experiences the turmoil of deposed rajahs, student revolutionaries, still devout Buddhists, and western-ized aristocrats.

Hom Minfong: *Sing to the Dawn*. Lothrop, Lee & Shep-ard, 1975. Determined to continue her education, Dawan, a young Thai girl, wins a scholarship to the city high school and faces her runner-up brother's resentment and her father's opposition to city life and further education for a girl.

Houston, James: *White Dawn: An Eskimo Saga*. Har-court, Brace Jovanovich, 1971. Havoc and tragedy result when a band of Eskimos discover three sur-vivors of a doomed boat and nurse them back to health.

Jarunkova, Klara: *Don't Cry for Me*. Scholastic Book Services, 1973. A Czech teenager seeks to find a place for herself among her peer society, which is in revolt against adult mores.

Jhabvala, Ruth P.: *Travelers*. Harper & Row, 1973. Modern-day India affects the lives of Lee, Margaret, and Raymond, each of whom has journeyed east in search of commitment.

Lingard, Joan: *Across the Barricades*. Thomas Nelson, 1973. Grosset & Dunlap. In contemporary strife-torn Belfast, the deepening relationship between Sadie, a protestant girl, and Kevin, a Catholic boy, results in bitter family opposition. (Sequel to *The Twelfth Day of July* and followed by *A Proper Place* and *Hostages to Fortune*.)

Oz, Amos: *Elsewhere Perhaps*. Harcourt Brace Jovanovich, 1973. A novel of life and love on a kibbutz—and of the special love that binds people together.

Paterson, Katherine: *The Master Puppeteer*. Thomas Y. Crowell, 1976. In 18th-century Osaka, Jiro, son of a starving puppet-maker, runs away from home to apprentice himself to Yoshida, the ill-tempered master of the Nanaza puppet theater.

————: *Of Nightingales That Weep*. Thomas Y. Crowell, 1974. In 12th-century Japan, during the Keike-Genji civil wars, Takiko, daughter of a famous samurai killed in the wars, is taken into court as a musician and personal servant.

Ruesch, Hans: *Back to the Top of the World*. Ballantine Books, 1974. An Eskimo man and wife find the ways of the white man unfathomable but amusing as they follow their own rituals and beliefs.

Townsend, John Rowe: *Good Night, Prof. Dear*. J. B. Lippincott, 1971. Sixteen-year-old Graham considers eloping to Scotland when his overbearing parents forbid his friendship with a waitress.

————: *The Summer People*. J. B. Lippincott, 1972. Dell. A teenage boy and girl whose parents hope they will someday marry seek romance elsewhere during their summer vacation at an English resort in 1939.

Wellman, Alice: *The Wilderness Has Ears*. Harcourt Brace Jovanovich, 1975. In a Bantu village in contemporary Angola, a 14-year-old American girl confronts the alien lifestyle and wisdom of the Bantu villagers.

Wojciechowska, Maia: *The Shadow of a Bull*. Atheneum,

1964. The son of Spain's greatest bullfighter believes he has no choice but to follow in his legendary father's footsteps, although he would prefer to be a doctor.

Wong, Jade Snow: *Fifth Chinese Daughter*. Harper & Row, 1950. A delightful account by an American-born Chinese girl of her family life in San Francisco, her education, and her career as a creative artist.

U.S. HISTORY

Baker, Betty: *The Dunderhead War*. Harper & Row, 1967. Seventeen-year-old Quince Hefferdorf and his Uncle Fritz, a German immigrant, accompany a wagon train from Missouri into Mexican territory during the opening stages of the war with Mexico.

Bolton, Carole: *Never Jam Today*. Atheneum, 1971. Madeline Franklin, a 1917 suffragette, pickets, goes to jail, and puts herself through college as her commitment to women's rights deepens.

Bontemps, Arna: *Black Thunder*. Beacon Press, 1968. Gabriel, a slave, leads a revolt against the plantation owners of Richmond, Virginia, in 1800.

Clapp, Patricia: *Constance*. Lothrop, Lee & Shepard, 1968. In diary form, Constance records the experience of living in Plymouth Plantation between her 14th and 20th years.

Collier, James L. and Christopher: *My Brother Sam Is Dead*. Four Winds Press, 1974. In a colonial town where revolutionary feeling is low, Sam Meeker joins the Minutemen, drawing his family into conflict.

Fast, Howard: *April Morning*. Bowmar/Noble, 1970. Bantam Books. The story of the battle of Lexington and of a boy who became a man on that April day which changed the lives of "plain people not used to war and death."

————: *The Hessian*. William Morrow, 1972. Bantam Books. A Hessian drummer boy is hidden by a family of Quakers until he is found by the authorities.

Fenton, Edward: *Duffy's Rocks*. E. P. Dutton, 1974. An Irish Catholic boy in the Pittsburgh area in the 1930s undergoes a painful adolescence.

Fisher, Leonard Everett: *The Death of Evening Star: The Diary of a Young New England Whaler*. Doubleday, 1972. When 11-year-old Jeremiah Poole ships on a whaler, he begins a diary to record life at sea during the 1840s.

Forbes, Esther: *Johnny Tremain*. Houghton Mifflin, 1943. Dell. Johnny is an arrogant apprentice to a silver-smith in pre-Revolutionary Boston until he burns his hand in an accident. Humbled, he becomes a messenger boy for the insurgent colonists.

Forman, James: *The Life and Death of Yellow Bird*. Farrar, Straus and Giroux, 1973. Chronical of the life of an Indian seer from the battle of Little Bighorn to that of Wounded Knee as he battles to save his people from the depredations of the white man.

Frazier, Neta Lohnes: *The Stout-Hearted Seven*. Harcourt Brace Jovanovich, 1973. An account of the Western migration of the Sager family on the Oregon Trail, constructed from diaries, letters, manuscripts, and interviews.

Houston, James: *Ghost Fox*. Harcourt Brace Jovanovich, 1977. Avon Books. Kidnapped by the Abnaki Indians in colonial times, 16-year-old Sarah Wells gradually adopts the Abnaki way of life and must eventually choose between being an Indian or returning to the life from which she was taken.

Hunt, Irene: *Across Five Aprils*. Follett, 1964. Gosset & Dunlap. Jethro, living on a southern Illinois farm during the Civil War, is intensely loyal to the Union, but also loves his rebel brother and sympathizes with a friend who is a deserter.

Johnston, Norma: *The Keeping Days*. Atheneum, 1973. Tish Sterling tells of seven months in the life of her family in Yonkers, New York, from June to December 1900. (Sequel: *Glory in the Flower*. Atheneum, 1974.)

Keith, Harold: *Rifles for Watie*. Thomas Y. Crowell, 1957. A Union soldier sees both sides of the war when he is befriended by the Rebel soldiers upon whom he is spying and witnesses the treachery of his own commander.

Kornfeld, Anita: *In a Blubird's Eye*. Holt, Rinehart and Winston, 1975. A lonely young girl growing up in the rural south of the 1930s hides a secret friendship with a black woman.

Latham, Jean Lee: *Carry On, Mr. Bowditch*. Houghton Mifflin, 1955. Nathaniel Bowditch, indentured at the age of 12, becomes captain of the ship at 20 due to his genius in mathematics, astronomy, and navigation.

Levitin, Sonia: *Roanoke*. Atheneum, 1973. An adolescent boy survives the fate of his fellow Roanoke settlers through his friendship with the Indians.

Peck, Robert Newton: *Fawn*. Little, Brown, 1975. Dell. The saga of a boy who cannot take sides during the French and Indian War.

Richter, Conrad: *Light in the Forest*. Alfred A. Knopf, 1953. Bantam Books. True Son, a white boy captured by Delawares and raised as an Indian, is forced to return to his own white family whom he no longer understands or loves.

Speare, Elizabeth George: *The Witch of Blackbird Pond*. Houghton Mifflin, 1958. When Kit Tyler comes from the Barbados to live with her Puritan relatives in colonial Connecticut, she is not prepared to accept the austere life of hard work—or to stand trial as a witch.

Steele, William: *The Wilderness Tattoo: A Narrative of Juan Ortiz*. Harcourt Brace Jovanovich, 1972. The early life of Spaniard Juan Ortiz, who was captured by the Florida Indians in 1527.

Van Every, Dale: *The Day the Sun Died*. Little, Brown, 1971. An exploration of the events which led up to the conflict between the army and the Indians at Wounded Knee.

Yep, Laurence: *Dragonwings*. Harper & Row, 1975. The Chinese immigrant experience in San Francisco's Chinatown in the early 20th century is seen through the eyes of 11-year-old Moon Shadow.

WORLD STORIES

Bacon, Martha: *In the Company of Clowns*. Little, Brown, 1973. An orphan raised in a convent sees a new side of life when he joins a touring comedy troupe in 18th-century Italy.

Barnes, Margaret C.: *Tudor Rose*. Macrae, 1971. A splendid portrayal of Elizabeth of York—daughter of a king, wife of a king, and mother of Henry VIII—during the War of the Roses in 15th-century England.

Beatty, John and Patricia: *King's Knight's Pawn*. William Morrow, 1971. When he travels to Ireland to serve under his soldier-godfather, young Christopher Barlow is witness to the massacre of the Irish by Cromwell's Roundheads.

Behn, Harry: *The Faraway Lurs*. Avon Books, 1976. In this Romeo and Juliet kind of story with a prehistoric setting, a boy and a girl of enemy tribes who fall in love are sacrificed by their people.

Benchley, Nathaniel: *Beyond the Mists*. Harper & Row, 1975. A shipwrecked merchant seaman in Norway meets Leif Ericson, who includes him on his next voyage of exploration.

————: *Bright Candles*. Harper & Row, 1974. The story of a teenage boy's participation in Denmark's Resistance during the Nazi occupation.

Bibby, Violet: *Many Waters Cannot Quench Love*. William Morrow, 1975. In 17th-century Cambridgeshire, a girl falls in love with the son of one of the hated Dutch engineers brought to drain the marshes for farmland.

Bolton, Carole: *The Search of Mary Katherine Mulloy*. Thomas Nelson, 1974. A girl fleeing from the tragedy of the Irish potato famine goes to find her lover in the new land of America.

Clifford, Eth: *The Wild One*. Houghton Mifflin, 1974. Santiago Ramon y Cajal, Nobel prizewinner for medicine in 1906, remembers his rebellious boyhood in Spain.

Degens, T.: *Transport 7-41-R*. Viking Press, 1974. Dell. A young girl discovers her own sense of values on the long slow journey from the Russian zone to the free city of Cologne after World War II.

Dickinson, Peter: *The Dancing Bear*. Atlantic Monthly Press, 1973. In 6th-century Byzantium a young Greek slave, his dancing bear, and an old holy man journey to rescue Lady Ariadne, who has been captured by invading Huns.

Forman, James: *My Enemy, My Brother*. Scholastic Book Services, 1972. Immediately after the war, a handful of young Jews who have survived Hitler's concentration camps set out on foot to make the long journey from Poland to Israel.

————: *Ring the Judas Bell.* Farrar, Straus and Giroux, 1965. Nicholos and his cynical sister are among the 30,000 Greek children kidnapped by the Communist Andarte after World War II.

Fox, Paula: *Slave Dancer.* Bradbury Press, 1973. Dell. When, in 1840, 14-year-old Jessie is impressed into service on a slave ship to play his fife so that the slaves can be made to dance for exercise, he learns the nature of the slave trade and his own response to it.

Heyman, Anita: *Exit from Home.* Crown, 1977. Opposing the demands of a dictatorial father, the oldest son of a Jewish family in Tsarist Russia follows his own commitment to social revolution.

Hill, Susan: *Strange Meeting.* Penguin Books, 1976. Two young British soldiers of opposite personalities develop a special friendship which helps each to survive World War I.

Holm, Anne S.: *North to Freedom.* Harcourt Brace Jovanovich, 1965. A dramatic story of a young boy who escapes from a concentration camp and has to learn the most elementary things about the world outside.

Hughes, Richard: *A High Wind in Jamaica.* Harper & Row, 1972. Children on a ship bound for England are captured by pirates.

Konigsburg, E. L.: *A Proud Taste for Scarlet and Miniver.* Atheneum, 1973. Eleanor of Aquitaine, queen of France and then of England, mother of Richard the Lion-Hearted and King John, recounts her life in the 12th century.

Moskin, Marietta: *I Am Rosemarie.* John Day, 1972. Scholastic Book Services. A 12-year-old Jewish girl learns about the ravages of war when the Germans occupy Holland and she is sent to a concentration camp.

Nostlinger, Christine: *Fly Away Home.* Franklin Watts, 1975. An account of living in Vienna at the end of World War II during the Russian occupation told from a child's point of view.

O'Dell, Scott: *The Hawk That Dare Not Hunt By Day*. Houghton Mifflin, 1975. Dell. A young British sailor is friend and companion to William Tyndale, who attempts to publish the Bible in English and is branded a heretic.

————. *The King's Fifth*. Houghton Mifflin, 1966. Dell. A 17-year-old cartographer awaiting trial for defrauding the king of Spain writes of his adventure in the land of the Seven Cities where gold madness seized the expedition and only Father Francisco and the Indian girl, Zia, escaped the contagion.

Plowman, Stephanie: *Three Lives for the Czar*. Houghton Mifflin, 1970. An account of the last years of Tsarist Russia against the panorama of the larger European scene during the First World War.

Rubin, Arnold: *The Evil That Men Do: The Story of the Nazis*. Julian Messner, 1977. Bantam Books. (Bantam edition entitled *Hitler and the Nazis*.) A journey into the dark world of the Holocaust.

Speare, Elizabeth George: *The Bronze Bow*. Houghton Mifflin, 1961. Daniel is as obsessed with hatred for the Romans and desire for vengeance as his sister Leah is with the "demons" of fear, until he meets a rabbi named Jesus.

Tunis, John R.: *His Enemy, His Friend*. William Morrow, 1967. A German sergeant in an occupied French village, when forced to carry out reprisals against the villagers, faces a choice between conscience and patriotic duty.

SPORTS STORIES

Ashford, Jeffrey: *Grand Prix Britain*. G. P. Putnam's Sons, 1973. Dick Knox finds that mechanical problems and dissension among his racing team offset any advantage he might have from racing on his native soil.

Brancato, Robin. *Winning*. Alfred A. Knopf, 1977. Bantam Books. Injured in a football game, Gary Madden finally faces the fact that he may never walk again.

Brashler, William: *The Bingo Long Traveling All-Stars and Motor Kings*. New American Library, 1976. Bingo Long, great black baseball player, angered by mistreatment by his manager, persuades his teammates to join him in barnstorming the country and challenging anyone to play baseball.

Cox, William R.: *Gunner on the Court*. Dodd, Mead, 1972. Two rivals for team leadership struggle to resolve their differences before the championship game.

Dygard, Thomas: *Running Scared*. William Morrow, 1977. Tension rises when a college football coach believes his job is on the line and his star quarterback develops a fear of running.

Fenner, Phyllis, ed.: *Lift Line*. William Morrow, 1976. Stories of downhill and cross-country skiing by John Updike, B. J. Chute, Rutherford Montgomery, and others.

Gault, William C.: *The Big Stick*. E. P. Dutton, 1975. Rusty Todd, a hot-tempered young hockey player from Minnesota, realizes that his uncontrollable outbursts are ruining his athletic career and personal life.

Gutman, Bill: *My Father, the Coach and Other Sports Stories*. Julian Messner, 1976. Ten basketball, baseball, football, and hockey stories involving young athletes who find themselves in critical situations calling for decisions and action.

Halacy, D. S. Jr.: *Surfer*. Macmillan, 1965. Pete Marlin must balance his interest in his combo group, his enthusiasm for surfing, and his need to excel in school if he is to manage college entrance.

Heath, William L.: *Most Valuable Player*. Harcourt Brace Jovanovich, 1973. Pete starts his senior year with a fine chance to get the most valuable player award but disaster threatens the night before the big game.

Honig, Donald: *Winter Always Comes*. Four Winds Press, 1977. Bonus baby Billy Prescott discovers that organized baseball is not all glamour when a hitting slump during his rookie year forces him to come to terms with the "real" world of professional sports.

Jackson, C. Paul: *Rose Bowl Pro*. Hastings House, 1970. Bo Greyam, star left halfback for Michigan State, wants to play professional football so badly that he allows his feelings to influence his play for his college team.

Jacobs, Karen Foler: *Girlsports*. Bantam Books, 1978. Girl athletes, aged 9 to 17, tell what it's like to compete, lose—and win!

Knudson, R. R.: *Fox Running*. Harper & Row, 1975. Avon Books. Fox Running, a young Zuni woman taught by her grandfather to run free in the desert, is recruited for the medal-minded Uinta University track team.

————: *Zanbanger*. Harper & Row, 1977. Zan tries out for the boys' basketball team.

Lipsyte, Robert: *The Contender*. Harper & Row, 1967. Bantam Books. Alfred, a black dropout, wants to be somebody so famous that he can return to Harlem in a big white car. Though not particularly promising, he enters the Harlem Training Center for Boxers hoping to become good enough to be a contender for the championship.

Ogan, Margaret and George: *Grand National Racer*. Westminster Press, 1977. A stock-car driver's rookie season.

Schulman, L. M., ed.: *Winners and Losers*. Macmillan, 1968. An anthology of sports fiction from baseball and football to jai alai and ping-pong that focuses on the player rather than the sport.

Towne, Mary: *First Serve*. Atheneum, 1976. Dulcie's development into a professional class tennis player changes her relationship with her sister Pat and upsets her parents' plans for the two girls.

Watkins, William J.: *A Fair Advantage*. Prentice-Hall, 1975. A hospitalized high-school wrestler reconstructs moments from his wrestling past.

Yee, Min S., and Donald K. Wright: *The Sports Book*. Bantam Books, 1976. Celebrates and explores America at play. More than 30 sports are highlighted in this book in a mixture of anecdotes, biographical sketches, commentaries, reminiscences, quizzes and articles.

6

The Popular Adult Book

For it is impossible that anything should be universally
tasted and approved by the multitude, though they are
only the rabble of the nation, which hath not in it some
peculiar aptness to please and gratify the mind of man.
—*Joseph Addison*

Most teenagers will move from the adolescent novel
to truly adult literature through the medium of the
popular adult novel. Some adolescents begin to feel
insulted by teenage material as early as the eighth or
ninth grade; others may still enjoy the adolescent novel
as seniors in high school. Probably the average age for
leaving the adolescent novel is 15 or 16, in the tenth
grade.

The change can be as dramatic as the adolescent's
discovery that the girls' or boys' departments no longer
have suitable clothing and a move must be made to
new stores, or new departments. The young adult feels
uncomfortable with the adolescent novel, finding it a
bit condescending, the language oversimplified, and
the view of life too centered on just the teenage world.
The vision of adulthood gained from the popular adult
novel may still be somewhat distorted, but the reader
does get the feeling of being grown up.

Before discussing the popular adult book, let us consider a small, distinguished handful of books that are
significant literature (chapter 8) but are not truly
adolescent *or* adult. These "in-between" books are more
mature in tone and in the experiences they detail than

teenagers are; yet they are read almost exclusively by teenagers. *A Separate Peace* by John Knowles is such a book. Soon after publication it was seized upon by English teachers looking for a literary work to replace *Ivanhoe* or *Silas Marner* in tenth-grade English classes. It was published as an adult work of fiction, but by now it is read almost exclusively by adolescents. The story is told in retrospect by Gene, returning after World War II to his New England preparatory school. This "double view" is more complicated than the directly narrated teenage novel reporting on present experiences. Gene relives a friendship with Finney which climaxed in the traumatic moment when Gene jiggled a tree limb just as Finney was diving, causing his friend to slip and injure himself. Indirectly this brought about his death. Gene, now an adult, is trying to find the "separate peace" that everyone must make with his feelings of guilt. The book is filled with adolescent happenings, but it builds toward an understanding beyond that in teenage novels.

In Sol Stein's *The Magician,* a 16-year-old sleight-of-hand enthusiast makes a fool out of Urek, a bully, at a school assembly and is later attacked and beaten by Urek. When charges are preferred, Urek is cleared through the manipulation of the law by a clever criminal lawyer. Laws set up to protect the innocent are used to free the guilty, thus condemning our trial system. The protagonist, as in *A Separate Peace,* is a teenager, but the theme and treatment of the events are adult.

A "'tween" book read by countless girls is Ann Head's *Mr. and Mrs. Bo Jo Jones.* This book was also published as an adult novel, but quickly became a teenage favorite. July and Bo Jo marry in high school after July becomes pregnant. The book recounts their struggles as July quits school and Bo Jo takes a full-time job. Their baby dies and the young couple's parents assume the two will get a divorce and take up the pattern of their former lives. But July and Bo Jo realize they cannot return to being dependent teenagers and decide to stick together and make their marriage last. The incidents and issues as well as the tone of the book align it with popular adult reading. It is marketed as such on paperback bookracks, and has been made into a motion picture for a general audience, but it is the teenage girl customer who is keeping the book alive.

The popular adult book is widely read and discussed; it often makes the best-seller list and is selected by a major book club. It may be made into a motion picture—and yet within a few years it usually fades into oblivion. It does not become a part of the continuing literary heritage that people cherish generation after generation.

Popular books have a gripping story to tell, with plenty of incident and action. The adult reader is kept reading in much the same way that a teen is charmed by a juvenile series. Thus *Jaws* begins with lovemaking on the beach, a midnight swim, a white form in the water, a tingling in the legs, and the discovery the next day of parts of the torso of a woman's body. Naturally the reader continues in horrified fascination.

The protagonist of such books is slightly larger than life—more beautiful, more suffering, more alive, more everything than most of us can hope to be. We are fascinated, just as the teenager is fascinated by Nancy Drew. Look at *The Thorn Birds,* a story of a family on a sheep station in the Australian Outback. Maggie is impossibly beautiful; she is long-suffering (throughout her entire life, as a matter of fact). She falls in love with a Catholic priest. She manages the home paddock better than any man. She bears two brilliant, startling children. And she is only one of a huge cast of intriguing characters. No wonder that buyers read all night to get through the book, and wish it was longer still.

Most popular adult books lack two qualities found in great literature: a significant and enduring theme, and a sensitivity to the flow of language. The popular adult book may hold individuals spellbound as they read, but once finished, they have no desire to read the story again. It is read for momentary enjoyment . . . a relaxing interlude.

What is missing from the popular adult book is the strange, moving quality that language can achieve in the hands of great writers. To see the difference, try reading material by two different writers treating the same experiences. Compare, for example, incidents about Lincoln in Irving Stone's *Love Is Eternal* with the similar happening in Carl Sandburg's *Abraham Lincoln: The Prairie Years*.

Popular adult books account for most of the leisure-time reading of the literate public, who will continue to read such books for the rest of their lives—and rightly so, for they express contemporary cultural life.

Teenagers read perhaps 10 to 20 percent of the popular adult books. While some of them are as transitory for teenagers as for adults, others will be read by generations of teens. *Love Story,* after being passionately read during a year or two, may have been discarded by the young along with the adults, but a few popular novels are still read by teens centuries later. Who but the young still read *The Count of Monte Cristo* or *Frankenstein?* Twentieth-century favorites like *Gone with the Wind, Rebecca,* and *Lost Horizon* are kept alive primarily by teenage readers. Of current books, one may predict continuing readership for *First Blood* by David Morrell and *Ordinary People* by Judith Guest. In the following discussion of pop books, we will concentrate on books that have lived at least one generation.

The adult story that appeals to a young girl usually has a girl or woman as the leading character—especially a woman of great strength of character, with a commanding personality like Scarlett O'Hara's in *Gone with the Wind*. The heroine should be important to the ongoing life around her—a young woman finding direction for herself, or an older woman on whom others depend.

Of course, *Gone with the Wind* is the most passionately read historical novel. One young girl I knew took six weeks to finish the book and at the end she said,

"Do you mind if I start over and read it through again?" This story has the fascination of the antebellum plantation life of the South. It is filled with descriptions of the white-columned houses, the scent of blossoms, the beautiful costumes of the women with their hoopskirts and voluminous petticoats, the beruffled, gallant men. Against this backdrop emerges Scarlett O'Hara—beautiful, capable, and ruthless—able to control the turbulent world around her during the social upheaval and changes wrought by the Civil War.

Girls like romantic books, which always include a love story but often include something more: a picture of life with a quality of mystery and a heightening of emotional response. Life in such romances is slightly unreal, like the scenes in a tapestry. One of the favorite romance writers is Mary Stewart, who has turned out a series of such books, each set in a fascinating part of Europe—the Greek islands, the Austrian Alps—and each centering on a nice but spirited English girl who finds herself involved in mysterious happenings and a love affair. She takes risks and moves toward danger with a kind of feminine James Bond determination. Part of the great charm of her books lies in the historical information Miss Stewart imparts and the quality of landscape in her settings. *Airs Above the Ground* is laced with much fascinating information about Lippizaner horses; in *This Rough Magic,* the author weaves in the details that have led people to choose Corfu as the setting of Shakespeare's *The Tempest.* Both books make the reader want to take off immediately for foreign countries.

Two writers of gothic romances are Victoria Holt (set in the past) and Phyllis Whitney (set in the present, but in an exotic setting). Both authors present ordinary well-bred girls who are suddenly pitched into a world of affluence, with some mystery and a romance.

Daphne du Maurier's *Rebecca* is everything that a girl wants in a romance. Rebecca, the dead wife of an English lord, exerts an all-pervasive influence from the grave over the affairs at Manderley and almost succeeds in wrecking her husband's second marriage. Only toward the end does the reader discover that Rebecca's husband despised her through their married life. This book of passion and mystery, in the dream setting of a country estate of the English aristocracy, is fascinating because the dominating character of the story is dead. Only step by step does the reader gain a picture of what she was really like.

Many young girls enjoy the stories of Edna Ferber, who also creates strong, often aggressive, women in interesting situations. She appeals to our romantic conception of a life filled with exciting problems; *Show Boat, Giant, So Big, Ice Palace,* and *Cimarron* succeed in capturing the romantic, almost legendary overtones of the Mississippi River, Texas, the Illinois prairies, modern Alaska, and the Oklahoma of pioneer days. Each book has a character who rises to the level of a folk story hero or heroine.

Robert Nathan's *Portrait of Jennie* is the kind of gentle, beautifully crafted romance that girls find appealing. A discouraged New York artist unexpectedly meets a quaintly old-fashioned little girl at twilight in Central Park. The child sings a haunting little song and is delightfully vague about who she is and where she comes from. In subsequent meetings, Jennie matures far faster than the time intervals given would permit. Ethan and Jennie's strange relationship grows into love and his failure as an artist turns to success. But the different time dimensions in which they live do not permit the pat happy ending that one might expect.

After reading such stories, a girl may go on to great romances like *Jane Eyre, Wuthering Heights,* and *Green Mansions.* Even if she doesn't, she knows the satisfactions that come from books which say that life is more intense, beautiful, and mysterious than we suspect.

The historical novel, like the romance, features a vivid main character, with fascinating, sometimes mysterious happenings. Supplementing these elements is a historical setting and often at least fairly accurate material about the period. Irving Stone has written a series of historical biographies, many of them centering on an American woman. In *Love Is Eternal* he tells of Mary Todd Lincoln, the southern belle who visits her sister in the frontier capital of Illinois and falls in love with the gaunt, rugged young Lincoln. Stone's story explains why such a woman should have married the young lawyer and why her later actions, particularly those as first lady, earned her the enmity of historians. His interpretations may be open to question, but the picture of Mary Todd he presents is convincing and intriguing. He has also written of Jessie Frémont in *Immortal Wife* and of Rachel Jackson in *The President's Lady*. His accounts of Michelangelo in *The Agony and the Ecstasy* and of Van Gogh in *Lust for Life* are worthwhile reading. For years, *Lust for Life* was the only book even dimly resembling an adequate biography of the tormented artist.

Girls like adult stories about a woman facing the tribulations of modern life. *Mrs. Mike,* by Benedict and Nancy Freedman, the story of Kathy, a 16-year-old Boston girl who is sent to Canada because of a lung difficulty, is a great favorite. Kathy is swept off her feet by a Royal Canadian Mounted Policeman and after marrying him faces a rugged, primitive life. Another favorite is *Winter Wheat* by Mildred Walker, in which, after spending a year at the University of Minnesota, the young heroine finds it difficult to accept her farming parents and her limited background.

Girls of 16 or 17 like many of the same books their mothers are reading, but not stories that detail the daily routine of a woman on a job or at home, true as it may be to the life the girl readers may later lead. They want a story that holds forth the promise of a splendid, exciting life.

Boys at this age choose adventure stories, especially those that describe the thoughts and feelings, the tension and pressures experienced by men in challenging, unusual situations. *Von Ryan's Express* is set in a prisoner-of-war camp in Italy. Ryan, a newly captured soldier, is the ranking officer in the camp. Although the men despise his rigid discipline, they are kept going by the sense of order it gives their lives. The book comes to a climax on a POW train taking the imprisoned men to a camp in Germany. Under Ryan, the men systematically kill the guards on the train and take it over. The strong personality of the leading character—a man almost inhuman in his denial of basic human emotions —seems the primary reason for the book's popularity.

The political intrigue novels of Alistair MacLean, Helen MacInnes, and John le Carré are very popular. Much of the desire for raw adventure is also filled by nonfictional accounts of feats of endurance and courage (chapter 13).

Teenagers are critical if not rebellious about the world as they perceive it. They go through a phase of reading books that show injustices happening to people because of race, religion, or economic position. These books are often so violent that they almost turn one's stomach. *First Blood* by David Morrell begins with a confrontation between Rambo, who has been a Green Beret in Vietnam, and Teasle, the sheriff of a small Kentucky town. Jailed, Rambo seizes a razor, kills a deputy, and escapes into the mountains surrounding the town. The hunter-hunted story makes it inevitable that the two will kill each other. Sympathy is built for Teasle and Rambo so that the book produces the same kind of catharsis in the reader that we associate with Greek tragedy. The book reads as a suspense story, but underneath, it is the social conditioning of the protagonists that appalls the reader.

Many books with social impact are autobiographical, like *Manchild in the Promised Land* by Claude Brown. *Roots* by Alex Haley roused the conscience of adults and teenagers as he traced his ancestry from capture in Africa through slavery in the United States to the present day. Arthur Hailey has written romantic but critical novels about hotels, airports, automobile plants, hospitals, banks.

The story set in the near future does not have to be science fiction, for the scientific conditions of life remain much as we know them; nor is it a story of a utopian society, since the social organization is not idealistically conceived. One of the earliest, *On the*

Beach, written by the prolific and imaginative Nevil Shute, tells of the last little group of humans as deadly radiation advances toward their remote stronghold. *Fail-Safe,* by Eugene Burdick and Harvey Wheeler, pictures the situation when the panic button is pushed and computers activate the bombers of the Strategic Air Command for an attack on Russia. Fletcher Knebel and Charles W. Bailey's *Seven Days in May* is similar, suggesting that even in the United States a group of the military could take over the government in a well-planned coup. These are terrifying books, but it should be reassuring that they are popular with the adolescent, for they show that in spite of his music, his dances, his clothing styles, and his dating habits, he is deeply concerned about the future and what may happen to his world.

Boys and girls like a story dominated by a central character with a vivid, strong personality, either good or evil. *Mutiny on the Bounty,* which Nordhoff and Hall based on the journals and newspaper accounts of the famous mutiny against Captain Bligh in the South Pacific, has the thrill and excitement of the usual adventure story at sea, but it also has Captain Bligh, a tyrant of indomitable personality who by sheer determination guides a boatload of men over 5000 miles of ocean to safety after they are set adrift by the mutineers. Equally exciting and commanding is Fletcher Christian, the man who is prevailed upon by the men to lead the mutiny. Jack Schaefer's *Shane* also centers on a pair of rugged individualists. Shane is a drifting gunman who becomes involved by chance in a battle between a western farmer and cattlemen who resent the newcomer's fencing in the formerly open range. The two men stand shoulder to shoulder in a final gunfight. Descriptions of personality and value differences give depth to the story, lifting it into the category of a psychological western, probably the first of the type.

The popular adult books that young people read change from generation to generation. A few, like *Lost Horizon,* will be favorites ten years from now, but most of the others discussed in this chapter will be dust-laden. The new favorites will have a family resemblance to books that the young adult is now reading, because they will be read for the same reason—primarily, for entertainment—and they will continue to represent the social thinking of the generation that produces them. Some argue that these books present only the illusion of maturity. But this, after all, is the pattern of growth: first come the bold, undifferentiated movements, then the process of slow, painful refining. So in reading the child needs first to gain a big, bold, often bald outline of the adult world and its ideas. Then, slowly and painfully, he will move on to literature that will help him refine and separate the dross from the precious metal.

Bibliography

Anson, Jay: *The Amityville Horror*. Prentice-Hall, 1977. Bantam Books. The strange, eerie experiences of a young family who buy a supposedly haunted house.

Bach, Richard: *Jonathan Livingston Seagull*. Macmillan, 1970. Avon Books. A popular philosopher's musings on the beauty of flights and personal freedom. The story is narrated by a youthful seagull striving to find his place in nature's great life scheme.

Ball, John: *In the Heat of the Night*. Harper & Row, 1965. Bantam. A black homicide detective from California becomes involved in solving a murder in the rural South.

Baldwin, James: *If Beale Street Could Talk*. Dial Press, 1974. New American Library. Young and black in New York, Fonnie and Tish discover that love and family ties can withstand inequality and sustain the next generation.

Benchley, Peter: *Jaws*. Doubleday, 1974. Bantam Books. A scenic resort town is terrorized by a great white shark. Nature conquers man until selfish human motives are set aside in pursuit of a community solution to the shark's dominance.

Bernays, Anne: *Growing Up Rich*. Little, Brown, 1975. Ballantine Books. Raised in upper-class New York City in the forties, Sally's world is torn by her mother's death. Surviving adolescence, she learns to cope with public school, new middle class values, and changing family relationships.

Bradford, Richard: *So Far From Heaven*. J. B. Lippincott, 1973. Pocket Books. A joyous romp with the Tafoyas, New Mexican Chicanos with a lust for life, larceny, and love. Illegal land speculation provides the action in this zany family story.

Bredes, Don: *Hard Feelings*. Atheneum, 1977. Bernie Hergrutter's season of personal growth takes him from Long Island to Chicago and back again as he learns about friendship, sex, love, and family.

Browne, Gerald A.: *Eleven Harrowhouse*. Arbor House, 1972. Dell. Diamonds are the plunder in this carefully crafted mystery. Chesser never loses his sense of humor as he steadily pursues romance and the big score.

Burdick, Eugene, and Harvey Wheeler: *Fail-Safe*. Mc-Graw-Hill, 1962. Dell. A missile raid warning proves a false alarm, but by accident one group of bombers misses the recall signal and heads on to Moscow.

Butler, William: *Butterfly Revolution*. Ballantine Books, 1975. A group of boys take over a summer camp and struggle among themselves for control.

Cook, Robin: *Coma*. Little, Brown, 1977. New American Library. Suspicious of a series of unexplained, but seemingly related hospital deaths, Dr. Susan Wheeler launches an unauthorized investigation that threatens to make her a victim, too.

Courlander, Harold: *The African*. Crown, 1977. Bantam Books. This novel recreates with powerful authenticity the details of African village life, the passage to America, and the cultural adjustment faced by a free African who was sold into slavery.

Cussler, Clive: *Raise the Titanic*. Viking Press, 1976. Bantam Books. An ill-fated ship with a priceless cargo has a second chance to make history as intrigue and international competition battle the ocean's depths.

Dickey, James: *Deliverance*. Houghton Mifflin, 1970. Dell.

A white-water canoe trip becomes a lesson in terror for four suburban men. Innocent of the powers of nature and backwoods solidarity, they must redefine personal life priorities merely to survive.

Doctorow, E. L.: *Ragtime*. Random House, 1975. Bantam Books. Houdini, Henry Ford, and Freud are three of the historical figures interacting with an immigrant family in this rhythmic study of America on the eve of the jazz age.

Drury, Allen: *Advise and Consent*. Doubleday, 1959. Avon Books. In this detailed fictional account of government process and people, congressional intrigue is triggered when the Senate is called upon to confirm the president's nomination of a new secretary of state.

Du Maurier, Daphne: *Rebecca*. Doubleday, 1948. Avon Books. The mysterious atmosphere of an old English estate, coupled with the peculiar behavior of the housekeeper, arouses a bride's suspicions about the death of her husband's first wife.

Durham, Marilyn: *The Man Who Loved Cat Dancing*. Harcourt Brace Jovanovich, 1972. Catherine Crocker flees from an unfeeling husband, only to be taken captive by four train robbers.

Edwards, Anne: *The Survivors*. Dell, 1969. Sole survivor of a mass murder that took six members of her family, Luane Woodrow relives the incident ten years later for a writer doing a story about the tragedy.

Fairbairn, Ann: *Five Smooth Stones*. Crown, 1966. Bantam Books. The long and complex story of David Champlin and his love affair with a white girl. In the tradition of *Gone with the Wind*.

Fields, Jeff: *A Cry of Angels*. Atheneum, 1974. Ballantine Books. Living in his great-aunt's boarding house, Earl confronts poverty, racism, love, and sorrow. Guided by Em Jojohn, a powerful but gentle Indian, Earl grows to appreciate the sheer pleasure of being alive.

Ferber, Edna: *Cimarron*. Doubleday, 1951. Fawcett Books. The pageantry of Oklahoma history is revealed through the lives of quixotic Yancy Cravat, Sabra (the southern belle he married), and their family.

————: *Giant*. Doubleday, 1954. Fawcett Books. The grandeur and harshness of the Texas landscale, the brashness and materialism of Texans are seen through the eyes of a rancher's bride.

————: *Ice Palace*. Doubleday, 1958. Fawcett Books. Two pioneering families in Alaska are followed through three generations.

————: *Showboat*. Fawcett Books, 1977. The life and loves of the wandering actors and actresses who perform aboard steamers on the Mississippi River during the 19th century.

————: *So Big*. Doubleday, 1951. Fawcett Books. A strong, determined woman rears her only son on a truck farm in the Midwest.

Forbes, Kathryn: *Mama's Bank Account*. Harcourt Brace Jovanovich, 1978. This is the original collection of vignettes about a Norwegian immigrant family that was ultimately developed into a stage play, TV show, and Broadway musical (*I Remember Mama*).

Fowles, John: *The French Lieutenant's Woman*. Little, Brown, 1969. New American Library. A study of 19th-century literary style in a contemporary novel. Society's standards are explained by a gregarious narrator in this unique morality tale.

Gaines, Ernest J.: *Autobiography of Miss Jane Pittman*. Dial Press, 1971. Bantam Books. Fictional memoirs of a 100-year-old ex-slave recalling her life on a plantation in Louisiana during and after the Civil War.

Gallico, Paul: *The Poseidon Adventure*. Dell, 1972. Turned upside down by a tidal wave, a liner is slowly being flooded and its passengers' climb to rescue is a race against time.

Gardner, John C.: *Grendel*. Alfred A. Knopf, 1971. Ballantine Books. The classic epic of English literature rewritten from the monster's point of view. An approach to Beowulf that questions the roles of hero and villain.

Gedge, Pauline: *Child of the Morning*. Dial Press, 1977. Popular Library. Reared by her pharaoh father to assume his throne upon his death, Hatshepsut—a real historical figure—has to contend with her weak half brother before she can realize her dream.

Gifford, Thomas: *The Wind Chill Factor*. G. P. Putnam's Sons, 1975. The Fourth Reich takes hold in Minnesota as an innocent American finds that his inheritance provides for a wealth of terror and intrigue on an international scale.

Goldman, William: *Boys and Girls Together*. Bantam Books, 1965. A whole generation of students—their passions, yearnings, and frustration—springs to life in this remarkable study of young men and women in college.

————: *Temple of Gold*. Dell, 1976. Raymond must salvage what is left of his self-respect when his best friend dies and he feels responsible.

Grady, James: *Three Days of Condor*. Dell, 1975. Code name Condor is trapped by double dealing in his covert organization. Maintaining a moral stance against mercenary agents proves to be a high-risk personal assignment.

Green, Gerald: *Holocaust*. Bro-Dart, 1978. Bantam Books. Beginning in 1935, not long before the enactment of the anti-Semitic Nuremberg laws, and ending in 1945 with the liberation of Auschwitz, this is the saga of two families, one Jewish and one German, and the effects of the holocaust on each.

Green, Hannah: *I Never Promised You a Rose Garden*. Holt, Rinehart and Winston, 1964. Living in a mythical world that both frightens and protects her, Deborah must confront her demons in order to regain her sanity.

Greenberg, Joanne: *In This Sign*. Holt, Rinehart and Winston, 1972. Avon Books. Through the story of one family, this novel movingly portrays the isolation of the deaf in trying to cope with the hearing world.

Guest, Judith: *Ordinary People*. Viking Press, 1976. Ballantine Books. After recovering from a suicide attempt, 17-year-old Conrad learns to recognize his own emotions and to share them with his family.

Hailey, Arthur: *Airport*. Doubleday, 1968. Bantam Books. An excitement-packed tale of 24 hours at a snowbound airport. A charming elderly stowaway, a mad bomber, a tormented general manager, and a conceited pilot meet crises and work their way towards solutions as the hours tick by.

Haley, Alex: *Roots*. Doubleday, 1976. Dell. Poignant and powerful narrative of the descendants of African slave

Kunta Kinte, and the family's history as slaves and as free Americans.

Harris, Marilyn: *Hatter Fox*. Random House, 1963. Abused by white society and its institutions, a young Indian girl withdraws from humanity. Dr. Teague Summer slowly brings her back, only to lose her again to callous misuse of power.

Harris, Thomas: *Black Sunday*. G. P. Putnam's Sons, 1975. Bantam Books. An embittered Vietnam veteran teams up with a bank of Palestinian terrorists in a maniacal plot to blow up the Super Bowl stadium.

Higgins, Jack: *The Eagle Has Landed*. Holt, Rinehart and Winston, 1975. Bantam Books. Winston Churchill is the intended victim of a highly trained German assassination team that infiltrates a British coastal town in the closing months of World War II.

Hilton, James: *Lost Horizon*. William Morrow, 1936. Pocket Books. A plane crash in the remote Himalayas brings a crew of jaded westerners face to face with utopia in an ageless Eastern society. Humanity's restless need to move and grow is explored in this confrontation with Shangri-la.

Jackson, Shirley: *We Have Always Lived in the Castle*. Penguin Books, 1970. Tainted by accusations of murder, members of the Blackwood family draw close for self-preservation. The sane and macabre worlds of the innocent and the condemned are switched in this frightening tale of revenge.

Joffo, Joseph: *A Bag of Marbles*. Houghton Mifflin, 1974. Bantam Books. Two young Jewish brothers flee occupied France during World War II and hide their identities for three perilous years.

Kaufman, Bel: *Up the Down Staircase*. Prentice-Hall, 1964. Avon Books. A collection of notes, memoranda, and letters is used to present the frustrating, fascinating first year of teaching in an overcrowded New York City high school.

Kellogg, Marjorie: *Tell Me That You Love Me, Junie Moon*. Farrar, Straus and Giroux, 1968. Popular Library. Three handicapped friends join in a communal living arrangement that defies convention and helps all three to grow and cope with the normal world.

Knebel, Fletcher, and Charles W. Bailey 2d: *Seven Days in May*. Harper & Row, 1964. Bantam Books. A military conspiracy to take over the White House threatens almost 200 years of tradition in this novel which raises many interesting questions about our political system.

Kozinski, Jerzy: *Being There*. Harcourt Brace Jovanovich, 1971. Bantam Books. An allegorical, deceptively simple story about a man with no discernible background, who is transformed into a national celebrity overnight, for no logical reason.

————: *The Painted Bird*. Houghton Mifflin, 1976. Bantam Books. This account of a small boy who was separated from his parents at the beginning of World War II traces his wartime wandering from village to village, horror to horror.

Le Carré, John: *The Spy Who Came In From the Cold*. Coward, McCann & Geohegan, 1978. Bantam Books. British secret agent Alec Leamas pretends to defect in order to destroy an East German who has killed the last British agent behind the iron curtain.

Lee, Harper: *To Kill a Mockingbird*. J. B. Lippincott, 1960. Popular Library. Bigotry in a southern town, justice and love in one southern family. Scout's child's-eye view reveals a special wisdom in her innocence.

Levin, Ira: *The Boys from Brazil*. Random House, 1976. Dell. Escaped Nazis living in Brazil are triggering a complicated plot that might establish a Fourth Reich through the cloning of Hitler.

Ludlum, Robert: *The Gemini Contenders*. Dial Press, 1976. Dell. Twin brothers represent good and evil in a suspense story of World War II. Based on little-known facts about the history of Christianity, the novel questions humanity's need for knowledge that may upset the balance of world power.

McCullers, Carson: *The Heart is a Lonely Hunter*. Houghton Mifflin, 1940. Bantam Books. Communication can be more than just words and in the friendship of a deaf-mute and a young girl it has to be, as they confront the subtle bigotry of a southern town.

McCullough, Colleen: *The Thorn Birds*. Harper & Row, 1977. Avon Books. A chronicle of the Cleary clan maturing in the Australian outback as their rough country progresses with the 20th century.

————: *Tim*. Harper & Row, 1974. Popular Library. A tender love story that explores the relationship between a retarded youth and a middle-aged spinster. Rejected by established society, Tim and Mary build a marriage on their own special strengths.

MacKenzie, Rachel: *The Wine of Astonishment*. Viking Press, 1974. Avon Books. The lives of Pliny Falls are so inextricably tied that the entire town suffers the consequences of Esther Handerson's relationship with a married man. A quietly tragic novel, narrated in 19th-century style.

Michener, James A.: *Centennial*. Random House, 1974. Fawcett Books. An epic account of the history of a small area of eastern Colorado, from its geological formation to its present force in politics.

————: *Hawaii*. Random House, 1959. Fawcett Books. Stories of many of the peoples of Hawaii—Polynesian, American missionary stock, Japanese, Chinese—are interwoven in a fast-paced narrative which spans the island's history.

Mitchell, Margaret: *Gone with the Wind*. Macmillan, 1936. Avon Books. Scarlett O'Hara, the ultimate southern belle, sees her beloved plantation, Tara, fall to the Union army's victory. Pursuing the love of Rhett Butler and an outmoded Dixie dream, she vows to survive the destruction of the Civil War.

Morrell, David: *First Blood*. M. Evans, 1972. Fawcett Books. Unable to settle back into society after a tour of duty in Vietnam, Rambo, trained as a killer, becomes the hunted. There is no moral solution in Teasle's pursuit of Rambo, only inevitable tragedy.

Nathan, Robert: *A Portrait of Jennie*. Alfred A. Knopf, 1949. Dell. A dreamlike quality pervades this account of a young painter whose success dates from his first meeting with the strange, time-defying Jennie.

Nichols, John: *The Sterile Cuckoo*. Avon Books, 1972. Hearing the name Pookie Adams should have warned Jerry that college was going to be more than classes, exams, and fraternity parties.

Osborn, John Jay, Jr.: *The Paper Chase*. Avon Books, 1973. The first year at Harvard Law forces Hart to question his goals. A cagey professor, a tender love affair, and the constant competition of his classmates lend hard and soft edges to academic life.

Pasternak, Boris: *Dr. Zhivago*. Pantheon Books, 1958. New American Library. A Russian doctor aches for his homeland, torn by revolution. At the same time, he must find peace from the personal torment he suffers because of his love for two special women.

Patterson, Sarah: *The Distant Summer*. Simon and Schuster, 1976. Pocket Books. As World War II devastates Europe, Kate falls in love with an RAF rear gunner. They must learn to live for the future in spite of their fear that each mission over Germany may be Johnny's last.

Plath, Sylvia: *The Bell Jar*. Harper & Row, 1971. Bantam Books. During a sultry summer in New York, Esther Greenwood works as a junior editor on *Mademoiselle*, quarrels with her mother and boyfriend, and gradually begins her tragic descent into madness.

Portis, Charles: *True Grit*. Simon and Schuster, 1968. New American Library. A different kind of western in the true Hollywood style which tells of the adventures of a 14-year-old girl who sets out for Indian Territory to avenge her father's death.

Potok, Chaim: *The Chosen*. Simon and Schuster, 1967. Fawcett Books. The sheltered world of Brooklyn's Hasidic community is both a heritage and a powerful restraint as two boys build a friendship amid tradition.

Price, Richard: *The Wanderers*. Houghton Mifflin, 1974. Avon Books. A raw survival story of gang life in the early sixties. Set in the Bronx, the subcultures of ethnic neighborhoods are shown to be unforgiving proving grounds for the rights of manhood.

Raucher, Herman: *Summer of '42*. Dell, 1978. Hermie's idyllic coastal summers become childhood memories in that one special season when he tastes first love and begins to see himself as a man.

Renault, Mary: *The Bull from the Sea*. Pantheon Books, 1962. Vintage Books. *The King Must Die*. Pantheon Books, 1958. Bantam Books. Two stirring historical novels based in the Greek legend of Theseus, who was sent to slay the Cretan Minotaur

Sarton, May: *As We Are Now*. W. W. Norton, 1973.

Aging and alone in a desolate senior citizens' home, Caro is not without spirit as she decides how to define her last days in a youth-oriented world. Her final statement is a warning to society.

Schaefer, Jack: *Shane*. Houghton Mifflin, 1954. Amsco School. A mysterious, gentle gunman helps the farmers in their fight with the cattlemen and becomes a hero to young Bob Starrett, who tells the story.

Schwarz-Bart, Andre: *The Last of the Just*. Atheneum, 1973. Bantam Books. This novel tells the story of the Levy family. It begins with a pogrom at York, England, in 1185 and ends in the Auschwitz gas chambers some 760 years later.

Segal, Erich: *Love Story*. Harper & Row, 1970. Avon Books. During their years at Harvard and Radcliff, Oliver and Jennie fall in love, though they come from very different backgrounds. Their early struggle as young marrieds is blighted by Jennie's untimely death.

Selinko, Annemarie: *Desiree*. William Morrow, 1953. Avon Books. Admittedly romantic and sentimental, this is about Napoleon and his first love, Desiree.

Shute, Nevil: *On The Beach*. William Morrow, 1957. Ballantine Books. The only survivors of an atomic war gather in Australia to await inevitable doom as deadly radiation moves toward them.

Smith, Betty: *A Tree Grows in Brooklyn*. Harper & Row, 1947. Growing up in a tenement, the daughter of immigrants, Francie Nolan adores her romantic, irresponsible father. She inherits the ability to dream from him, but it is her mother's fortitude that sees the Nolans through crisis and death, and guides Francie into adolescence.

Stein, Sol: *The Magician*. Dell, 1972. A victim of violence and twists in the judicial system, Japhet must resort to similar manipulation when his instinct for self-preservation catches in the web of the law.

Stewart, Mary: *Airs Above the Ground*. William Morrow, 1965. Fawcett Books. A romantic thriller, set against the background of an Austrian circus featuring the famed Lippizaner stallions.

————: *This Rough Magic*. William Morrow, 1964. Fawcett Books. A young English actress visiting on the Greek island of Corfu becomes involved in a strange adventure with a retired Shakespearean actor, a friendly dolphin, and a romantic hero.

Stone, Irving: *The Agony and the Ecstasy*. Doubleday, 1965. New American Library. This biographical novel about Michelangelo emphasizes the disappointments and triumphs of his art and personal life.

————: *Love Is Eternal*. Doubleday. New American Library, 1972. A fictionalized biography of Mary Todd Lincoln, the aristocratic southern gentlewoman who opted to marry the uncouth, gawky Lincoln and desperately tried to change him.

————: *Lust for Life*. Doubleday, 1954. Pocket Books. A biographical novel based on the stormy personal life and career of the painter Vincent Van Gogh, ending with his suicide at age 37.

————: *The President's Lady*. Doubleday, 1959. New American Library. Rachel Jackson's life was saddened and perhaps shortened by an ugly scandal kept alive by her husband's political enemies.

Swarthout, Glendon: *Bless the Beasts and Children*. Doubleday, 1970. Five boys, all losers, have been sent to a western camp to make men of themselves. Once together, they brilliantly, comically save themselves and some noble buffalo threatened by hunters.

Tey, Josephine: *Daughter of Time*. Berkley, 1975. A suspenseful novel that unravels the mystery of Richard III and the murder of the princes in the Tower.

Trumbo, Dalton: *Johnny Got His Gun*. Bantam Books, 1970. A casualty of war, one nameless youth represents all senseless destruction as he struggles to communicate despite the loss of his face and limbs.

Updike, John: *Rabbit Run*. Alfred A. Knopf, 1960. Fawcett Books. The gray monotony of a Pennsylvania coal town masks Rabbit Angstrom's options after high school. Trapped by his own lack of imagination, he tries to find personal space in a world void of choices.

Walker, Mildred: *Winter Wheat*. Harcourt Brace Jovanovich, 1966. An introspective story of a Montana girl who blames her parents when her fiancé breaks their engagement because of the difference in their backgrounds.

Warren, Robert Penn: *All the King's Men*. Random House, 1960. Bantam Books. A fictionalized study of Louisiana power and politics in the 1930s. Democratic concepts are challenged by the rise and fall of Willie Stark as the depression blankets the South.

West, Jessamyn: *The Massacre at Fall Creek*. Harcourt Brace Jovanovich, 1975. The wanton destruction of Indian nations is painfully detailed in this courtroom exposé of white power abuses in the settlement of the American West.

Westheimer, David: *Von Ryan's Express*. Doubleday, 1964. New American Library. One thousand war prisoners in Italy are loaded into boxcars to be sent to Germany. A sharp American colonel engineers their escape.

Wilder, Thornton: *Theophilus North*. Harper & Row, 1973. Avon Books. A young tutor touches the lives of the rich and the struggling lower classes during the 1920s. Theophilus grows wiser and his pupils stronger after his summer with them in historic Newport, Rhode Island.

Wouk, Herman: *The Winds of War*. Little, Brown, 1971. Pocket Books. Rumblings of political tension in Europe and Asia begin to affect the members of the Henry family. Student or sailor, all are drawn into the chaos that follows Pearl Harbor.

7

Reading Rights

The fact is that censorship always defeats its own purpose, for it creates, in the end, the kind of society that is incapable of exercising real discretion . . . In the long run it will create a generation incapable of appreciating the difference between independence of thought and subservience.

—Henry Steele Commager

The only freedom deserving the name is that of pursuing our own good in our own way, so long as we do not attempt to deprive others of theirs . . . Mankind are greater gainers by suffering each other to live as seems good to themselves, than by compelling each to live as seems good to the rest.

—John Stuart Mill

There is no such thing as a moral or an immoral book. Books are well written or badly written.

—Oscar Wilde

All kinds of people demand the right to limit the reading of the young. Feminists demand that the picture of passive females be eliminated from children's reading. Gays object to unfavorable presentations of homosexuality. Some religious groups want to censor stories centering on divorce, remarriage, and rape among teens. Elements of the political body wish to eliminate books showing a political system other than our own. Each ethnic group is testy about any suggestion of human faults and failings of its members. Some parents' groups are militantly against sex appearing in stories for teens. And there are those who insist that some twenty obscene or profane words be eliminated from the language.

If we are honest with ourselves, we will probably admit that at some time with some teenage book we feel the instincts of the censor. We get the feeling that some word, scene, or idea should be eliminated.

The prevalence of attempts to censor books attests to the widespread, deep-felt belief that literature is potent in affecting attitudes, beliefs, and perhaps behavior. People have attempted to censor dictionaries for including such words as "fuck" or "whore." They apparently believe that a word alone will incite people to action.

It is not surprising then that people feel the young should read only limited materials so they will not pick up attitudes, language, or behavior patterns considered harmful to themselves or society. The shielding of the young is a deep instinct in most of us. We limit our children's environments to guard them from natural hazards; as adults they will live with them freely. It is an easy step to believing that adults should exercise careful control of what the young may read.

The two most often censored items in books are language and sex.

LANGUAGE

Throughout written history, all peoples have had taboo words. Many of them have a long history. The words, few in number, are generally used to express strong emotion, but often their use is confined to certain settings—such as by men in a locker room. First, there are words used in religion but also used secularly to express an emotion: "God," "hell," "damn," "bloody." These are the "profane" words, to which religiously oriented groups object both in oral use and in print. Second are the words labeled obscene. These are common terms for bodily functions: "fuck," "shit," "pee," etc. Some people demand loudly that these words be eliminated from the language, especially that of the young. Recently, a third group of words has been attacked by women's and ethnic organizations. Women would rule out the masculine morpheme in words referring to both sexes: "*man*kind," "chair*man*," "*king*dom," "*father*land." One ethnic group demands that "black" or "Afro-American" be substituted for "colored," "negro," or "nigger" in literature even though at certain historical times the latter were the terms used. Another ethnic group insists that "Native American" be used for "Indian" in books and stories, in spite of the fact that all people born in America are natives of the country. Those who decry linguistic censorship by one kind of pressure group are often guilty of the same kind of censorship in some other area.

People have always needed words to express strong emotion. They may be used, too, to express inner rebellion against the limitations of society, family, jobs, fate. The words serve as a kind of safety valve, releasing pressure when it becomes intolerable. Obviously, writers interested in presenting a realistic picture of life will reproduce the speech that their characters would actually use. Most adults would find it hard not to titter if war-hardened heroes in the midst of battle used expletives such as "mercy me," "shucks," "oh, my," and "tush-tush," yet these same adults may want the language in teen books watered down just that way.

The adults' fear seems to be that young readers will imitate the language of the characters in books or that they will be indiscreet in using such words. Some religious people believe strongly that users of profanity are taking the Lord's name in vain and condemning themselves to eternal damnation: hence their concern when their own teens use profanity.

Research in vocabulary indicates the surprising fact that if we do not know a word, we tend to neither hear it nor see it. You may recall that when you have just learned a new word, suddenly you encounter it everywhere. Obviously it was there all the time. Fussing about words may be one of the best ways to ensure that the young learn them if they don't already know them.

Most teens encounter few profane or obscene words, in books, to which they have not been exposed in daily life. In literature the use of such words helps delineate character or situation. For example, in *The Catcher in the Rye,* Holden Caulfield says he has a "lousy" vocabulary. Salinger (and Caulfield) are not recommending a poor vocabulary to the reader. The impact of profanity in literature on the young is recognition of the kind of situation in which people use taboo language. We quoted Commager in the epigraphs to this chapter as saying that people will through reading become capable of "exercising real discretion." They will not be more apt to imitate profanity they have read than to imitate Shakespearean blank verse after reading *Hamlet.*

SEX IN BOOKS

Sexual relationships between men and women account for a major portion of the great literature of the world. Almost no literature is without some element of sexuality. Controversy revolves around three aspects: the pornographic as opposed to the literary, the depiction of sexual details, and the age and level of development of the reader.

The Distinction between Pornography and Literature

The government has tried, somewhat unsuccessfully, to define pornography. The word stems from the Latin and means literally "writing about prostitutes." The dictionary defines it as writing intending to incite lascivious actions. Thus the intent of the writing is crucial. Depiction of explicit sexual actions in literature does not make it pornographic unless there is intent to incite lascivious action. Pornography is almost always subliterary, and the writer has no interest in evoking real feelings about life. The book is formulistic. One has only to examine a few porn magazines to see endless repetition of the same situations, the same poses. Pornography tends to become dull because of this repetition. The sex acts portrayed are seldom beautiful or realistic; they emphasize the biological, and there is no suggestion of a warm, loving relationship between the people engaged in the sexual acts.

Most books in school libraries that are criticized by would-be censors are far from being pornographic. One sometimes suspects that the individual calling *The Catcher in the Rye* or *Catch-22* pornographic has never seen real hard-core pornography.

Years ago I. A. Richards spelled out four dimensions of meaning of a piece of literature: the plain sense, the attitude of the writer toward the plain sense, the attitude of the writer toward the reader, and the intention of the work.

Objections to a novel usually stem from people reading it as though it were expository prose in which "plain sense" is all-important. They seem unaware of the need to grasp the writer's attitude toward what is happening, and toward the reader; thus they fail to grasp the intent of the book. It is a misreading of the writer's purpose not unlike that of the listener to a sermon on man's vices who came away feeling that they sounded pretty attractive.

If you examine *The Catcher in the Rye* using all four of Richards's criteria for literary understanding, you will see the effect of the book quite differently from looking at only the surface story. Though the narrative is in the first person, Salinger communicates his feeling about the events of the story and his attitude toward the reader, which add up to his apparent intent in writing the book. These can be objectified somewhat as follows: Here is a confused kid from a wealthy family whose parents are too busy to pay much attention to him. He is growing up in a world whose value system seems to him crassly materialistic. He has instincts toward the pure and the good, but his concepts are too naive to survive in the real world. He finds other people phony, but does not recognize the phoniness in himself. The story is a document of great compassion toward a boy's growing up in the modern world. Holden would like to change humanity. In this sense he has sometimes been called a Christ figure, since he desires to expiate the sins of the world. Certainly the reader of the book does not come away thinking that Holden's life is something she/he wants to emulate. It is particularly ironic that he should be labeled harmful by some religious groups.

Details of Sex in a Book

In the last half of this century there has been a steady move toward more explicit physical details about sex in all books, including children's and adolescents'. Sexual themes developed slowly in adolescent books. Madeleine L'Engle used them in *The Small Rain* in the 1940s; Henry Felsen's *Two and the Town* in the 1950s and James Summer's *Limits of Love* were other early attempts. But there were seldom explicit details; as in movies "edited for TV," sex might be suggested by characters' removing a bit of clothing, or perhaps lying side by side in bed after the act.

In today's books little is left to the imagination. Menstruation, erection, masturbation are discussed by characters and described in detail. Girls worry about achieving orgasm, though here the physical sensations are seldom given. French kissing and oral sex are recorded. Though there are several adolescent books dealing with homosexual relations, none has as yet given explicit descriptions of the acts of homosexual lovemaking.

Do such sex scenes in teenage books serve a purpose? As late as the 1930s a major document in the teaching of English said that explicit sexual description could never be artistic. The principal defense is that they are necessary for the reader's understanding of the character, or of the relationship between the young people, or for the aesthetic impact of the book.

The detailing of sex in literature stems from the tradition of realism that has governed prose fiction for the last 200 years. The teenage book was birthed to

give teens a mirror of themselves. Since sexual maturation is reached in the teens and since it plays such an
important part in psychological development, it is
obvious that no book can deal realistically with teenage life and bypass it. Books that presented teen life as
concerned only with sports, proms, family relations,
and vocation were dealing with only part of life. Many
feel that such books omitted the most crucial part of it:
the drive toward sexual fulfillment. It is natural that in
the drive toward realism as a literary code writers
should push toward depicting more intimate details of
life. The countermovement in literature is discussed in
chapter 15, on science fiction.

All societies have to come to terms with the sexual
urges of the young. Some have institutionalized them
since primitive times through socially approved permissiveness. The young, after undergoing puberty rites,
were turned loose like colts in a pasture. Only when
pregnancy occurred did the adults step in and sanction
the union by marriage. Other cultures have pretended
that such urges were nonexistent, turning their backs
on the games of the young. A few have tried to restrict adolescent sexual activity through taboos, and
through systems of rigidly separating the sexes.

Our society has changed. Sex education in junior
high schools is a form of institutional recognition of
sexual activity among the young. There is increasing
permissiveness toward sex experiences before marriage.
Writers are not leading society, but following it.

One might wish for books that deal more with the
emotional and less with the biological aspects of sex,
as do Norma Klein's *Hiding* and George Bower's *November, December,* as compared to the more explicit
Judy Blume's *Forever* and M. E. Kerr's *I'll Love You
When You're More Like Me.*

Age of the Reader

The cry is often heard: "They shouldn't know about
such things yet." No one argues against restricting a
teenager from drinking or driving before a certain age,

so it is not surprising that some feel that age should determine what people should read. Undoubtedly some literal and imaginative experiences can be traumatic to the very young. An acquaintance, taken through a slaughterhouse at the age of 8, was so traumatized that she has refused to eat meat ever since. The fear that too early a presentation of only the physical side of sex may traumatize the teenager about sex is understandable.

There is a cliché that readers get from a book what they bring to it. The level of experiential development of readers determines their understanding of what the writer is evoking. Teens, because of their limited background, will fail to understand much of adult experience. This can often be seen in teaching Shakespeare: the plain sense of the story is grasped, but the problems and emotions of a Lear, Othello, Hamlet, Macbeth, Brutus are incomprehensible to most adolescents.

Young readers usually do not understand situations in a book for which they are not ready. Recently a sixth grader read *Forever,* Judy Blume's explicit book about the sexual experiences of teenagers. She thought the book was rather "dumb," and couldn't understand why the girl was so mean to the boy in the story. This is an aspect that probably never occurred to the adults who were shocked that a sixth grader was reading the book. Years ago when *A Tree Grows in Brooklyn,* a rage among teenagers, was severely questioned by adults, the usual response of girl readers was: "Isn't it wonderful that Francie could have lived in such abominable circumstances and have come out such a beautiful person?" Perhaps this is a misreading of the book, but it shows that the impact of a book on a young reader is often different from what an adult reader thinks it will be.

If given freedom of choice, readers of all ages discard books that are beyond their experiential range, or if they struggle through them, interpret them within the limits of their own perceptions. Difficulties arise, as with Shakespeare, when adults try to force works on the young before they are ready for them.

TODAY'S PRACTICE

I have found it useful when considering literature for classroom use to divide books roughly into four categories.

Books Assigned for Group Reading and Discussion

These materials should not be above the maturity level of the class. They should be free from situations that may be traumatic for some students because of religion, ethnic background, or family problems, and that might embarrass members of a mixed class in open discussion. Their content should eventuate in significant understandings.

Books on a List for Individual Reading

Such a list contains books recommended for independent reading. Everyone is expected to find something on it on his/her level, but no one is required to read any one title. Titles should be related to the educational objectives of the class; they should include different sexual protagonists, of different levels of maturity, of differing racial or ethnic settings.

Books Available in the School Library with Open Access

These are books that would not be placed on a list for a particular assignment in class. Such books may be either too juvenile or too advanced in tone and experiential level. Any student may choose what to read to satisfy the requirements of the unit.

Books Outside the Immediate Confines of the School

Of the millions of books available, the school (or any collection, except the Library of Congress) deals with only a few thousand. Students may find and choose to read books from this pool to fulfill an assignment.

I firmly believe that students should not be forced
to read materials that they or their parents find ob-
jectionable on moral or religious grounds. But equally
they do not have the right to make this judgment for
other members of a class.

Certain principles begin to emerge concerning teenagers and their rights to read:

1. *A book must be looked at as a total experience,
not dissected into parts.* In art, the whole is greater
than and often different from the sum of its parts. So
in literature, the language, the situations, the descriptions are not of significance in themselves; but together
they build toward the impact of the book on the reader.

2. *Literature should not be judged by the same
standards as factual exposition.* Tone is as important
as plain sense in distilling literary intent. The most
flagrant example in which tone was not considered was
the furor that erupted over Jonathan Swift's "Modest
Proposal" in the 18th century. Readers failed to recognize the bitter irony of his tone and reacted only to the
appalling details. Similar failure to assess authors' intent accounts for most censorship disputes between
parental groups and teachers or librarians.

3. *Real literature, real works of art, tend always to
be forging new insights, new connection in life as we
perceive it.* Therefore, new forms seem shocking.
Wordsworth and Coleridge shocked the reader brought
up on 18th-century models, and Shelley and Byron
were condemned not only for their works but for their
life-styles. Genteel people did not go to Ibsen plays in
Norway. The multiple image painting of Andy War-
hol, which at first seemed bizarre, has moved into the
position of a recognized friend. Marshall McLuhan
has posed the idea that we live our lives, not in the
present, but in the immediate past. Only the poets see
and can show us the present as it really is: this is one
of their functions in the scheme of social living. Therefore, the best books will probably always stir up objections.

4. *No one has a right to impose his choice in reading
on others.* An individual has the right to refuse to read

certain books, but not to prevent you or me from reading them if we so desire. A parent or legal guardian of a teenager can limit the reading of his child, but should not be permitted to limit the reading of other people's children by forcing the removal of a book from the school library. Recently in two places, teenagers have brought suits under the umbrella of freedom of speech when literary works that they wished to read were removed from library shelves. They won.

5. *Maxim Gorky said years ago that real literature could be nothing but moral.* If a writer is wrestling with his existence and relationships and emotions, if he is honestly trying to record what he feels and hears and sees in a structured form, the result will be true. The problem comes in formulistic writing—the kind defined as subliterature. Unfortunately, the line between the two is not always clear.

The National Council of Teachers of English and the American Library Association have evolved a procedural plan for dealing with objections raised about books.

1. No action is taken without a signed written objection. A form which can be duplicated is sent to complainees as a way to record their points of view.

2. The written form is given to a standing committee to evaluate the merits of the complaint. The committee usually consists of several teachers, a librarian, an administrator, often a lay person or two, and a student. The complaint is adjudicated by a jury, not by a single individual or two or three self-appointed censors. Justice sometimes miscarries in a jury system, but it is still the best system that people have devised to settle a problem.

We decry the attempts of the Russians, the Chinese, the South Africans to control the reading of their people. We pride ourselves on offering refuge to writers like Solzhenitsyn when they are forced to flee their country for what they have written. The right to free access to ideas and books is fundamental in a free society. Any attempt to restrict the reading of the young by arbitrary standards moves toward a society of controlled communication. It is more important to help the young learn to evaluate what they read than to arbitrarily determine what they can read. As President Dwight D. Eisenhower said in a speech at Dartmouth College: "Don't join the book burners. Don't think you are going to conceal thoughts by concealing evidence that they ever existed."

8

Significant Modern Literature

> Old books, as you well know, are the books of the
> world's youth and new books are fruits of its age.
> —*Oliver Wendell Holmes*

A handful of the books published each year are hailed
by critics as modern classics. It is difficult to define a
modern classic precisely, but it is generally thought
of as an enduring work of literature, distinguished by
skillful and original writing, in-depth character portrayal, intricate plot design, provocative use of symbol,
and subtle, often poetic use of language.

To the adolescent, modern classics express an ap-
pealingly contemporary point of view. According to a
survey made by the National Council of Teachers of
English among several thousand award-winning students in English, of the 40 titles most often mentioned
as having the greatest impact, two-thirds were written
during the 20th century, and more than half of these
since World War II. With few exceptions, they had
been acclaimed by critics.

Each generation of adolescents selects a group of
titles or authors as their own. These become the idols
that one must have read and must admire to be "in
the know." In the 1920s young adult intellectuals read
Edna St. Vincent Millay and Sinclair Lewis. In the
1930s they were enthusiastic about James T. Farrell,
Thomas Wolfe, and Ernest Hemingway. In the 1940s
preferences were less distinct, perhaps because of
youth's involvement in World War II; Norman Mailer

probably came close to becoming such an idol, as did Ayn Rand. In the 1950s T. S. Eliot, Dylan Thomas, and Albert Camus were among youth's most admired authors. The 1960s brought Salinger, Golding, Orwell, Updike, and Heller to the forefront. And the beginning of the 1970s found Hermann Hesse, Kurt Vonnegut, Jr., and Richard Brautigan as the "in" authors.

Idols change from generation to generation, but they have qualities in common. They tend to be writers who challenge the conventional assumptions of the period, who glorify the individual and his individuality as he struggles against the intolerable web of contemporary society. They write books that may shock older readers in idea, situation, or language. Each generation's idols express the adolescent's rebellion against adult society and his struggle to find a more satisfying direction or pattern for himself.

Teenagers, even intellectual ones, do not read all the contemporary books and authors considered significant, but make a selection. There are few, for example, who read Doris Lessing, John Barth, or Joyce Carol Oates, who are perhaps some of the finest writers of our time. Very few read Mann's *The Magic Mountain* or Hemingway's *The Sun Also Rises*. Reading interests of the bright are about the same as those of the average.

The bright may read significant literature, but basically they respond to works whose themes are those discussed in chapter 3. Young people are interested in reading about the adolescent experience. This is why *Of Human Bondage* has had a great impact on several generations of bright 17-year-olds. The reader watches Philip Carey grow up from 12 to 30 during the 1890s and 1900s. Philip's clubfoot colors all his relations with people, but his journey toward maturity is the journey shared by most young intellectuals. He struggles with his religious beliefs, discovers the world of ideas, pursues the dream of an artist's bohemian life, tries to probe and understand the bittersweet torments of love, and finally faces the necessity of vocational choice, settling on medicine. At the end of the book he marries a well-balanced girl and is ready to take over a country doctor's medical practice; he becomes respectable. No other book of the 20th century seems to have captured so well the storm and torments accompanying the young adult's struggle to find direction.

Interest in adolescent confusion accounts for the fantastic popularity of J. D. Salinger's *The Catcher in the Rye*. Holden Caulfield, the hero, is trying desperately to find something clean, pure, and beautiful in life, but his tentative attempts are met by pretense, filth, or phoniness. He is a tangled mass of confusion about his sexual desires, his vocational aims, his family, his relationships with his peer group. Holden, more than any other character in American literature since Huck Finn, portrays the innermost doubts, fears, guilt, and aspirations of the adolescent male.

Carson McCullers's beautifully crafted *The Member of the Wedding* is the story of Frankie Addams, a 12-year-old girl who is desperately looking for the "we of me." Frankie's brother is about to get married and the young girl conceives the strange desire to go with the honeymooners on their wedding trip. She tries to grow up by adopting the trappings of maturity: putting on lipstick, going to the Blue Moon tavern, making a date with a soldier. Through these incidents the author captures the confusion of a young girl as she finds herself confronting new emotions, a developing body, and changing status.

Perhaps the greatest literary work to explore adolescence is James Joyce's *A Portrait of the Artist as a Young Man*, which tells of Stephen Dedalus's slow rebellion during his growing years against school, religion, family, and country as he searches for self and comes to an artistic awakening. Few teens will undertake the book voluntarily, but properly guided they are usually very stimulated by it.

Herman Hesse's *Demian*, an intriguing book widely read by European teens in the 1920s, was not discovered by American teenagers until sometime in the sixties. The book begins in late childhood when Sinclair is exploited by a bully, and Demian, an older boy in the school, helps him free himself. Sinclair tries to find himself as he passes through the stages of adolescence by trying alcohol, sex, gambling and the arts. The book is rich in symbolism, but is generally read by young adults as a straightforward account of growing up.

Books that are bizarre and off-beat, presenting human life in extreme fringe situations, appeal to young adults. The extreme situation is a metaphor for the general status of human beings in the modern world. One of the most provocative is Franz Kafka's *Metamorphosis*. Gregor Samsa awakens to find he has changed into an enormous insect. The short, deceptively simple novel is built around incidents that show him becoming less human and more buglike. Family and friends are horrified by his form. Every reader brings different insights to the story, which is a statement of modern man's sense of intense alienation.

Ralph Ellison's *Invisible Man* is a mixture of realism and the bizarre, with obvious symbolic intentions. The unnamed narrator is expelled from a black college for reasons he doesn't understand and begins a fantastic journey through New York City. Finally he retreats to an underground hideaway in Harlem and becomes, in effect, invisible.

Another unusual book which appeals to teenagers is *Lord of the Flies* by William Golding, about a group of boys isolated on a tropical island after a plane crash. They divide into two groups: one seeks to set up an ordered civilization based on justice and right; the other group reverts to primitive savagery. Bit by bit savagery gains control; those who support rationality and morality are nearly overwhelmed. Only the arrival of a navy ship prevents the annihilation of the forces of good. The real impact of the story is subjective, as the reader gradually becomes aware that Golding is not commenting about the nature of children, but about humanity in general. He is suggesting that the evil in human life is an active force that must be met with a united front, or humanity is doomed. The appalling events in the book are plausible enough to set readers wondering, thinking, probing their own thoughts and attitudes. The significance of the book lies in its title: the devil Beelzebub in early Middle Eastern cultures was the dispenser of flies.

Many modern classics deal with individuals trapped by the web of society or by something in their own natures that they cannot resolve. Such are the books of Graham Greene, which are often laid in exotic places in Africa, Indochina, Mexico, South America. *A Burnt-Out Case* tells of a successful architect who has the "disease of civilization (wealth, fame)" and has become a burnt-out case. He tries to lose himself in a leper colony in Africa, but life's demands reach out for him like a vine's tendrils.

Albert Camus's *The Stranger* also presents an internal struggle. The setting is Algeria, where Meursault, a young Frenchman, kills an Arab in a moment of sun-blindness on the beach. He is arrested, convicted, and about to be executed. His strange refusal to make any defense of his actions and his seeming lack of feeling are the essence of existential modern man, that is, a person who has freedom of choice but no rational criteria for choosing. He is isolated in the web of his own perceptions and sensations. The story is told in brittle, clear language and is often read in advanced French classes at the high-school level.

Another book of inner anguish is the beautiful South African novel *Cry the Beloved Country* by Alan Paton. A black priest goes on a mission to Johannesburg to find out what has happened to his son and his sister. He discovers that his sister has become a prostitute and his son has murdered a white man. His anguish in the face of a hopeless situation is akin to that of the heroes and heroines of ancient Greek tragedy.

The Russian novel *One Day in the Life of Ivan Denisovich* by Aleksander Solzhenitsyn is widely read. The short book recounts in simple, direct prose, a day in the life of a political prisoner in a Siberian labor camp. Ivan Denisovich Shukhov is unjustly accused of being a spy and condemned to hard labor by the Stalinist regime. The day is in the dead of winter and the book records the endurance, the courage, the cruelty of the camp in which the hero's great achievement is that he has survived another day. At the book's end, it has been "a day without a dark cloud. Almost a happy day" and there are only "three thousand six hundred and fifty-three days" more to be endured.

Bigger Thomas in Richard Wright's *Native Son* is a character in fiction who seems to epitomize the black's situation in American society. An uneducated boy from Chicago's South Side, he gets a job as a chauffeur for a wealthy white family who pride themselves on their liberal point of view. On his first day he drives the daughter of the family to her college classes; she gets drunk and has to be carried to her room. Fearing discovery and to prevent her screaming, Bigger put a pillow over her face and accidentally smothers her. Horrible as the act is, Bigger is really the victim of a society that has made him a second-class citizen subject to insurmountable fears when dealing with whites.

Modern classics, because they deal with fundamental issues at the heart of modern life, are often dark and depressing. Characters are caught in a social milieu that engulfs them. They work not for goals but simply to survive in an uncaring if not hostile environment. No wonder one group of teenagers, surveyed about what they would like to see in literature, said they wanted something that suggested there was something to live for.

Only occasionally in recent literature have writers presented a positive feeling about life. Willa Cather is one of the exceptions. The recurring theme that runs through her works is the impact of the old, deep European culture on the American frontier. In *The Song of the Lark,* a girl reared in the bleakness of an eastern Colorado town discovers music and becomes one of the great opera singers of her time. In *Death Comes for the Archbishop,* Father Latour, a highly cultured Frenchman, comes to Santa Fe in the 19th century to reestablish the Catholic faith in the vast territory of the Southwest. *My Ántonia* traces the life of a high-spirited Bohemian girl whose parents homestead in

Nebraska. We see Ántonia's youth in a sod shanty, her adulthood as a hired girl, and her maturity as a farm wife surrounded by children.

Of Hemingway's works, *The Old Man and the Sea* may be popular among teens because it seems to affirm the dignity of an individual's life and struggles. Santiago, a broken old fisherman, engages in an epic struggle with a huge marlin. After hours of battle he succeeds in catching the monster, only to have his catch devoured by sharks. Santiago's will to fight and subdue the gigantic fish, though in retrospect it may seem irrational and useless, somehow epitomizes the elusive thing called spirit in people. Here is positive action, in the pitting of oneself against natural forces.

Something of the same kind of theme in John Steinbeck has made him almost a cult figure among young readers. It is not *The Grapes of Wrath* that they particularly prize, though this has the strength of Ma Joad as a positive force. The books teenagers particularly like are *Tortilla Flat, Cannery Row,* and *Of Mice and Men.* In these, Steinbeck has captured a kind of joie de vivre among those whom society rejects.

Each generation of sensitive adolescents favors some writer their parents do not approve of or understand. Because they feel that no one before them has faced the same problems, the same feelings, the same world that they face, they look for authors who help them express their uniqueness. It is their own world for which adolescent readers search, even though it is, at heart, mostly the same world that people have always struggled to understand. The significant writer for adolescents is the one who reacts to the factors in their world and makes a meaningful synthesis.

Bibliography

Agee, James: *A Death in the Family.* Bantam Books, 1971. The recognition of grief and human emotions that touch one family in the face of a father's death are recorded in this moving novel on a universal theme.

Baldwin, James: *Go Tell It On The Mountain*. Dial Press, 1953. Dell. A frank picture of black migrants to Harlem as they attempt to find meaning through religion.

Bellow, Saul: *The Adventures of Augie March*. Viking Press, 1953. Avon Books. A boisterous, jubilant novel of a young man's coming of age. Chicago is the classic national setting, but Augie takes his experiences from coast to coast in pursuit of his slice of the American dream.

Buck, Pearl: *The Good Earth*. Pocket Books, 1975. The cycles of life touch a simple Chinese family in the early 20th century. Land as power is the symbol of man's worth in this Nobel prizewinner's novel that has meaning for all societies.

Camus, Albert: *The Plague*. Alfred A. Knopf, 1948. Vintage Books. Locked into an Algerian city because of an epidemic of bubonic plague, a doctor narrates this existential survival story. Relationships are forced by the disease. Those remaining as the pestilence kills must face and accept the very essence of their lives.

——: *The Stranger*. Alfred A. Knopf, 1946. Vintage Books. A classic work by the important existentialist philosopher. The story of Meursault, a young Frenchman in Algeria, who does nothing to prevent his own execution.

Cather, Willa: *My Antonia*. Houghton Mifflin, 1918. A study of the gradual incorporation of a charming, original immigrant girl into the nondescript culture of the emerging American nation. America's heartland has been defined by this analysis of the "melting pot."

Dreiser, Theodore: *An American Tragedy*. New American Library, 1973. Clyde Griffiths, poor but with social aspirations, realizes that he cannot continue his romantic pursuit of wealthy Sondra Finchley as long as Roberta Allen, who bears his child, lives.

Ellison, Ralph: *Invisible Man*. Random House, 1951. A novel of black identity told through the thought processes of the nameless protagonist. Confronting the hatred and racism of mid-20th-century society, Ellison's character must take responsibility for his niche in time.

Farrell, James T.: *Studs Lonigan*. Avon Books, 1973. A three-part novel tracing the rise of a classic American character. Lonigan, like Bellow's Augie March of a later era, battles his way up from the squalor of the Chicago slums.

Faulkner, William: *The Sound and the Fury*. Random House, 1966. Set against the decay of the post-Civil War South, this stunning four-part narrative traces the dissolution of the Compson family.

Fitzgerald, F. Scott: *The Great Gatsby*. Charles Scribner's Sons, 1925. A sharp view of the empty value system embodied by wealthy jazz age Americans between the world wars. Nick Carraway tells the story of Daisy Buchanan, her husband Tom, and the mysterious Jay Gatsby who lives for a glorious dream, and dies alone.

Forester, C. S.: *The African Queen*. Modern Library, 1940. Caught in the African jungle as German forces advance, a spinster missionary and a rough-hewn boat pilot join forces to reach the open waters of Lake Victoria. A high adventure with touches of comedy and romance.

Golding, William: *Lord of the Flies*. Coward, McCann & Geohegan, 1978. Capricorn Books. A shipwrecked band of British schoolboys becomes a microcosm of 20th-century society. Stranded on an island, they revert to primitive instincts, abusing power and preying on the weak among them in a battle for survival of the fittest.

Greene, Graham: *A Burnt-Out Case*. Penguin Books, 1977. A famous architect goes to live in a leper colony in the Congo to escape the spiritual alienation of his "normal" existence.

Heller, Joseph: *Catch-22*. Simon and Schuster, 1961. Dell. War is the ultimate macabre comedy as Captain Yossarian and his fellow flyers attempt to cope with ridiculous rules and regulations at their North African battle station during World War II.

Hemingway, Ernest: *A Farewell to Arms*. Charles Scribner's Sons, 1929. A young couple escape the rigors of World War I only to experience deep personal tragedy.

————: *The Old Man and the Sea*. Charles Scribner's Sons, 1952. A spare tale of a Cuban fisherman's conquest of a gigantic deep-sea prize. The simplicity of one man's struggle against nature takes significance from the act of pursuit, rather than the ultimate possession of the fish.

Hersey, John: *Hiroshima*. Alfred A. Knopf, 1946. Bantam Books. The author's visit to Hiroshima results in a moving account of the effect of the atomic blast on the lives of the survivors.

Hesse, Hermann: *Demian*. Harper and Row, 1965. Bantam Books. Sinclair's adolescence is torn by his attempt to balance the sensual, realistic side of his nature with his idealism and mystical yearnings.

————: *Siddartha*. New Directions, 1951. Bantam Books. The Eastern philosophy of the inner man is studied in this German author's story of a youth in search of personal truths.

James, Henry: *The Turn of the Screw*. 1898. Perhaps the greatest ghost story ever written, this terrifying tale depicts an atmosphere of sinister evil, into which innocent children are drawn.

Joyce, James: *A Portrait of the Artist as a Young Man*. Viking Press, 1964. Penguin Books. The universal anxieties of adolescence are detailed by the master Irish writer. Stephen Dedalus is a youth torn by his own needs and the expectations of others as he stumbles toward manhood.

Kafka, Franz: *Metamorphosis*. Schocken Books, 1968. Bantam Books. The bizarre story of a young man's gradual evolution as an insect. Not science fiction, Kafka's allegory represents the inevitability of man's manipulation by fate and circumstance.

Kesey, Ken: *One Flew Over the Cuckoo's Nest*. Viking Press, 1962. New American Library. Randle Patrick McMurphy is a boisterous, lusty, life-loving rebel who challenges the dictatorship of Big Nurse in a mental institution. What starts out in fun becomes a battle to the finish.

Knowles, John: *A Separate Peace*. Macmillan, 1960. Bantam Books. A young man revisits the prep school where as a student he was involved in the death of his best friend.

Koestler, Arthur: *Darkness at Noon*. Macmillan, 1941. Bantam Books. Based on the Stalinist purge trials of

1937, Koestler's novel haunts the reader with an inner view of the manipulative power of totalitarian government.

Lawrence, D. H.: *Women in Love*. Viking Press, 1920. Penguin Books. Two working-class sisters seek compatible mates in this study of structured British society. Youthful ideals are gradually replaced by mature vision as the women accept responsibility for their own identities.

Lewis, Sinclair: *Main Street*. Harcourt Brace Jovanovich, 1950. New American Library. Faced with what she considers to be a cultural wasteland, college-educated Carol attempts to enrich her neighbors' lives. Middle America is bared to its solid, if uninteresting, core in this classic novel.

Llewellyn, Richard: *How Green Was My Valley*. Macmillan, 1941. Dell. The harsh life of a Welsh coal mining family is detailed in this powerful tale about human devotion to simple moral values and dreams of a better future.

McCullers, Carson: *Member of the Wedding*. Houghton Mifflin, 1946. Bantam Books. The literal understanding of a child's mind is probed in this sensitive study of Frankie's realization that she must wait to grow up, as have all women before her.

Mailer, Norman: *The Naked and the Dead*. Holt, Rinehart and Winston, 1977. New American Library. Characters representing the American "melting pot" attempt to sort out their roles in World War II. Mailer's men are the human toll in the callous political manipulation of nations in conflict.

Malamud, Bernard: *The Fixer*. Farrar, Strauss and Giroux, 1966. Pocket Books. Wrongly accused of a heinous crime, a Russian peasant pays the penalty for his government's need of a victim. Although he retains his dignity in the face of official accusation, the awesome power of anti-Semitism remains frighteningly real.

Maugham, W. Somerset: *Of Human Bondage*. Modern Library, 1959. Pocket Books. Tortured by a handicap that makes him different from other people, Philip Carey looks forward to the maturity that will bring him independence. A victim of his own innocence, he finally reevaluates his aspirations and settles for a satisfying if unglamorous life as a country doctor.

Nordhoff, Charles and James N. Hall: *Mutiny on the Bounty*. Little, Brown, 1932. Pocket Books. The fictional re-creation of a British warship crew's revolt in the 1780s. Fletcher Christian and Captain Bligh embody good and evil in this taut adventure about human conflict on the high seas.

Orwell, George: *Animal Farm*. Harcourt Brace Jovanovich, 1954. New American Library. Farmer Jones's animals revolt and set up a socialist state ruled by the pigs.

Paton, Alan: *Cry the Beloved Country*. Charles Scribner's Sons, 1961. The simple life of an African minister is destroyed when he follows his family to Johannesburg. Prejudice and inequality haunt gentle characters trying to maintain their self-respect in a harsh confrontation with apartheid.

Remarque, Erich Maria: *All Quiet on the Western Front*. Little, Brown, 1929. Fawcett Books. Fighting for the kaiser's forces in World War I, a young German student represents the common man as victim. Although he has no quarrel with his enemy, Paul must defend the concept of national honor, sacrificing his spirit and ideals.

Roth, Philip: *Goodbye, Columbus*. Houghton Mifflin, 1959. Bantam Books. Neil Klugman is searching for personal direction after a hitch in the army. He is absorbed, used as a summer toy, and cast back into reality by Brenda Potamkin. The Potamkins represent the excesses of the nouveaux riches.

Saint-Exupery, Antoine de: *Wind, Sand and Stars*. Harcourt Brace Jovanovich, 1949. Excitement, philosophy, and a sense of wonder in the early days of flying.

Salinger, J. D.: *The Catcher in the Rye*. Little, Brown, 1951. Bantam Books. The *Everyman* of modern adolescents. Holden Caulfield carves a path through the censor's fences to literary history. This lost youth has become the world's symbol for the anxieties and inner turmoil of teenagers in their struggle for maturity. It's also a very funny and real story.

————: *Franny and Zoey*. Little, Brown, 1961. Bantam

Books. The crises, triumphs, and tragedies of the younger members of the Glass family, chronicled with compassion and humor in two novellas.

Saroyan, William: *The Human Comedy*. Harcourt Brace Jovanovich, 1944. Dell. A California family quietly copes with the details of daily life while the world around the town of Ithaca deals with the larger issues of World War II. The perspectives of different ages lend balance to the picture of a world in turmoil.

Solzhenitsyn, Aleksandr: *One Day in the Life of Ivan Denisovich*. E. P. Dutton, 1963. Bantam Books. A prisoner of conscience, Ivan is a workhorse of the Russian state in a Siberian exile camp The systematic dehumanization of men for the goals of the Communist ideal is exposed and condemned.

Steinbeck, John: *The Grapes of Wrath*. Viking Press, 1939. Penguin Books. The Joad family survives despite death, harassment, and apparent defeat as they attempt to escape the Oklahoma dust bowl in the 1930s.

————: *Of Mice and Men*. Viking Press, 1937. Bantam Books. Gentle Lenny, large and warm, is slow to think and comprehend. Although George tries to protect him, more ordinary people who cannot tolerate Lenny's differences make him a victim of their rules.

————: *The Pearl*. Viking Press, 1947. Bantam Books. The enduring fable of a poor fisherman who finds a priceless pearl.

Waugh, Evelyn: *The Loved One*. Little, Brown, 1977. Satirical story of a famous Los Angeles cemetery and of the people who run it. Biting and harsh but always funny.

White, Terence H.: *The Once and Future King*. G. P. Putnam's Sons, 1958. Berkley. The magnificent legend of King Arthur retold as a novel for modern readers. Arthur's anguish over war, the love story of Guinevere and Lancelot, and the evil machinations of Mordred comprise the story of Camelot. (The sequel is *The Book of Merlyn*, University of Texas Press, 1977. Berkley.)

Wilde, Thornton: *Bridge of San Luis Rey*. Harper & Row, 1967. Avon Books. A Franciscan friar inquires into the lives of five people killed in the collapse of an ancient bridge in colonial South America to discover if it was an accident or divine plan.

————: *Theophilus North*. Harper & Row, 1973. Avon Books. Theophilus becomes enmeshed in the lives of the people in a small Rhode Island town in the 1920s.

Wolfe, Thomas: *Look Homeward, Angel*. Charles Scribner's Sons, 1929. One of the many autobiographical novels that chronicle a young man's loss of innocence during the first half of the 20th century. Eugene Gant suffers the typical self-doubts that plague all adolescents until he feels secure enough to leave home.

Wright, Richard: *Native Son*. Harper & Row, 1940. A "nigger" in a white man's world, Bigger Thomas unintentionally commits a murder in a moment of panic, and is then frustrated into a repetition of the act. A gripping novel of failed dreams and suffering.

9

The Classics

A classic is something that everybody wants to
have read and nobody wants to read.
—*Mark Twain*

"Who knows only his own generation remains forever
a child" is carved in stone over the entrance to the
library at the University of Colorado. But teenagers
are contemporary-minded and overwhelmingly prefer
modern writers and modern books. So what about the
works of literature from earlier times? What about the
classics? In American education in literature, a primary objective has been transmission of the cultural
heritage. Traditionally, survey courses in English and
American literature, organized chronologically, have
been required for students in the upper years of high
schools. Background in older literary works was a
recommended part of one's cultural baggage. All people should have their imagination fired by Captain
Ahab and Huck Finn. But few educators could agree
on what works qualify as classics.

Teachers often feel that young people will find, read,
and understand contemporary literature on their own,
so the school should present the literature which they
are not apt to read. They feel that studying the classics
will provide criteria by which students can judge contemporary literature. This is sound enough, but it fails
to take into account the psychology of the adolescent
and his attitude toward reading. It assumes that the
reader is a static entity who can be molded from the

outside, rather than a developing organism who grows from within.

The classics need to be looked at in terms of what adolescents are seeking and are ready to understand. Going back to the maps of adolescents' strivings and interests described in chapters 2 and 3, where in early literature do we have a content that is congruent with them? There, we have a chance of eliciting a positive response even though the language is often difficult.

It is a cliché that the classic "has stood the test of time," meaning that it has survived while nearly all its contemporaries have been forgotten. To survive, a book must have certain qualities: it must confront the reader with one of the eternal dilemmas of human life. It may show the pettiness and absurdities of human beings, point out the transfiguring beauty of love, make the reader aware of the ironies in human existence, show how the human spirit transcends the immediate bounds of suffering, depict the individual's feelings of alienation and loneliness. Great literature may provide a vision of a better world that people might achieve except for their own natures, or present the conflict between the laws of the social order and the natural law the individual feels within himself. Literature, as long as it has existed, has expressed these yearnings of the human spirit as it struggles to find value in experiences. The book that becomes a classic has as its theme a profound, mature, and significant appraisal of human life.

The classic is enriched by timeless symbols. The story, its images, its details, transcend the age in which they were conceived and can be understood by generations of readers. The stories of Mary and Martha, of the prodigal son, of the Good Samaritan in *The Bible* carry the same basic understandings across cultural boundaries and across 2,000 years. For each generation, for each reader, the story has a specific meaning. For different readers Captain Ahab's pursuit of the great white whale, Moby Dick, may represent man's search for God, labor's fight against capital, man's pursuit of woman, the fight of science against the humanities, the struggle of society against individual freedom. The writer's symbolism expresses the deepest, most unresolved problem troubling the reader.

A classic has not only ageless symbolism but a magnificence of structure that cannot be catalogued and dissected and yet produces an elusive, deep satisfaction. The choice of words, the ordering of details, the use of symbols, seem exactly right for the theme the writer is developing. A reader may return to a classic, and each time he will take pleasure in its language and perhaps find new interpretations of its meaning.

There is no doubt that the classics represent man's finest use of language; but it is also true that classic literature is one of the most difficult, most subtle, and most mature expressions of human beings, so it is no surprise that an understanding and enjoyment of the classics comes, if at all, fairly late in a reader's growth.

Recently a class of 75 college seniors and graduate students were asked when they began reading the classics on their own. One or two indicated that they read some Dickens with enthusiasm in late childhood (junior high school). A few said that they enjoyed dramatizing *A Midsummer Night's Dream* in ninth grade. A few more mentioned becoming interested in Victorian novels in the last years of high school. But the majority indicated that they were sophomores or juniors in college before they came to a real, inspired liking for the classics.

Still, parents and teachers persist in feeling that even though adolescents don't like or understand classics they are "good for them" and teenagers "will someday be glad they were forced to read them." The records of thousands of readers indicate that this is not true. You usually thoroughly dislike what you are forced to read and cannot understand, rather than being allowed to grow slowly toward an enjoyment of the classics through the reading patterns sketched in earlier chapters of this book.

We will describe some classics that have appeal for some adolescents at some step in their reading maturation.

FROM THE ANCIENT WORLD

The most important book in Western culture is *The Bible*. It was once almost the only book available; readers immersed themselves in its pages, reading and rereading the old, familiar stories. It might almost be called a complete library, for within its covers are adventure stories, and stories of daily life, romance, history, law, philosophy, and poetry. Because *The Bible* was an integral part of people's lives, its rhythms of language influenced the style of great writers and speakers for centuries; thus a thorough understanding of Western art forms and culture requires some familiarity with *The Bible*. Many adolescents decide at some point to read the entire *Bible*. Usually they set themselves a quota of reading for each day, but like most self-improvement programs, this one bogs down in good intentions before many days pass. Therefore it may be helpful to suggest a selected reading program from *The Bible*, perhaps Genesis, Exodus, Ruth, Samuel, and one of the four Gospels. This will give the young person a body of basic stories that have been echoed throughout the writings and thinking of the Western world.

The teenage reader has recently rediscovered ancient Greek tragedies. For years they were available only in literal, labored translations; but in the last 20 years there have been a number of new translations, in which the similarity between the Greeks' problems and ours is strikingly revealed. Because of the stark simplicity of the plots, adolescents find the plays easy to comprehend. One of the better collections is *Ten Greek Plays*, a paperback anthology of representative plays by Aeschylus, Sophocles, and Euripides, with one comedy by Aristophanes. Probably most adolescents discover Greek tragedy when they read *Oedipus Rex* or *Antigone*, the two greatest plays of Sophocles, or the *Medea* of Euripides.

The long epic poems of Homer, *The Iliad* and *The Odyssey*, are fine adventure reading for adolescents if good contemporary translations are used. *The Iliad* recounts the events of the Trojan War, caused when Paris of Troy eloped with Helen, the wife of the Greek Menelaus. *The Odyssey* is the poetic account of Ulysses's adventures during his long, wandering return from that war. Like *The Bible*, the two epics are fundamental background for anyone who wants to understand Western literature. Homer's two stories have had a resonating impact on the writers of the world, and there are many references to them in contemporary works.

Some young people are fascinated by the stories of Greek mythology. This interest develops in late elementary school or early in junior high school—or even as late as college, when the young person becomes seriously interested in the study of literature. Of the many volumes dealing with the Greek myths, one of the most authoritative is Edith Hamilton's *Mythology*. An interest in myth is worth encouraging, for the ancient myths are referents of modern allusions.

FROM ENGLISH LITERATURE

English literature provides a wealth of classics for the young reader. The sensitive and intelligent teen will be enthralled by the tales of King Arthur and his Round Table. The most satisfying account is in a modernized version of Malory's *Le Morte d'Arthur*. Some of Chaucer's witty *Canterbury Tales* also have appeal in modernized versions. A few teenagers will find Shakespeare rewarding. The plays that are most comprehensible to adolescents are *Romeo and Juliet*, a story of adolescent love and marriage; *The Taming of the Shrew*, the madcap, slapstick comedy of a man who tames a shrewish wife with crude practical jokes and physical intimidation; and *The Merchant of Venice*, a drama of life's injustices and men's trickery. A few sensitive girls will find *A Midsummer Night's Dream* delightful, while some of the boys will enjoy the histories. But the great tragedies are difficult reading for most high-school students (with the possible exception of *Julius Caesar*); and the great comedies require so much explanation that they cease to be amusing. Of course, many English teachers do make Shakespeare exciting for young people in the classroom.

Robinson Crusoe, a marvelous adventure tale by Daniel Defoe, is primarily a boy's book. Defoe intended to demonstrate that a civilized man cast into a primitive society could solve his problems through reason, but the average reader enjoys the story for the details of Crusoe's survival: how he builds a hut, finds food and clothing, protects himself from attack.

Jane Eyre, Wuthering Heights, and *Green Mansions* are 19th-century novels with similar appeal. *Jane Eyre* and *Wuthering Heights* were written by the Brontë sisters, daughters of a remote country minister, who poured into the books all their mystical, romantic longings for a life burning with intensity. *Green Mansions,* by W. H. Hudson, a botanist, has a very different story. A man is captured by a primitive tribe of Indians in the jungles of South America and discovers a mysterious woman who inhabits a sacred grove.

Charles Dickens holds charms for the maturing reader, who is impressed by Sydney Carton's self-sacrifice in the romance of the French Revolution, *A Tale of Two Cities,* and finds *David Copperfield* appealing for its picture of the hero's journey into manhood. But perhaps *Great Expectations* is most popular with the adolescent. Pip, an orphan boy, is suddenly befriended by a mysterious benefactor and taken from his lowly life with Joe and Biddy to become a young gentleman living in London. He gradually finds himself too refined for his old friends and his old ways of life. Not only is Dickens concerned with universal human emotions and situations, but he fills his novels with galleries of colorful characters and fascinating events.

Because Robert Louis Stevenson is so much a children's favorite, we forget that he is a classic writer. Because he chose as his subject high adventure, mysterious characters, plots and counterplots, his superb artistry is often overlooked. *Treasure Island* is a beautifully crafted work, and *Kidnapped, The Master of Ballantrae,* and *Dr. Jekyll and Mr. Hyde* are masterpieces. In Stevenson's novels, as in Dickens's, the excitement of the story often carries the young reader through the complex sentences and elaborate vocabulary.

Joseph Conrad stands at the line of demarcation between two styles of writing: the Victorian (involved stories with strange and complex characters) and the modern (stories that probe deeply into psychological problems). Most popular with young adults is *Lord Jim,* the story of a young seaman who chooses in an emergency to save his own life rather than the lives of his passengers. Jim has a deep need to expiate his sense of guilt—to find some way that he can live with himself. The story takes place in the Indian Ocean and the tropical jungles of southern Asia. It is intriguing not only because of the moral problem involved, but for its romantic setting.

FROM AMERICAN LITERATURE

Adolescent boys often discover the tales of James Fenimore Cooper. While Cooper's stories are quaint and old-fashioned, they have an undeniable charm. In the 19th century they reflected what Europeans believed was true about the American Indian, and to this day they color Europeans' judgment of America. *The Last of the Mohicans* and *The Deerslayer* are filled with the tense struggle of the new settler against the wilderness and the red men who inhabited it.

Nathaniel Hawthorne's *The Scarlet Letter* is a favorite of older adolescent readers. In one study, it was the only noncontemporary work among the top 20 chosen by a group of bright 11th- and 12th-grade students. It has the dark somber quality of Puritanism. Its portrayal of people who transgress the code of their society and live with a sense of guilt is absorbing and provocative.

Herman Melville, one of the two or three most

important American novelists, is not widely read by young people. His epic, *Moby Dick,* is generally considered too long and difficult. Perhaps most popular is *Billy Budd,* his last work. Through complex prose it tells of a handsome, morally upright young sailor who is impressed into the British navy and comes face to face with evil in the person of one of his superior officers, by whom he is ultimately destroyed. This situation—one of man-created injustice—confounds a young reader, yet *Billy Budd,* like similar stories, is a favorite.

Of the great American writers, Mark Twain is the adolescent's favorite. From the good-hearted humor of *The Adventures of Tom Sawyer* or the more serious *The Prince and the Pauper,* he may move on to the fun of *Life on the Mississippi, Innocents Abroad,* and *Roughing It.* Later he may enjoy *A Connecticut Yankee in King Arthur's Court,* which usually appears to teenagers as a simple frolic through the Middle Ages: they miss the vitriolic attacks that Twain makes on the Church. Some may delight in *Pudd'nhead Wilson,* an elaboration on the theme of *The Prince and the Pauper.* But sooner or later they will read Twain's masterpiece, *The Adventures of Huckleberry Finn.* This is not merely a sequel to *Tom Sawyer,* as many assume, but a seriously crafted novel dealing with a multitude of themes, beautifully expressed through the visions of Huck as he floats down the Mississippi River on a raft. It can be enjoyed by the youngster simply as a good story; then it is best to put it aside for several years, for in this book Twain has presented two visions of the world, neither of which a reader can see at the in-between stage when she or he is neither child nor adult.

Stephen Crane's short novel *The Red Badge of Courage* is perhaps the most intense study of a young boy's conception of war and his reactions under fire. Its emotional impact reaches the sensitive adolescent reader, but for many the story is so deceptively simple that it leaves them unmoved.

Edgar Allan Poe is a perennial favorite with junior-high-school students. Young people glory in the bizarre, the scary, the mysterious. This is when they enjoy a good horror movie or delight in an eerie television program. No writer has produced these feelings more skillfully than Poe. It is logical to use this interest of youngsters to introduce them to the writer of some of the greatest horror stories ever created.

FROM EUROPEAN LITERATURE

Some European classics (here we exclude those written in English) are available through translation, but the American reader is often unaware of the best-loved European literature. Everyone talks about *Don Quixote,* the strangely moving Spanish work whose central character is a man who prefers to live in the age of knighthood instead of his own time. The hero tries to interpret everything that happens to him within the context of his imagined world. A complete translation runs to almost a thousand pages. Most readers find a shortened or retold version more palatable and come to know the gallant, impractical Don in such a version.

Two great favorites of 15- and 16-year-old readers are Alexandre Dumas's *The Count of Monte Cristo* and *The Three Musketeers,* which are considered classics here more than they are in France. These sophisticated stories of intrigue offer exciting fare. A long French novel often read by sensitive adolescents is Victor Hugo's *Les Miserables,* which depicts the miseries of the lower classes in France. Since young adults are looking for a code of values in their reading, this exposure of social injustice affects them deeply. Emile Zola's gripping novel *Germinal* appeals for the same reason. But the French work to which adolescents most often lose their hearts is Rostand's *Cyrano de Bergerac.* The long-nosed Cyrano is a great spirit imprisoned in the body of a clown. The reader can visualize renunciation, fidelity, romance, the grand gesture—everything that helps to make humanity a little closer to the angels.

Of the great Russian novels, *Crime and Punishment* by Dostoevski is the one most often read by adolescents. It begins as a young student carries out a strange whim, murdering an old, repulsive pawnbroker. Most of the novel takes place after the crime as he wrestles with his guilt. Tolstoi's *Anna Karenina,* Turgenev's *Fathers and Sons,* and Gogol's *Dead Souls* are also favorites.

Great literature is written by mature artists about mature concerns; only a few classics center on the subjects closest to the adolescent's heart: adventure, mystery, teenage problems, romance.

The classics are the pinnacle of man's literary achievement, so it is natural to want our children to appreciate and value the views of life they present. In our eagerness to share the best of the adult world with teenagers, we sometimes pressure them into reading experiences that can repel and frustrate. They are not yet adults, ready for adult concerns. They have no background of experience to aid them in interpreting great adult literature. If we want our children someday to appreciate the classics, we must build reading ladders toward this goal, allowing young people's tastes to mature and mellow at their own pace. When they have learned to enjoy, savor, and react to the best of contemporary literature, they will be ready and eager to meet that great and wonderful body of older works waiting just beyond their reading horizon.

Bibliography

Most of these classics are available in several editions, including paperback. No dates are given for the ancient classics; date of first publication (or of first complete manuscript) is given for English, American, and European classics.

FROM THE ANCIENT WORLD

The Bible. Editions include the *Anchor Bible* (Doubleday), *The Bible as History* (Bantam), *Good News for Modern Man* (American Bible Society), and *New Testament in Modern English* (Macmillan).

Aeschylus: *Agamemnon*. Tragic drama of a man torn by his loyalties as ruler, soldier, and husband.

————: *Prometheus Bound*. In a sense both thief and soothsayer, a young man attempts to mediate between the gods and earthly need.

Aristophanes: *Complete Plays of Aristophanes*. Witty commentaries on the society of his time that have an application today.

Euripides: *Medea*. The drama of a wife and mother who in seeking revenge proves how fine is the line between love and hate.

Homer: *The Iliad*. Detailed account of the Trojan War.

————: *The Odyssey*. Epic tale of Ulysses's homeward journey after the Trojan War.

Lind, Levi R., ed.: *Ten Greek Plays: In Contemporary Translations*. Houghton Mifflin, 1957. In modern, often poetic translations, the volume contains *Prometheus Bound* and *Agamemnon* by Aeschylus; *Antigone, Oedipus Rex*, and *Philocietes* by Sophocles; *Alcestis, Suppliants, Andromache*, and *Bacchae* by Euripides; and *Lysistrata* by Aristophanes.

Plato: *The Republic*. Socrates's dialogues on justice, order, and the individual.

Sophocles: *Antigone*. Tragic drama depicting a conflict between filial love and royal decree which results in death for those involved.

————: *Oedipus Rex*. Man's blindness is shown in this drama as the hero tries to escape the fate prophesied by the Delphic oracle and brings disaster to his family and country.

See also:

Hamilton, Edith: *The Greek Way*. W. W. Norton, 1948. Avon Books. One of the best interpretations of ancient Greek civilization for the general reader

————: *Mythology*. Little, Brown, 1942. New American Library. A readable retelling of the ancient Greek myths that have become a part of Western culture.

FROM ENGLISH LITERATURE

Austen, Jane: *Pride and Prejudice.* 1813. Social falsity and reliance on appearances are corrected in time to assure two marriages.

Bronte, Charlotte: *Jane Eyre.* 1874. A dark mystery stands between a shy governess and the unconventional employer whom she loves.

Bronte, Emily: *Wuthering Heights.* 1847. A London waif accepts a family's affections, only to repay them in later years with heartbreak.

Bunyan, John: *Pilgrim's Progress (From This World to That Which Is to Come).* 1678–1684. An allegory tracing a young man's odyssey from the City of Destruction to the Gate of Heaven.

Carroll, Lewis (Charles Lutwidge Dodgson): *Alice's Adventures in Wonderland.* 1865. A young girl literally falls into a world of fantastic make-believe.

Chaucer, Geoffrey: *Canterbury Tales,* c. 1395. Life and thought in medieval England are portrayed through a series of entertaining stories told by imaginary pilgrims on the way to Canterbury.

Conrad, Joseph: *Lord Jim.* 1900. A young seaman commits an act of cowardice and spends the rest of his life struggling to atone for this error and to regain his self-respect.

Defoe, Daniel: *Robinson Crusoe.* 1720. An island castaway and his native companion mix ingenuity and adventure in making a civilized life for themselves.

Dickens, Charles: *David Copperfield.* 1850. Dickens tells the story of David, an orphan who is thrust from person to person until he matures, marries unsuccessfully, and becomes a writer.

————: *Great Expectations.* 1861. Pip's life is changed by a strange circumstance. He grows to manhood expecting a great inheritance and marriage with his childhood sweetheart. Neither expectation is fulfilled.

————: *A Tale of Two Cities.* 1859. Charles Darnay is convicted by the French Revolutionists for a crime of his ancestors and is sentenced to the guillotine. He is saved by his friend, Sydney Carton.

Galsworthy, John: *The Forsyte Saga.* 1906–1921. A trilogy which depicts the materialism and confused affections in the life of a "successful" London family.

Goldsmith, Oliver: *She Stoops to Conquer*. 1773. Charles Marlowe, a shy suitor, is tricked into a series of errors, but wins the young heiress in spite of them.

————: *The Vicar of Wakefield*. 1776. A series of turns, both tragic and fortunate, punctuates the life of a gentle, gullible clergyman and his family.

Hudson, W. H.: *Green Mansions*. 1904. Romance and untimely loss in the South American jungles. Powerfully descriptive.

Kipling, Rudyard: *Kim*. 1901. A young Irish boy in colonial India is involved with a native mystic and the Secret Service.

Malory, Sir Thomas: *Le Morte d'Arthur*. 1468. The life of King Arthur and related legends.

Scott, Sir Walter: *Ivanhoe*. 1819. A romance of chivalry and intrigue set in the time of Richard the Lion-Hearted and Robin Hood.

Shakespeare, William: *Complete Works of Shakespeare*. 1590–1613. Many editions. Paperback editions of individual plays are also numerous.

Stevenson, Robert Louis: *Dr. Jekyll and Mr. Hyde*. 1886. Early science fiction dealing with man's goodness, his latent evil, and his transformations by drugs.

————: *Kidnapped*. 1886. In Scotland during the 18th century, David Balfour is kidnapped on his uncle's orders. He survives a sea wreck and, with a Jacobite ally, is chased across the highlands until together they force his uncle to return his inheritance.

————: *The Master of Ballantrae*. 1889. Scotland's revolt against England in the 1740s is the background for a story of bitter hatred between two brothers.

————: *Treasure Island*. 1883. A young boy narrates this colorful tale of pirates, buried treasure, and a nearly successful mutiny.

Swift, Jonathan: *Gulliver's Travels*. 1726. A satirical fantasy of Gulliver's capture by the tiny Lilliputians and later by the gigantic Brobdingnags. Finally he lives with the Houyhnhnms, rational horses who are the masters of irrational human beings.

Thackeray, William Makepeace: *Vanity Fair*. 1848. Becky

Sharp, an ambitious woman, moves up the social scale through her wits. Set in early 19th-century London.

Wells, H. G.: *The War of the Worlds*. 1898. A Martian invasion which, in a 1938 radio adaptation, caused real panic throughout the United States.

Wilde, Oscar: *The Picture of Dorian Gray*. 1891. A young man's moral degeneration is strangely and faithfully chronicled in his portrait rather than his face.

Wyss, Johann: *Swiss Family Robinson*. 1820. An English family is marooned on a deserted island where they salvage what they can from their wrecked ship, build a tree house, and set up a survival existence.

FROM AMERICAN LITERATURE

Cooper, James Fenimore: *The Deerslayer*. 1841. Natty Bumpo, a young hunter, lives with the Delaware Indians fighting against the Hurons and resisting the romantic inclinations of Judith Hunter.

————: *Last of the Mohicans*. 1826. The French and Indian War is the background for the romantic story of Indian-white relations in the forests of New York State.

Crane, Stephen: *The Red Badge of Courage*. 1895. A study of fear as it affects the life and romantic presuppositions of a young Union soldier in the Civil War.

Hawthorne, Nathaniel: *The House of the Seven Gables*. 1851. For 200 years the Pyncheon family has suffered from the curse laid on their house, but young Phoebe Pyncheon falls in love and dispells the curse.

————: *The Scarlet Letter*. 1850. This story explores both on a literal and a symbolic level the effect on a Puritan community of Hester Prynne's adultery. Guilt, evil, and courage are the components of the story.

James, Henry: *The American*. 1877. Contrasts between simplicity and sophistication are developed in this novel of an American in 19th-century Paris.

————: *The Portrait of a Lady*. 1908. Isabel Archer, a wealthy young American, weds an English dilettante in hope of finding the best men and ideas abroad. James incisively contrasts American and British types and social mores.

London, Jack: *Martin Eden*. 1909. A young writer discovers that success assures "friendships" of which failure only dreams.

————: *The Sea Wolf*. 1904. During a long sea voyage a young man is shanghaied into service by a ruthless captain.

Melville, Herman: *Billy Budd*. 1851. Impressed into sea service, Billy Budd finds his youthful innocence sharply contrasted by the evil of the master-at-arms. When he strikes down his persecutor, he meets with swift maritime justice.

————: *Moby-Dick*. 1851. A strange sea captain involves his crew in a mystical pursuit of the great white whale, Moby Dick. Only the narrator survives.

Norris, Frank: *The Octopus*. 1901. California ranching and railroad interests are presented in an intense power struggle.

Poe, Edgar Allan: *Short Stories*. 1833–1849. Poe is a master at detailing inner and imagined horror.

Sinclair, Upton: *The Jungle*. 1906. Set in Chicago of the early 1900s, this story shows the terrible sanitary and labor conditions and exploitation in the stockyards.

Stowe, Harriet Beecher: *Uncle Tom's Cabin*. 1852. A significant abolitionist document, this novel delineates the horrible conditions of the Negro under slavery.

Thoreau, Henry David: *Walden*. 1854. Chronicle of the author's two-year search for values as he lived alone at the edge of Walden pond.

Twain, Mark (Samuel Langhorne Clemens): *The Adventures of Huckleberry Finn*. 1884. Huck Finn runs away with Jim, an escaped slave, and makes a long trip on a raft down the Mississippi River.

————: *The Adventures of Tom Sawyer*. 1876. The free and easy life of a boy in Hannibal, Missouri, at the end of the 19th century.

————: *A Connecticut Yankee in King Arthur's Court*. 1889. The satiric misadventures of a man who finds himself transported backward in time.

————: *Innocents Abroad*. 1869. A hilarious account of Americans in Europe.

————: *Life on the Mississippi*. 1884. A humorous, often poetic account of Twain's years as a steamboat captain on the Mississippi River.

————: *The Prince and the Pauper*. 1881. Two boys exchange roles for a brief and revealing education.

————: *Puddin'head Wilson*. 1894. A black and a white baby are interchanged at birth. Twain shows that basically there are no real differences in people except those that society imposes on them.

————: *Roughing It*. 1872. Stories and incidents that Twain put together from his experiences as a newspaper reporter in the gold mining towns of the Far West.

Wharton, Edith: *The Age of Innocence*. 1920. Conflict between love and convention in the New York society of the 1870s.

————: *Ethan Frome*. 1911. A reversal of personalities marks this ironic novel of a triangular love affair in a New England village.

FROM EUROPEAN LITERATURE

Balzac, Honore de: *Pere Goriot*. 1835. The story of an avaricious father, from Balzac's immortal Human Comedy series.

Cervantes, Miguel de: *Don Quixote*. 1615. An attempt to recapture chivalry and romance transforms the life of an angular country gentleman. See Leighton Barret's edition for junior-high readers (Alfred A. Knopf).

Chekhov, Anton: *The Cherry Orchard*. 1904. A once wealthy family, unable to cope with the onslaught of time, loses both pride and property in this Russian drama.

Dante (Alighieri): *The Divine Comedy*. 1321. An epic, allegory, and critique in which the poet traces a detailed passage through hell and heaven. See the translation by John Ciardi (W. W. Norton).

Dostoevski, Fyodor: *The Brothers Karamazov*. 1880. A many-sided narrative defines complex relationships among a father and his four sons.

————: *Crime and Punishment*. 1866. A detailed psychological study of a young man's crime, guilt, and ultimate contrition.

Dumas, Alexandre: *The Count of Monte Cristo*. 1844. Politics, imprisonment, escape, discovery, and retribution mark the life of a mysterious stranger.

————: *The Three Musketeers*. 1844. The friendship and adventurous exploits of four young swordsmen in 17th-century France.

Flaubert, Gustave: *Madame Bovary*. 1856. Boredom and unhappiness lay siege to a pathetic, discontented wife of a country doctor.

Goethe, Johann Wolfgang von: *The Sorrows of Young Werther*. 1787. A young romantic becomes hopelessly entangled in his own speculations.

Gogol, Nikolai V.: *Dead Souls*. 1842. An archswindler tries to buy up the dead serfs who are still legally alive until the next census, and uses them as collateral to buy land.

Hugo, Victor: *Les Miserables*. 1862. The theft of a loaf of bread plagues the life and fortunes of a man who struggles for dignity.

Khayyam, Omar. *The Rubaiyat*. c. 1000. Translated by Edward FitzGerald, 1859. A series of Persian quatrains dwelling on the beauties and satisfactions of a sensual life.

Molière: *The Misanthrope*. Sharply incisive comedy dealing with human pretension.

Rostand, Edmond: *Cyrano de Bergerac*. 1897. In this remarkable play, a dashing poet and would-be lover encounters problems because of his long nose.

Tolstoi, Leo: *Anna Karenina*. 1875. Two love matches are contrasted in this study of a young woman's inability to accept life as it is.

————: *War and Peace*. 1877. Napoleon's invasion of Russia and the lives of many people, both foolish and wise, are interwoven in this monumental work.

Turgenev, Ivan: *Fathers and Sons*. 1862. A portrayal of the conflicts between the old aristocracy and the new democratic intelligentsia in Russia during the 1860s.

Voltaire: *Candide*. 1759. An unlikely series of misadventures leads a young man to doubt his tutor's belief that all is for the best in this best of all possible worlds.

Zola, Emile: *Germinal*. 1885. A study of the bitter sufferings of workers in the French mines and their attempt to organize a strike.

10

Poetry

> Poetry is the silence and speech between a wet struggling root of a flower and sunlit blossom of that flower.
>
> —*Carl Sandburg*

We live in an age of prose, not of poetry; our culture has affected the reading preferences of this generation so that most of our published literature for the past 200 years has been prose. Yet we know that poetry is a natural form of expression for human beings. Delight in the rhythmic arrangements of words is as old as communication itself. In the long history of man, poetry has been the most common literary form. The great historical traditions are embedded in such poetic epics as *The Iliad,* the *Ramayana,* and the *Kalevala.* Until prose came into its own around the 18th century, people used poetry to express their ideas and interpret the events in their lives. There is, then, nothing unnatural about poetry and nothing that makes it inherently more difficult to comprehend than prose.

Most people read poetry at times. It may be a casual glance as they thumb through a magazine and their eye falls on a poem that they skim before turning the page. It may be while they are browsing through a shelf of books and a thin, beautifully bound volume lures them to look inside because of its rich appearance. It may be while hunting for a poem to use for a Thanksgiving program. Or perhaps they are preparing an assignment for a class and find that reading one poem leads to another. The impact of a poem can be out of proportion to the amount of time spent reading it. A remembered line from a poem helps one interpret a moment of beauty, a feeling about a person, the reaction to birth or death, the inevitability of change. There are times when we would be lost indeed if we could not dip into the reservoir of images brought to life by the poets.

Today's teenagers may be more receptive to poetry than students have been for several generations. The popularity of folk and rock music has made culture heroes out of musician/songwriters such as John Denver and Bob Dylan. Some of their lyrics are rich in poetic imagery, intricate rhythms, and ideas of deep significance to young audiences. In response, young people increasingly experiment with their own poems and songs, giving voice in verse to their major concerns. Some resourceful teachers use rock lyrics and poetry written by adolescents in the classroom as an introduction to the more formal poetic tradition.

Certain cultures and periods of history have been especially endowed with the gift of poetry. One of the richest, steadiest outpourings of poetry has been from the British Isles. The English—a nation of merchants, sailors, and industrialists—seem hardly the stuff from which poets spring, and yet for a thousand years they have produced great poets, reaching peaks in the 16th and early 17th centuries (the period of Queen Elizabeth I) and in the 19th century.

American poetry has benefited from this rich poetic heritage. American poets have contributed substantially since 19th-century New England. Many stimulating ideas about our culture today and man's relationship to it are expressed by the prolific, vibrant poets of our generation.

Several standard collections of English poetry present well-selected samplings from our poetic tradition. The fashion for this kind of collection was set in 1861 by a professor in England, Francis T. Palgrave, who worked with Lord Tennyson and other literary friends to winnow the best lyric poems written in English after

1550. He was interested in individually fine poems, not in poets. His preferences and tastes have proved remarkably enduring, for Palgrave's *Golden Treasury,* which is chronologically organized, has become a "must" in many libraries. Since Professor Palgrave died in 1897, his collection has been edited and added to by able persons. It remains a fine collection of English verse.

The Oxford Book of English Verse is a larger but still one-volume standard collection which samples both English and American poetry. It can serve the family as a collection of a large body of poems that students may be looking for, as well as a volume in which to browse. Stevenson's *The Home Book of Verse* is also excellent.

Young readers may at first be intrigued by light verse. In a survey of high-school students by the University of Iowa, young people cast their votes for humorous verse. They wanted nonsense rhymes. It is true that in most schools the poetry presented tends to be serious and removed from modern concerns. In the words of one boy, "There is too much stuff about clouds and daffodils."

To satisfy this interest in lighthearted rhymes William Cole has collected 500 pages of delightfully funny verse in *Fireside Book of Humorous Poetry.* Most of it is modern. It tickles your funny bone through an incongruity, a ridiculous rhyme, an unexpected or concocted word, an unusual rhythmic pattern. The poems are organized around such themes as "The Other Animals," "Bores and Boars," "Races, Places, and Dialects," and "In Praise and Dispraise of Love." Readers who dip into this book will feel compelled to keep turning the pages.

A perennial favorite humorous verse form is the limerick, a five-line form in which the first, second, and fifth lines have one rhyme while the third and fourth lines have another. The pattern lends itself to zany combinations of ideas.

Adolescents say they like humorous poems best, but when asked to list their favorite poems, they cite nar-

rative poems, such as "The Highwayman," "The
Raven," "Casey at the Bat," "The Cremation of Sam
McGee," "Paul Revere's Ride," and "The Rime of the
Ancient Mariner." Today's interest in folksinging
springs from the human impulse to tell and listen to
a story in verse. The novice balladeer begins with
familiar songs that have sifted down from one generation to the next. But sophisticated modern balladeers
do what great folksingers have done through the ages:
they sing of the events of their own times: racial in-
tegration, political issues, contemporary wars, burnings
and marches, human tragedies. The ballad has always
been an instrument of social criticism—a way for those
on the street to express their indignation at the events
in their culture which are controlled by a few status
figures.

Because of this interest in storytelling poems, it is
important to provide the young reader with a standard
collection of folk ballads. MacEdward Leach's *Ballad
Book,* an excellent collection, contains 250 English,
Scottish and American ballads, giving variant forms of
each. It is a good source book where the budding folk-
singer can find the words to some standard folk songs.
Other youngsters will enjoy fast-moving stories whose
action is heightened by rhythm and rhyme. A big collection is Duncan Emrich's *American Folk Poetry,*
consisting of lyrics of typical children's games and
songs, calls for folk dances, old American hymns and
carols, and occupational songs. Some are familiar,
some are strange and unknown, but they are all real
folk songs.

Other Americana is found in *The Gift Outright,* a
collection by Helen Plotz, with poems representing the
diversity of the American experience. There are sections on Columbus, on Indians, and on settlers. A part
deals with what poets have said about the regions of
America, and the book concludes with attempts to express the "Idea of America."

Elinor Parker's *One Hundred Story Poems* is a
balanced selection of the most familiar old ballads,
some of the best 19th-century narrative poems, and a

few modern pieces such as "Dunkirk." The stories are grouped by themes such as "Poems About History," "Poems About the Sea," and "Kings, Knights, and Heroes." Her *One Hundred More Story Poems* contains less familiar narratives and is somewhat easier and more suitable for younger readers.

It may be a commentary on the times that there are few book-length narrative poems on contemporary subjects. The long poem seems to have passed with the Victorians. Most of their favorites—*The Lady of the Lake, Evangeline, The Idylls of the King*—have a Victorian style that most adolescent readers categorically reject. The best long narrative poem of this century may be *John Brown's Body* by Stephen Vincent Benét, which tells the story of the Civil War through the experiences of two young men, one from the North and one from the South. The story is so vivid that the reader forgets that he is reading poetry, although actually the verse form increases the emotional impact.

Modern verse is often the most significant for the adolescent. Poetry of the past often touches on only a few basic subjects: love, nature, and religion. But modern poetry is not bound by such limits: it runs the gamut of modern life from automobile wrecks to astronauts, from disassembling guns to motorcycle rumbles, from heroism to peace marches. Whitman expressed the spirit of modern poetry when he talked of sounding his "barbaric yawp over the roofs of the world." So today's poetry experiments with language and content, often seeming as confused and barbaric to the uninitiated as modern life itself.

Poets in every age have experimented, and what seems strange in one age becomes commonplace in the next. When Coleridge, Byron, Shelley, and Wordsworth were first published they were considered unpoetic and incomprehensible by staid readers, and the Victorians were not sure that Browning was quite respectable. The chances are good that the adolescent reader will have less difficulty making sense out of today's verse than teachers and parents do.

Two of the best collections of modern poetry were

edited by Louis Untermeyer: *Modern American Poetry*
and *Modern British Poetry,* available in two volumes,
or combined in one; there is a shortened version of
each for secondary-school use. The American volume
starts with Walt Whitman; the British, with Thomas
Hardy. The verse is arranged by poet in roughly
chronological sequence.

Modern poetry chosen for teenagers appears in such
shorter anthologies as *Reflections on a Gift of Watermelon Pickle* and *Some Haystacks Don't Even Have
Any Needle,* edited by Stephen Dunning, Edward Lueders, and Hugh Smith. These are printed in a sleek
contemporary format, with handsome photographs and
reproductions of modern paintings. In the themes and
styles chosen, as well as in appearance, they make it
clear that poetry is for today.

Zero Makes Me Hungry by Edward Lueders and
Primus St. John is a startling book which presents new
poetry grouped in untitled sections. The book is vividly
printed: some pages are vibrant orange, yellow or
green; others are edged with border designs in primary colors. The book is eye-catching as well as mind-
catching.

Richard Peck's *Sounds and Silences* is a large collection of contemporary poetry, most of it American,
arranged thematically under such topics as "Family,"
"Identity," "Dissent," and "Recollection." In another
exciting book of contemporary poetry, *To See the
World Afresh,* multi-ethnic poets deal with common
human experiences.

Many volumes of poetry are assembled around a
topic, or by a selection of writers from a given group.
A recent paperback collection, *A Geography of Poets,*
celebrates the rise of regionalism in poetry in the last
two decades. The editor, Edward Field, organizes the
selections according to the region where the poets live.
The poets include such well-established names as Adrienne Rich, John Ashbery and Muriel Rukeyser, along
with poets whose work has never been previously
anthologized. The result is a startlingly fresh and
eclectic collection.

Many collections are based on ethnic backgrounds. Arnold Adoff in *Celebrations* has put together a volume of more than 500 pages of work by black writers. Poets are arranged chronologically from duBois in the 19th century to Julian Perry, who was born in 1952. Lee B. Hopkins's *On Our Way* contains 22 poems ranging from young unpublished black writers to well-established poets like Gwendolyn Brooks and Langston Hughes. Poems are grouped by themes such as "Blackness," and "Soul Love." In *African Voices,* Howard Sergeant has selected from African poetry written in English.

There are collections on almost any subject: science, holidays, drug addiction, magic and spells, love, religion, and so on. Two unusual anthologies feature poetry about sports, or as one editor designates her volume, *The Sport of Poetry. Sprints and Distances* and *Hosannah the Home Run* cover sports from fishing to boxing. *Hosannah* has work by poets of all eras, from Virgil to a contemporary basketball player, to illustrate the long history of physical activity as a subject for poetry.

Only occasionally are teenagers interested enough in a poet to want a whole volume of his/her work. Certainly they do not want whole books devoted to Donne, Pope, Wordsworth, or Tennyson. Once in a while a contemporary poet becomes almost a cult figure. Earlier in the century these were Kahlil Gibran, Edna St. Vincent Millay, and Dylan Thomas. Recent favorites have included Rod McKuen and three women: Sylvia Plath, Nikki Giovanni, and Maya Angelou.

The average reader reads much less poetry than prose in a lifetime, but poetry is still of great importance. It is a source of rich pleasure and gives a heightened awareness to the nuances of living. Therefore, it seems worthwhile to help young people discover this form of expression. Life is deepened and enriched when one can find the exact words to capture the essence of a moment. To use the language of poetry to express a reaction is immensely rewarding: to think of that blue-and-gold fall day as "the season of mellow fruitfulness"; of the soft winter snowfall as "a walk with velvet shoes"; of someone's restless drive as that "of a motor-cycle rumble." The words of the poets increase our own awareness and understanding of ourselves and of the moment.

Bibliography

GENERAL COLLECTIONS

Adoff, Arnold, ed.: *Celebrations*. Follett, 1977. Comprehensive collection of black writers, from the 19th century to the present day.

————: *The Poetry of Black America: Anthology of the 20th Century*. Harper and Row, 1973. More than 600 poems by some 140 writers, from W. E. B. Du Bois to today's poets.

Auslander, Joseph, and F. E. Hill, eds.: *Winged Horse*. Haskell House, 1968. An old favorite among students and teachers as a source for the best traditional poetry. Poems arranged chronologically from Chaucer and medieval ballads to modern poets such as Robert Frost and Carl Sandburg.

Brewton, John and Sara: *Laughable Limericks*. Thomas Y. Crowell, 1965. Limericks arranged under 13 subject headings from "Bug" to "Science" and "Courtship."

Cole, William, ed.: *Fireside Book of Humorous Poetry*. Simon and Schuster, 1952. A large collection of well-selected humorous verse.

Creekmore, Hubert, ed.: *Little Treasury of World Poetry*. Charles Scribner's Sons, 1952. Translations into English of outstanding poetry written in foreign languages, as far back as early Babylonian times.

Gardner, Helen: *The New Oxford Book of English Verse*. Oxford University Press, 1972. Representative English poems written by established poets between the years 1250 to 1950—arranged chronologically.

Palgrave, Francis T., ed.: *Golden Treasury*. Macmillan, 1944.

Reit, Ann, ed.: *Alone Amid All This Noise*. Four Winds Press, 1976. Women poets through the ages.

Stevenson, Burton E., ed.: *The Home Book of Verse*. Holt, Rinehart and Winston, 9th ed., 1953. An older but excellent large, standardized collection of favorite poetry arranged by topic.

COLLECTIONS OF MODERN POETRY AND INDIVIDUAL POETS

Adoff, Arnold, ed.: *It is the Poem Singing into Your Eyes*. Harper & Row, 1971. Teenagers write their own poems.

Aiken, Conrad, ed.: *Twentieth Century American Poetry*. Modern Library, 1963. Compact volume of carefully chosen poems which represent many types of modern poetry.

Angelou, Maya: *Just Give Me a Cool Drink of Water 'Fore I Diiie*. Random House, 1971. The author of *I Know Why the Caged Bird Sings* has written a group of passionate and intense poems on a variety of subjects.

————: *Oh Pray My Wings are Gonna Fit Me Well*. Random House, 1975. Bantam Books. The 36 poems in this collection are eloquent evidence of Maya Angelou's continuing celebration of life.

Atwood, Ann: *Haiku Vision*. Charles Scribner's Sons, 1977. Beautifully illustrated, this pulls together feeling and seeing in the classic haiku style.

Bankier, Joanne, et al., eds.: *The Other Voice*. W. W. Norton, 1976. Twentieth-century women's poetry from all over the world.

Benét, Stephen V., ed. by J. L. Capps & C. R. Kembles: *John Brown's Body*. Holt, Rinehart and Winston, 1969. An epic that recounts the events leading up to John Brown's raid and his execution.

Brooks, Gwendolyn: *The World of Gwendolyn Brooks*. Harper & Row, 1971. An excellent collection of her poems.

Carruth, Hayden, ed.: *The Voice that is Great Within Us*. Bantam Books, 1970. This volume includes seldom anthologized poems by major American poets of the modern period, with special emphasis given to new poets.

Cole, William, ed.: *Book of Love Poems*. Viking Press,

1965. Old favorites in this modern context resume their freshness and sincerity. None of the triteness and sentimentality that so often characterizes books of poetry about love.

Cullen, Countee, ed.: *Caroling Dusk*. Harper & Row, 1974. Black poetry written before 1927.

cummings, e. e.: *95 Poems*. Harcourt Brace Jovanovich, 1958. His original patterns and stylistic verse.

Dickinson, Emily: *Final Harvest*. Little, Brown, 1962. Displays the complete range of her poetry.

Dunning, Stephen, et al., eds.: *Reflections on a Gift of Watermelon Pickle*. Lothrop, Lee & Shepard, 1967. Contemporary and controversial language, varied and pithy subject matter, photographs reflect the spirit of the poetry.

————: *Some Haystacks Don't Even Have Any Needles*. Lothrop, Lee & Shepard, 1969. The old themes of love, loneliness, anger, and compassion are set in a context that ranges from wild to tender.

Field, Edward, ed.: *A Geography of Poets*. Bantam Books, 1979. This collection of contemporary American poetry reflects the current trend toward regional awareness and cultural diversity. More than 200 poets are included.

Fleming, Alice: *Hosannah the Home Run: Poems about Sports*. Little, Brown, 1972. Poetry about all kinds of sports, ranging from Virgil's Aeneid through Izaak Walton, Lord Byron, and Walt Whitman to basketball pro, Tom Meschery.

Gibran, Kahlil: *The Prophet*. Alfred A. Knopf, 1923. Inspirational words from a thinker.

Giovanni, Nikki: *The Woman and the Men*. William Morrow, 1975. Wise and witty observations about the relations between the sexes.

Gregory, Horace, and Marya Zaturenska: *Silver Swan*. Macmillan, 1968. Poems mysterious and romantic.

Hesse, Hermann: *Poems*. Farrar, Straus and Giroux, 1970. Translated by James Wright, who selected these poems with the special insight of a fellow poet.

Hopkins, Lee B., ed.: *On Our Way*. Alfred A. Knopf, 1974. A short collection of poetry by previously unpublished as well as established black writers.

Howe, Florence, and Ellen Bass, eds.: *No More Masks!*

Doubleday, 1973. Poems by 20th-century American women.

Hughes, Langston: *Selected Poems*. Alfred A. Knopf, 1959. Vintage Books. These are chosen from the poet's earlier works.

Jordan, June: *Things That I Do in the Dark*. Random House, 1977. A gifted black poet writes powerfully, evocatively and realistically.

Kherdian, David: *Poems Here and Now*. Greenwillow Books, 1976. Most express happiness, surprise, and delight.

Larrick, Nancy, ed.: *Crazy to be Alive in Such a Strange World*. M. Evans, 1977. Humorous and ironic, these poems deal with people of varied background and age.

————: *On City Streets*. M. Evans, 1968. Significant poetic interpretations of the wonder, tragedies, pleasures, and sorrows of urban life.

————: *Room for Me and a Mountain Lion*. M. Evans, 1974. Poetry that sings in praise of open space.

Livingston, Myra C., ed.: *A Tune Beyond Us*. Harcourt Brace Jovanovich, 1968. An uncommonly fresh and rewarding anthology with selections from the 8th century to the present.

Lueders, Edward, and Primus St. John, eds.: *Zero Makes Me Hungry*. Lothrop, Lee & Shepard, 1976. Contemporary poetry packaged eye-catchingly with modern graphics.

McCullough, Frances M., ed.: *Earth, Air, Fire and Water*. Coward McCann and Geohegan, 1971. Contemporary poets.

McGinley, Phyllis, ed.: *Wonders and Surprises*. J. B. Lippincott, 1968. A wide variety of poems geared to please nearly everybody.

Merriam, Eve: *Rainbow Writing*. Atheneum, 1976. Fun moments, insights, and feelings in her individual style.

Millay, Edna St. Vincent: *Poems Selected for Young People*. Harper & Row, 1929. Among her 60 poems in this book are "Renascence," "The Harp Weaver," selected sonnets, and many of the poet's loveliest nature poems.

Moore, Lilian, and Judith Thurman: *To See the World Afresh*. Atheneum, 1974. A collection of multi-ethnic modern poetry grouped under such themes as "The Muscles of Your Heart," "A Human Face," or "Leaving the Roots On."

Morrison, Lillian, ed.: *Best Wishes, Amen*. Thomas Y. Crowell, 1974. Verses as autographs, autographs as verses.

————: *Sprints and Distances*. Thomas Y. Crowell, 1965. Poetry of sports; runs the gamut.

Nash, Ogden: *Pocket Book of Ogden Nash*. Pocket Books, 1962. The skilled humorist has collected his best and funniest.

Peck, Richard: *Pictures that Storm Inside My Head*. Avon Books, 1976. Poetry about inner feelings, worries, stresses.

————, ed.: *Sounds and Silences*. Dell, 1970. A thematic arrangement of contemporary American poetry.

Plath, Sylvia: *Colossus and Other Poems*. Alfred A. Knopf, 1962. Vintage Books.

Poe, Edgar Allan: *Complete Tales and Poems*. Random House, 1975. Contains such famous poems as "The Raven" and "Annabel Lee."

Randall, Dudley, ed.: *The Black Poets*. Bantam Books, 1971. An outstanding, comprehensive anthology of black poetry.

Rich, Adrienne: *The Dream of a Common Language: Poets 1974–1977*. W. W. Norton, 1978. Her poetry explores woman-to-woman relationships, mothers and daughters, sister-siblings, lover and lover, friendships, and the spirit sisters of a collective past and future.

Stevenson, Burton, ed.: *Home Book of Modern Verse*. Holt, Rinehart & Winston, 2d ed., 1953. An extension of *The Home Book of Verse*, devoted to contemporary verse written for the most part in traditional forms.

Swenson, May: *Poems to Solve*. Charles Scriber's Sons, 1969. Understanding the meanings, unlocking the secrets of poems.

Thurman, Judith, ed.: *I Became Alone*. Atheneum, 1975. A collection of the work of five women poets.

Untermeyer, Louis, ed.: *Fifty Modern American and British Poets, 1920–1970*. Longman, 1973. An excellent standard collection.

Ward, Herman M., ed.: *Poems for Pleasure*. Hill & Wang,

1963. Choices were made by 10th- and 11th-grade classes. Organized in a carefully disorganized fashion.

Whitman, Walt: *Leaves of Grass*. Cornell University Press, 1961. Facsimile of the 1855 edition of what is perhaps the best-known book of poetry by an American.

Williams, Emmett, ed.: *An Anthology of Concrete Poetry*. Ultramarine, 1967. Poems are graphics, graphics become poetry.

Williams, Oscar, ed.: *The Pocket Book of Modern Verse*. Washington Square Press, rev. ed., 1972. From Walt Whitman to Dylan Thomas, more than 500 English and American poets.

Yeats, William Butler: *Selected Poems*. Macmillan, 1962. A good introduction to this great nineteenth-century poet.

NARRATIVE POETRY

Adams, Helen: *Selected Poems and Ballads*. Helikon Press, 1975. Strange, wild, eerie poems.

Emrich, Duncan, ed.: *American Folk Poetry*. Little, Brown, 1974. Contains games, songs, folk-dance calls, and old American hymns and carols.

Leach, MacEdward, ed.: *Ballad Book*. A. S. Barnes, 1955. Some 250 English, Scottish, and American ballads, with variant forms.

Parker, Elinor, ed.: *One Hundred Story Poems*. Thomas Y. Crowell, 1951. An excellent collection ranging from some old ballads and 19th-century narrative favorites to a few modern ones.

————: *One Hundred More Story Poems*. Thomas Y. Crowell, 1960. Less well-known narrative poems, suitable for junior-high-school students.

Plotz, Helen, ed.: *As I Walked Out One Evening*. Greenwillow Books, 1976. Many ballads, some old, some new.

————: *The Gift Outright*. Greenwillow Books, 1977. A collection of poetry representing the diversity of the American experience.

Untermeyer, Louis, ed.: *Story Poems*. Washington Square Press, 1957.

NATIVE AMERICAN POETRY

Levitas, Gloria, et al., eds.: *American Indian Prose and Poetry*. G. P. Putnam's Sons, 1975. Contains stories, poems, chants, and songs.

Niatum, Duane, ed.: *Carriers of the Dream Wheel*. Harper & Row, 1975. Contemporary native American poetry.

POETRY FROM OTHER COUNTRIES

Allen, Samuel, ed.: *Poems from Africa*. Thomas Y. Crowell, 1973. A collection of modern and traditional poetry.

Behn, Harry, ed.: *More Cricket Songs*. Harcourt Brace Jovanovich, 1971. Translations of Japanese haiku.

Carlisle, Charles R., ed.: *Beyond the Rivers*. Thorp Springs, 1977. An anthology of 20th-century Paraguayan poetry.

Rexroth, Kenneth, ed.: *One Hundred More Chinese Poems*. New Directions, 1970. Love and the turning year.

Rus, Vladimir, ed.: *Selections from German Poetry*. Harvey House, 1966. Bilingual. These poems have been selected for their intrinsic interest and ease of understanding in translation.

St. Martin, Hardie, ed.: *Roots and Wings*. Harper & Row, 1976. Modern Spanish poetry. A bilingual edition.

Sergeant, Howard, ed.: *African Voices*. Lawrence Hill, 1974. A collection of African poetry originally written in English.

11

Biography

There is no such thing as a great man or a great woman. People believe in them, just as they used to believe in unicorns and dragons. The greatest man or woman is 99 per cent just like yourself.
—*George Bernard Shaw*

Biography stands in a somewhat uneasy position between the imaginary and the factual, between fiction and history. Its practitioners have said that this is what makes it one of the most delicate, demanding jobs in writing. One writer has said, "There is a real model back of every word painting that a biographer creates. But the novelist is limited only by his own vision. No one but Thackeray knows how accurately he 'caught' Becky Sharp in his portrait of her in *Vanity Fair*."

We think of biography as real or true and classify it as nonfiction. The word means "life writing." This seeming reality attracts young people to biography. Every teacher has been stopped short by a student asking about a novel, "Is this true? Did it really happen?" This reflects the need of young people for the real and the true.

As we develop we move through stages of concern with the self and the nonself. In late childhood there is a burst of curiosity about the world "out there." Children experiment with and manipulate the "out there," trying to come to terms with it. One form of manipulation is collecting and classifying, as attics are filled with aborted collections of stamps, coins, ceramic

dogs, and baseball cards . . . all begun in late childhood. At the same age comes a desire to read what is
real, what actually happened. Children "collect" the
lives of presidents and their wives or the lives of scientists or baseball players. Those in parochial schools
eagerly read the lives of the saints.

Adolescence is a period of intense preoccupation
with self; interest in the life stories of others declines.
Teens want accounts of people who are almost mirror
images of themselves . . . and this kind of protagonist
is more often found in fiction. As people become mature, their interest in nonfiction grows again; many
adults read only biography and history. So the reading
of biography rises sharply in late childhood, recedes in
the teen years, and rises again in adult life.

Adults, like teens, are convinced that they are reading the truth in a biography. But what is truth? Biographers are more like portrait painters than photog-
raphers. They can never be completely objective in
presenting another's life, no matter how hard they try.
As storytellers they see pattern and form in the life and
tend to select materials to highlight their perceptions.
No one's life is lived without emotion, and biographers
often have to attribute emotions to their subjects for
which there is no documentation.

Near the beginning of the Gospel of Luke is the
statement: "It seemed good to me to write an orderly
account for you, most excellent Theophilus, that you
may know the truth concerning the things of which
you have been informed." Usually we see only the
surface of people's lives, but we are curious to know
what they are really like. What did Nixon say and do
during the Watergate cover-up? Was Tsar Nicholas II's
family all killed by the revolutionaries? What were
Napoleon's acts during his defeat at Waterloo? How
does a major-league football player feel and behave
before a big game?

You can see that biography and history have much
in common. Biography deals with how individuals
think and act; history, more with how groups act.

Readers turn to biography not only for facts but

from sheer curiosity about the great and famous. As Shakespeare wrote: "What great ones do, the less will prattle of." Because of our instinct for gossip, we enjoy seeing how "they" handle the routine affairs of their lives. Do they get headaches and diarrhea? Do they worry about bills? Do they change the baby's diapers or go on picnics? And what about their sex life? We eagerly read accounts by servants or secretaries about what remarkable people, who were their employers, were like behind the scenes. We delight in biographies by mistresses who reveal the secret love affairs of the famous. Biography has something in common with the gossip columns in the daily papers.

The motive for biography is often to explore the mysteries of human behavior. Thus biography has much in common with a psychological case study. Why do people do what they do? What are the underlying needs, pressures, and circumstances that influence an individual's actions? What in a Nixon accounts for a Watergate cover-up? Can we explain the incongruities in the character of Lincoln? What drives an individual to overcome great odds in sports? How can you explain the change in Eleanor Roosevelt from a retiring, gawky housewife and mother into a poised, outgoing world figure? Was Hitler mentally unbalanced? Some people continue to intrigue biographers and readers for generations. There is always some new biography of Alexander the Great, Napoleon, Washington, Jefferson, Lincoln—not to mention artists like Shakespeare, Michelangelo, and Beethoven, or scientists like Einstein and Freud. The desire to know *why* helps encourage teenagers to read biographies of folk heroes such as sports or rock stars.

Biographers may also be motivated by a desire to commemorate an individual who was important to them, echoing Kipling's words: "Lest we forget—lest we forget." It is like the use of tombstones, printed memorial services, and effigies to extend the impact of a person beyond death. William Allen White's sketch of his daughter, "Mary White," has made this school-

girl who died in an untimely accident remembered
through the century.

Writers also write biography for didactic purposes,
the subject serves as a model that we should emulate
or eschew. Plutarch in his paired lives of Greek and
Roman statesmen had an instructive purpose in mind.
The four biographies of Jesus in *The Bible* are not only
commemorative accounts but teaching vehicles. The
biographies of the saints used in parochial schools set
up images to be emulated. All of us remember the
tales of Washington's honesty and Lincoln's rise to
fame through hard work and self-education. And who
has not learned Longfellow's injunction: "Lives of
great men all remind us we can make our lives sub-
lime"?

DESCRIPTIONS OF BIOGRAPHY

A number of descriptions are used to differentiate
forms and purposes of biographies. "Juvenile" and
"junior biographies" are not biographies of children
but biographies written for children under 12 and
teenagers respectively. The junior biography is usually
short (150 to 250 pages). The best biographers include Nina Baker, Olivia Coolidge, Jeannette Eaton
and Manuel Komroff. Autobiographies, often by people with special but transient interest to teens—TV
personalities, rock stars, contemporary sports figures
—are apt to be "as told to" a professional writer. Individual titles have a life expectancy of only a year
or two.

"Fictionalized biography" includes scenes and dialogue which probably happened but cannot be backed
by documentary evidence. The writer's source may be
a creative insight into the behavior of human beings.
Actually, no biography is completely free of such fic-
tionalization.

The "definitive biography" aims at giving all the
known facts about the person, including a complete,

scholarly report of the extant material. Definitive biographies of artists are exemplified by Carlos Baker's biography of Ernest Hemingway and Leon Edel's four-volume life of Henry James.

"Interpretive biography" looks for a pattern in a life, selecting facts that emphasize the author's contentions. It may even omit nonsupportive information.

"Objective" or "factual biography" records the documented information about a life in chronological order. The author does not interpret or criticize, and there is no attempt to show direction or cause-effect relationships. It is not necessarily definitive.

"Monument biography" minimizes the faults and maximizes the virtues of the subject. Junior biography has tendencies in this direction. "Gargoyle" or "debunking biography" takes the opposite approach. There was a wave of gargoyle biographies during the early part of this century, especially of national figures. Recently James Roosevelt wrote something close to a gargoyle book in his account of FDR and Eleanor Roosevelt (*My Parents: A Differing View*).

"Critical biography" attempts to assess the value of a person's contribution to society or lifework. Scholars in literature and the arts often write such biographies. Or a Roosevelt or a Gandhi may be evaluated against the background of his time, from the perspective of later history.

"Collected biography" contains short accounts of people who have something in common. Plutarch's *Lives of the Noble Greeks and Romans* is a series of short biographies pairing a Greek with a Roman in comparable fields. Paul De Kruif's famous *Microbe Hunters* contains short accounts of medical researchers. John F. Kennedy in *Profiles in Courage* selected a group of congressmen who took an unpopular stand and risked their careers for what they thought was right. Other biographical collections cover business tycoons, athletes, artists, writers, religious leaders, outstanding women, ethnic groups, or the handicapped.

Teens want the same qualities in biography as in fiction. They seek real-life stories about heroes and heroines who resemble the characters in their favorite fiction. Boys prefer to read about men; girls about women. Both sexes want a fictionalized biography rather than a factual account. They enjoy undocumented dialogue, thoughts and feelings of the subject. The short biography is preferred; seldom do teens have enough interest in a person to read a long, detailed account. Adolescents are more interested in the youth of subjects than in their mature lives. They want to know what famous people were like as teenagers and how they achieved their success.

Teenagers are interested in people with interests like theirs. They want to read about sports, music, and entertainment personalities. The teenager interested in dance, science, or government will read biographies of successful people in their fields. Other popular subjects are adventurous activities—those of a mountain climber, outlaw, criminal, spy, or government agent— and traumatic situations such as living with an incurable handicap or disease.

Teenagers like monumental biographies in which the subject is heroized. They want to identify with someone they can admire, to find the same kind of heroes in real life that they found in subliterature and in animal stories.

There are not nearly as many classic biographies as classic works in fiction, poetry, or drama. A few are easily called to mind: Plutarch's *Lives*, the four Gospels in *The Bible*, Boswell's *The Life of Samuel Johnson*, Franklin's *Autobiography*, Strachey's *Eminent Victorians*, Sandburg's *Abraham Lincoln*, and Lincoln Steffens' *Autobiography*.

Of the 500 to 600 biographies published in the United States each year, and almost as many published in England, the teenager will only read 25 or 30 at most. Which 25 or 30 people in the whole course of human history would we as adults most like teenagers to know about in depth? One school has guided biography choices through a series of free reading units at each grade level. One grade reads lives of scientists; another, creative artists; another, modern statesmen or ethnic leaders; still another, heroes of the ancient world. Thus students can be led to widen their knowledge of human achievement in varying areas without dictating that they read specified books.

Bibliography

Adams, Alexander: *Sitting Bull: An Epic of the Plains.* G. P. Putnam's Sons, 1974.

Adler, Bill, and Jeffrey Feinman: *Woody Allen: Clown Prince of American Humor.* Pinnacle Books, 1975.

Albrecht, Mary Ellen, and Barbara L. Stern: *The Making of a Woman Cop.* William Morrow, 1976.

Ali, Muhammad, and Richard Durham: *The Greatest: My Own Story.* Random House, 1975. Ballantine Books.

Ashe, Arthur, and Frank Deford: *Arthur Ashe: Portrait in Motion.* Ballantine Books, 1976.

Baker, Nina: *Juarez, Hero of Mexico.* Vanguard, 1942.

————: *He Wouldn't Be King: The Story of Simon Bolivar.* Vanguard, 1941.

————: *Garabaldi.* Vanguard, 1944.

————: *Lenin.* Vanguard, 1945.

————: *Nickels and Dimes: The Story of F. W. Woolworth.* Harcourt Brace, Jovanovich paperback, 1966.

Benchley, Nathaniel: *Humphrey Bogart.* Little, Brown, 1975.

Bernstein, Burton: *Thurber: A Biography.* Dodd, Mead, 1975. Ballantine Books.

Bontemps, Arna: *Free at Last: The Life of Frederick Douglass.* Dodd, Mead, 1971.

Bradley, Bill: *Life on the Run.* Times Books, 1976. Bantam Books.

Braymer, Marjorie: *Walls of Windy Troy. A Biography of Heinrich Schliemann.* Harcourt Brace Jovanovich, 1966.

Buck, Pearl S.: *My Several Worlds.* Pocket Books, 1975.

Carpenter, Humphrey: *Tolkien.* Houghton Mifflin, 1977. Ballantine Books.

Carrighar, Sally: *Home to the Wilderness.* Houghton Mifflin, 1973. Penguin Books.

Cash, Johnny: *Man in Black*. Zondervan, 1975. Warner Books.

Cavett, Dick, and Christopher Porterfield. *Cavett*. Harcourt Brace Jovanovich, 1974. Bantam Books.

Chamberlain, Wilt, and David Shaw: *Wilt: Just Like Any Other 7-Foot Black Millionaire Who Lives Next Door*. Macmillan, 1973. Warner Books.

Chaplin, Charles: *My Life in Pictures*. Grosset & Dunlap, 1975.

Chisholm, Shirley: *Unbought and Unbossed*. Houghton Mifflin, 1970. Avon Books.

Christopher, Milbourne: *Houdini: The Untold Story*. T. Y. Crowell, 1969. Pocket Books.

Clapp, Patricia: *Dr. Elizabeth: A Biography of the First Woman Doctor*. Lothrop, Lee & Shepard, 1974.

Coolidge, Olivia: *Tom Paine, Revolutionary*. Charles Scribner's Sons, 1969.

————: *The Apprenticeship of Abraham Lincoln*. Charles Scribner's Sons, 1974.

————: *The Statesmanship of Abraham Lincoln*. Charles Scribner's Sons, 1976.

————: *Gandhi*. Houghton Mifflin, 1971.

Creamer, Robert: *Babe: The Legend Comes to Life*. Simon and Schuster, 1974. Pocket Books.

Davis, Clive, and James Willwerth: *Clive: Inside the Record Business*. William Morrow, 1975. Ballantine Books.

De Mille, Agnes: *Speak to Me, Dance With Me*. Popular Library, 1974.

Dreyer, Peter: *A Gardener Touched with Genius: The Life of Luther Burbank*. Coward, McCann & Geohegan, 1975.

Durocher, Leo, and Ed Linn: *Nice Guys Finish Last*. Simon and Schuster, 1975. Pocket Books.

Eaton, Jeanette: *Gandhi: Fighter Without a Sword*. William Morrow, 1950.

————: *Lone Journey: The Life of Roger Williams*. Harcourt Brace Jovanovich paperback, 1966.

Eiseley, Loren: *All the Strange Hours: The Excavations of a Life*. Charles Scribner's Sons, 1975.

Ellington, Duke: *Music Is My Mistress*. Doubleday, 1973.

Fields, W. C.: *W. C. Fields by Himself: His Intended Autobiography*. Prentice-Hall, 1973.

Flexner, James Thomas: *The Traitor and the Spy: Benedict Arnold and John Andre*. Little, Brown, 1975.

———: *Washington: The Indispensable Man*. Little, Brown, 1974.

Fonteyn, Margot: *Margot Fonteyn: Autobiography*. Warner Books, 1977.

Frank, Anne: *Anne Frank: The Diary of a Young Girl*. Doubleday, 1967. Pocket Books.

Frazier, Walt, and Joe Jares: *Clyde: The Walt Frazier Story*. Grosset & Dunlap, 1972.

Friedman, Myra: *Buried Alive: The Biography of Janis Joplin*. William Morrow, 1973.

Gerson, Noel B.: *The Swamp Fox: Francis Marion*. Mockingbird Books, 1975.

Goolagong, Evonne, and Bud Cullins: *Evonne! On the Move*. E. P. Dutton, 1975.

Gregory, Dick: *Up From Nigger*. Stein & Day, 1976. Fawcett Books.

Gunther, John: *Death Be Not Proud*. Harper & Row, 1971.

Guthrie, Woody: *Bound For Glory*. E. P. Dutton, 1976. New American Library.

Hayward, Brooke: *Haywire*. Alfred A. Knopf, 1977. Bantam Books.

Heidish, Marcy: *A Woman Called Moses (Harriet Tubman)*. Houghton Mifflin, 1976. Bantam Books.

Hemingway, Ernest: *A Moveable Feast*. Charles Scribner's Sons, 1964. Bantam Books.

Herndon, Venable: *James Dean: A Short Life*. Doubleday, 1974. New American Library.

Higham, Charles: *Kate: The Life of Katharine Hepburn*. W. W. Norton, 1975. New American Library.

Hoffmann, Banesh, and Helen Dukas: *Albert Einstein: Creator and Rebel*. Viking Press, 1972. New American Library.

Hughes, Langston: *I Wonder as I Wander*. Hill & Wang, 1964.

Jackson, Jesse: *Make a Joyful Noise Unto the Lord!* (Mahalia Jackson). Thomas Y. Crowell, 1974. Dell.

Jenner, Bruce, and Philip French: *Decathlon Challenge: Bruce Jenner's Story*. Prentice-Hall, 1977.

Keller, Helen: *The Story of My Life*. Doubleday, 1954. Dell.

Kennedy, John F.: *Profiles in Courage*. Harper & Row,

1964. The story of a group of senators who took an unpopular stand in American history.

Ketchum, Richard M.: *Will Rogers: The Man and His Times*. Simon and Schuster, 1975.

Killilea, Marie: *Karen*. Prentice-Hall, 1962. Dell.

King, Billie Jean, and Kim Chapin: *Billie Jean*. Harper & Row, 1974. Pocket Books.

King, Coretta S.: *My Life with Martin Luther King, Jr.* Avon Books, 1970.

Komroff, Manuel: *Julius Caesar*. Julian Messner, 1955.

————: *Marco Polo*. Archway.

————: *Walt Whitman, The Singer & The Chains*. Folcroft, 1973.

Kramer, Rita: *Maria Montessori: A Biography*. G. P. Putnam's Sons, 1977.

Kroeber, Theodora: *Ishi: Last of His Tribe*. Parnassus Press, 1964. Bantam Books.

Kruif, Paul De: *Microbe Hunters*. Harcourt Brace Jovanovich, 1932. Short biographies of the lives of biology scientists who have tracked down the cause of major diseases.

Landon, Margaret: *Anna and the King of Siam*. John Day, 1944. Pocket Books.

Lash, Joseph P.: *Eleanor and Franklin* (Roosevelt). New American Library, 1973.

Leitner, Isabella: *Fragments of Isabella: A Memoir of Auschwitz*. Thomas Y. Crowell, 1978.

Libby, Bill: *O.J.: The Story of Football's Fabulous O. J. Simpson*. G. P. Putnam's Sons, 1974.

Lipsyte, Robert: *Free to Be Muhammad Ali*. Harper & Row, 1978. Bantam Books.

Lund, Doris: *Eric*. J. B. Lippincot, 1974. Dell.

Maas, Peter: *Serpico*. Viking Press, 1973. Bantam Books.

McCabe, John, and Al Kilgore: *Laurel and Hardy*. Ballantine Books, 1976.

McKuen, Rod: *Finding My Father*. Coward, McCann & Geohegan, 1976. Berkley, 1977.

McLellan, David: *Karl Marx*. Viking Press, 1975. Penguin Books.

Malcolm X and Alex Haley: *Autobiography of Malcolm X*. Grove Press, 1965.

Mays, Willie: *Willie Mays: My Life In and Out of Baseball*. E. P. Dutton, 1966.

Mead, Margaret: *Blackberry Winter: My Earlier Years.* William Morrow, 1972.

————: *Letters from the Field, 1925–1975.* Harper & Row, 1968.

Meeropol, Robert and Michael: *We Are Your Sons: The Legacy of Ethel and Julius Rosenberg.* Houghton Mifflin, 1975. Ballantine Books.

Meltzer, Milton: *Langston Hughes: A Biography.* Thomas Y. Crowell, 1968.

Milford, Nancy: *Zelda: A Biography* (Zelda Fitzgerald). Harper & Row, 1970. Avon Books.

Miller, Merle: *Plain Speaking: An Oral Biography of Harry S. Truman.* Berkley, 1974.

Morris, Jeannie: *Brian Piccolo: A Short Season.* Rand McNally, 1971. Dell.

Mosley, Leonard: *Lindbergh: A Biography.* Dell, 1977.

Parlin, John: *Amelia Earhart.* Garrard, 1962. Dell.

Pele and Robert L. Fish: *My Life and the Beautiful Game.* Doubleday, 1977. Warner Books.

Percival, John: *Nureyev: Aspects of a Dancer.* G. P. Putnam's Sons, 1975. Popular Library.

Plath, Aurelia S., ed.: *Letters Home* (Sylvia Plath). Harper & Row, 1975. Bantam Books.

Quinlan, Joseph and Julia: *Karen Ann: The Quinlans Tell Their Story.* Doubleday, 1977. Bantam Books.

Rather, Dan, and Mickey Herskowitz: *The Camera Never Blinks.* William Morrow, 1977. Ballantine Books.

Richter, Hans Peter: *I Was There.* Holt, Rinehart and Winston, 1972. Dell.

Rivera, Geraldo: *A Special Kind of Courage.* Simon and Schuster, 1976. Bantam Books.

Rodgers, Richard: *Musical Stages: An Autobiography.* Random House, 1975. Jove/HBJ.

Sakai, Saburo: *Samurai!* Bantam Books, 1978.

Saroyan, William: *Places Where I've Done Time.* Dell, 1973.

Sayers, Gail and Al Silverman: *I Am Third.* Viking Press, 1970. Bantam Books.

Scaduto, Anthony: *Bob Dylan.* New American Library, 1973.

Schickel, Richard: *The Disney Version.* Simon and Schuster, 1968. Avon Books.

Schwarzenegger, Arnold and Douglas K. Hall: *Arnold:*

The Education of a Body Builder. Simon and Schuster, 1977.

Schweitzer, Albert: *Out of My Life and Thought.* Holt, Rinehart and Winston, 1972. New American Library.

Scott, John Anthony: *Woman Against Slavery: The Story of Harriet Beecher Stowe.* Thomas Y. Crowell, 1978.

Scott, John Anthony, and Milton Meltzer: *Fanny Kemble's America.* Thomas Y. Crowell, 1973.

Smith, Lacey Baldwin: *Elizabeth Tudor: Portrait of a Queen.* Little, Brown, 1975.

Sorrentino, Joe: *Up From Never.* Bantam Books, 1978.

Specht, Robert: *Tisha: The Story of a Young Teacher in the Alaska Wilderness.* St. Martin's Press, 1976. Bantam Books.

Steinbeck, John: *Travels with Charley.* Viking Press, 1962. Bantam Books.

Steiner, Nancy Hunter: *A Closer Look at Ariel: A Memory of Sylvia Plath.* Popular Library, 1974.

Sterling, Philip: *Sea and Earth: The Life of Rachel Carson.* Thomas Y. Crowell, 1970. Dell.

Stone, Irving: *Clarence Darrow for the Defense.* Doubleday, 1949. New American Library.

————: *Jack London: Sailor on Horseback.* Doubleday, 1978. New American Library.

Strachey, Lytton and Peter Smith: *Eminent Victorians.* Harcourt Brace and Jovanovich, 1969. Interpretative biographies of 4 major figures of Victorian England, a cardinal, a nurse (Florence Nightingale), a doctor, and a general.

Sullivan, Tom, and Derek Gill: *If You Could See What I Hear.* Harper and Row, 1975. New American Library.

Ten Boom, Corrie: *The Hiding Place.* Fleming H. Revell, 1974. Bantam Books.

Ullmann, Liv: *Changing.* Alfred A. Knopf, 1977. Bantam Books.

Vonnegut, Mark: *The Eden Express: A Personal Account of Schizophrenia.* Bantam Books, 1976.

Wagenheim, Kal: *Clemente!* Washington Square Press, 1974.

White, Florence M.: *Cesar Chavez: Man of Courage.* Garrard, 1973. Dell.

Wojciechowska, Maia: *Till the Break of Day.* Harcourt Brace Jovanovich, 1972.

CLASSIC BIOGRAPHY

Boswell, James: *The Life of Samuel Johnson.* Oxford University Press, 1970. New American Library.

Bowen, Catherine Drinker: *John Adams and the American Revolution.* Atlantic Monthly Press, 1950. Grosset & Dunlap.

Chute, Marchette: *Shakespeare of London.* E. P. Dutton, 1950.

Curie, Eve: *Madame Curie.* Pocket Books, 1963.

Douglass, Frederick: *The Life and Times of Frederick Douglass.* Thomas Y. Crowell, 1966. Collier Books.

Forbes, Esther: *Paul Revere and the World He Lived In.* Houghton Mifflin, 1962.

Franklin, Benjamin: *Autobiography.* Yale University Press, 1964. New American Library.

Ludwig, Emil: *Napoleon.* Pocket Books, 1953.

Morison, Samuel Eliot: *Christopher Columbus, Mariner.* Little, Brown, 1955. New American Library.

Plutarch: *Lives of the Noble Greeks and Romans.* E. P. Dutton, 1957, 3 vols.

Sandburg, Carl: *Abraham Lincoln: The Prairie Years* and *The War Years.* Harcourt Brace Jovanovich, 1970. Dell.

Steffans, Lincoln: *Autobiography of Lincoln Steffens.* Harcourt Brace Jovanovich, 1968.

Strachey, Lytton: *Queen Victoria.* Harcourt Brace Jovanovich, 1949.

Twain, Mark: *Autobiography* (ed. Charles Neider). Harper & Row, 1959.

Washington, Booker T.: *Up From Slavery.* Doubleday, 1933. Bantam Books.

12

Drama

A dramatist is one who from his earliest years has
found that sheer gazing at the shocks and counter-
shocks among people is quite sufficiently engrossing
without having to encase it in comment.
                                    —*Thornton Wilder*

Drama rises from two innate desires: the desire to
mimic and the desire to narrate. People may have imi-
tated animals first, as part of the hunt. Later they used
their bodies to reenact their exploits, just as they used
the walls of caves to paint stories of them. Then drama
may have become ritualized to celebrate life-forces perceived in the world or to honor great persons at their
deaths. Dance, pantomime, and music probably pre-
ceded the spoken word and dialogue.

The word "drama" comes from the Greek and
means "a thing done." The theater is "a seeing place";
and "audience," from Latin, means "those who listen."
Thus drama is to be watched and listened to.

Reading plays is difficult, since they were meant to
be seen and heard. Like reading architects' plans, a
musical score, a dress pattern, or a recipe, it requires
an imaginative leap in transforming the marks on
paper to another medium.

Teens don't read plays on their own, but if encouraged and taught how to read them, they will find plays
a significant literary experience. Teaching 11th-grade
English classes a few years ago, I found that *Death of a
Salesman* was the most remembered work.

Teenagers should be taught to read drama for pleasure as well as to get insights. Most have little access to real stages and must see versions on TV and in movies, or read plays. They find a play short compared to a novel; it is nearly all dialogue, which young readers find easier to read than narrative prose. It deals straightforwardly with issues of human relationships, interactions, emotions, situations that make for discussion.

Drama has no narrator to tell the reader who the characters are, what they are doing, where they are, how they got there. The purer the drama, the less information is given—for example, in a Greek tragedy or a Shakespearean play.

There are some hints in the *dramatis personae*. In modern plays there are detailed descriptions of the set, and stage directions which may be informative to the reader. But these details are appendages and are often merely technical. The reader has to figure out the ages of the characters, their relationships, appearances, and personalities. This can be done by the teenage reader, just as teenagers did in the thirties and forties by ear when listening to radio drama.

Many teenagers don't know the conventions of printed drama. Unless informed by a teacher, they don't usually understand the difference between the speaker's name printed on the page and what the speaker says, or between dialogue and the stage directions that are italicized and/or put in parentheses.

Most adolescents fail to recognize the scene as the unit of construction in a play. A scene is an interchange between a group of people on the stage. Even if the location is unchanged, whenever a character exits or enters, there is a new scene. It would help if, like the classic French playwrights, we indicated scenes this way in English-language plays. Then readers could keep track of who is onstage, and be aware of how each scene, no matter how short, has an issue and a climax.

The best help for teenagers reading drama comes through classroom enactment of scenes or "beats" (segments of action). Small groups of students are given copies of a scene. They discuss the characters involved, the business, the voice tonalities, and then cast and act out the scene. They may experiment with alternative versions. They are not preparing a performance, but trying to create the scene as they feel it would be acted on stage.

Libraries should shelve many individual contemporary plays as well as the ubiquitous collections. *Literary Cavalcade,* a periodical published by Scholastic Magazines, features a script (sometimes cut slightly) of a recent play in almost every issue. Over the years, these add up to an impressive collection of plays that will interest young people.

The body of junior drama doesn't match the large body of junior novels. The strong movement in children's theater has not led to a comparable adolescent theater.

The plays teens read are usually plays written for adult audiences. Except for Greek tragedies and Shakespeare (chapter 9), they are 20th-century plays.

The young teenager begins with comedy. *You Can't Take It with You* is hilarious to 13- and 14-year-olds, who love the zaniness of the Vanderhof family, who are all doing their own thing, from making fireworks to studying ballet to writing plays. It offers a secret vision of a life that we would all like but do not quite dare to have. It appeals to the junior high schooler who feels the constraints of family. The topical allusions to the 1930s do not seem to bother the contemporary teen.

Arsenic and Old Lace by Joseph Kesselring may be the best American farce ever written. The two elderly ladies who help their unhappy visitors by giving them poison in their elderberry wine never fail to delight young readers.

Older teens still enjoy comedy. Shaw, especially his *Pygmalion,* has a wide readership. Recently the comedies of Neil Simon, dealing with young adults caught in the web of modern city life, have had great appeal, especially *Barefoot in the Park. The Match-*

maker by Thornton Wilder, later the musical *Hello,
Dolly,* reads very well; the machinations of the invincible Dolly seem to delight readers as well as theater-goers.

Many plays, though written for adult audiences, are
about teenagers and adolescent problems. *Romeo and
Juliet* and its modern counterpart *West Side Story* deal
with an ill-fated teenage love affair. *Ah, Wilderness!*
by Eugene O'Neill probes the rites of passage of a
teenager: his desires and insecurities, his fumbling approach to sex, his embarrassment before his family. *The
Diary of Anne Frank* is as appealing as a play as was
the original diary, though the emphasis is different.
Reading the diary, you can almost forget the war, so
wrapped up do you get in the emotional turmoil Anne
is undergoing as she moves through puberty. In the
play the characters' desperate situation is ever present,
since the setting and actions underline the tensions.

Equus, a recent play, has co-protagonists: a 17-year-old boy and a psychiatrist, who tries to unravel the
boy's feelings that led him to blind six horses. As we
watch, the characters are psychologically stripped and
their innermost horrors revealed. At the climax, the
teenager is physically and psychologically naked on the
stage. The play holds the same fascination for older
teens as do novels centering on mental aberrations such
as *One Flew Over the Cuckoo's Nest* and *I Never
Promised You a Rose Garden.* Tennessee Williams's
The Glass Menagerie and Paul Zindel's *The Effect of
Gamma Rays on Man-in-the-Moon Marigolds* deal
with teenage girls, though the main character in each is
a domineering mother.

Some of the most provocative plays deal with societal problems. The problem play was developed in the
late 19th century by Henrik Ibsen, who in a long life,
was as prolific as Shakespeare. Several of Ibsen's plays,
though a century old, ring so true that they could have
been written about today's social problems. *An Enemy
of the People* shows a small town whose economy
depends on baths, which some claim to have medicinal
properties. When Dr. Stockmann discovers that they

are polluted and insists they be closed, he creates an uproar. He is vilified by his friends and neighbors and is drummed out of town. The situation is applicable to contemporary events. Peter Benchley uses almost the same issue in *Jaws:* if news gets out about the shark, the summer resort business will be ruined. Ibsen's *A Doll's House* is probably a more powerful statement of the plight of women than anything that has been produced by the recent women's movement.

A favorite 20th-century play of social implications is Arthur Miller's *The Crucible,* set during the witch-hunts in colonial New England; teenage girls accuse the stalwart citizens of witchcraft and enjoy the excitement they are causing and the power they have over adults. The play is relevant to many personal and social issues today. It is a kind of universal statement about witch-hunts yesterday and today.

Another favorite is a play about a black family, *A Raisin in the Sun.* The Youngers have finally gotten enough together to move into a middle-class neighborhood, where they face antagonism from their white neighbors. But the play is more than a racial confrontation; it deals with family tensions brought about by differences in age and personalities.

Readers have said that they learned English history from Shakespeare. Other historical plays have a similar function, especially the many semibiographical plays centered on a historical figure. Outstanding is *A Man for All Seasons,* which details the struggle between Thomas More and Henry VIII over the king's divorce and split with the Roman Catholic Church. Maxwell Anderson wrote moving plays of *Elizabeth the Queen* and *Mary of Scotland.* Robert Sherwood wrote of Lincoln's formative years in *Abe Lincoln in Illinois.*

Teenagers enjoy plays which, like *Equus,* lay bare the inner turmoil of people. Lillian Hellman's *The Little Foxes* strips away the characters' facade and reveals the appalling nastiness of a decaying southern family. Tennessee Williams in a number of plays (*A Streetcar Named Desire; Cat on a Hot Tin Roof*) also portrays southerners who rip away one another's pretenses step

by step. Perhaps the classic example of this kind of play
is Edward Albee's *Who's Afraid of Virginia Woolf?*,
which portrays superficially genteel people who play a
series of games with one another that gradually strip
them until there is no shred of self-respect left. Friedrich Durrenmatt's plays are terrifying. *The Visit* begins
as a wealthy woman returns to her hometown. Con-
trary to the townspeople's expectations, she has come
to wreak vengeance and to destroy the town, which she
does by playing on the corruption inherent in each
human being.

Drama has been the primary vehicle for the presentation of existentialism—the view that nothing exists
beyond one's own existence and there is no rational
way for making choices. Young intellectuals are attracted to plays which have almost every unit focused
on the modern philosophical cast of thought, such as
Jean-Paul Sartre's *No Exit* and Samuel Beckett's *Waiting for Godot*. An English play in the same vein is
Tom Stoppard's *Rosencrantz & Guildenstern Are Dead*,
which takes place backstage as the two actors wait to
go onstage in *Hamlet*.

Cult readers are those who become passionately involved with a writer or a book that breaks old forms
and concepts. In the drama, this has recently meant
the theater of the absurd. High-school drama class
favorites include Albee's *The Zoo Story* and *The Sandbox*, and Harold Pinter's *The Caretaker* and *The Dumb
Waiter*, in which characters seem to talk aimlessly.

But teenagers are still romantic and perhaps the
continuing favorite of them all is Thornton Wilder's
Our Town. The nostalgia of small-town life at the turn
of the century still evokes a response. Wilder captures
the dailiness of a life that has not changed for many
people. The use of the stage manager as a major character and the setless stage still seem innovative.

Viewing a play is the most vivid literary experience.
The author does not intrude an interpretation of what
we see and hear. There is no commentator; only action
and reaction. The immediacy of drama is what makes
it one of the oldest surviving literary forms. The issues

between people stand out starkly. From the hints given by the dialogue the teenage reader of plays comes to visualize the characters, hear their voices, watch their movements, even think about their lighting. Through this process he can come to the understanding about living that the actions encapsulate.

Bibliography

Albee, Edward: *The Sandbox*. New American Library, 1964. A couple go to the beach with the wife's aged, rebellious mother.

———: *Zoo Story*. Coward, 1960. A mentally disturbed man who cannot communicate with a man reading a newspaper on a park bench resorts to violence.

———: *Who's Afraid of Virginia Woolf?* Atheneum, 1962. An idyllic campus setting becomes a cage for two college professors and their wives as the four fight to expose one another's vulnerabilities. Albee bitterly condemns the charade of contemporary achievement.

Anderson, Robert: *Tea and Sympathy* (in *Famous American Plays of the 1950s*, ed. Lee Strasberg). Dell, 1962. A sensitive study of emerging manhood amid the rituals of a boy's prep school. Tom Lee's maturity is measured by his capacity for love rather than his ability to be a conquering athlete.

Beckett, Samuel: *Waiting for Godot*. Grove Press, 1964. A theater of the absurd classic that magnifies the emptiness of human life with humor and pathos. Two friends wait for their existence to be verified by the tangible arrival of a third, ever elusive character.

Bolt, Robert: *A Man for All Seasons*. Random House, 1962. Sir Thomas More's fatal conflict with King Henry VIII of England.

Chayefsky, Paddy: *Twelve Angry Men* (in *Great Television Plays*, ed. William I. Kaufman). Dell, 1969. Locked in a jury room on a sweltering day in New York City, a mix of men, ranging from mediocre to moral, must face their prejudices as one among them forces all to fairly judge an accused youth.

Christie, Agatha: *The Mousetrap and Other Plays.* Dodd, Mead, 1978. Dell. Ten guests invited to a luxurious retreat begin to understand that their unknown host is among them, intent on murder. Who will survive his macabre parlor games?

Durrenmatt, Friedrich: *The Visit.* Grove Press, 1962. A billionairess offers a fortune to her hometown in return for the life of the man who had seduced her as a young person, and demonstrates that moral rectitude is only skin-deep.

Gibson, William: *The Miracle Worker.* Alfred A. Knopf, 1957. Bantam Books. Incorrigible Helen Keller, blind, deaf, and mute since infancy, fights all attempts to civilize her. The patience, understanding, and sheer determination of teacher Annie Sullivan break through Helen's darkness as she learns to communicate.

Goodrich, Frances and Albert Hackett: *The Diary of Anne Frank.* Random House, 1956. The play, while faithful to the original diary, makes the reader more conscious of the confinement of the family and the tenseness of the situation.

Hansberry, Lorainne: *A Raisin in the Sun.* Random House, 1969. New American Library. A chance to break out of the ghetto syndrome motivates the Younger family to integrate a white neighborhood. Hopes, dreams, and frustrations are exposed as each family member forges an identity that will guarantee dignified survival in contemporary America.

Hart, Moss, and George Kaufman: *You Can't Take It With You* (in *Comedies of American Family Life,* ed. Joseph E. Mersand). All the members of a zany family do exactly what they please, from ballet to making fireworks.

Hellman, Lillian: *The Little Foxes and Another Part of the Forest.* Penguin Books, 1976. Decaying social and moral values seen through the eyes of a southern family with a last, desperate hold on an elite past.

Ibsen, Henrik: *A Doll's House* (in *Four Great Plays*). Bantam Books, 1959. A pioneer work that questioned male dominance in genteel society. Nora dared to challenge Torvold's authority in their marriage, de-

claring her independence as she slammed the door
on servitude and opened the gates of feminist expression.

————: *An Enemy of the People* (in *Four Great Plays*).
Bantam Books, 1959. The heroic struggle of a noble
man against the ignoble leaders of a community.

————: *Hedda Gabler*. Avon Books, 1975. A drama of an
ambitious young woman who attempts to control the
destinies of two men by a series of unsuccessful
intrigues.

Kesselring, Joseph: *Arsenic and Old Lace* (in *Three Plays
About Crime and Criminals*, ed. George Freedley).
Washington Square Press, 1965. A young man's aunts
have a charming habit of disposing of callers with a
gentle dose of poison. His befuddled attempts to correct their sinister doings lead to a hilarious climax.

Laurents, Arthur: *West Side Story*. Dell, 1963. A modern
musical version of Shakespeare's tragedy *Romeo and
Juliet* (with which it is bound in this edition). Maria
and Tony's love is doomed by the cultural differences
between whites and Puerto Ricans in New York's
deteriorating tenements.

Lawrence, Jerome, and Robert E. Lee: *Inherit the Wind*.
Bantam Books, 1969. Clarence Darrow and William
Jennings Bryan battle in court over the theory of
evolution in the famed Scopes monkey trial.

Luce, Clare Boothe: *The Women* (in *Plays by and About
Women*, eds. Victoria Sullivan and James V. Hatch).
Random House, 1973. Written by a woman about the
powers and pitfalls of feminist sisterhood, this biting
satire takes pointed shots at the sacred cows of business and politics during the thirties.

Luce, William: *The Belle of Amherst*. Houghton Mifflin,
1976. A one-woman show; this dialogue between
Emily Dickinson and her silent but participating
audience brings life to the writings of a passionate
and creative 19th-century poet.

Miller, Arthur: *All My Sons* (in *Six Great Modern Plays*,
ed. Laurel Editions Editors). Dell, 1964. Chris must
face the realities of his father's compromise of morality for money during World War II. Exposing vast
profits from the spoils of war, Miller also confronts
the decline of American family values.

————: *The Crucible.* Viking Press, 1953. Bantam Books. Based on the Salem witch trials, but written in response to the excesses of the McCarthy era, Miller focuses on the horrors of political accusation and the casual acceptance of hearsay evidence that ruins human lives.

————: *Death of a Salesman* (in *The Portable Arthur Miller*). Viking Press, 1971. Penguin Books. A modern tragic figure, Willy Loman drags his sample cases through the American landscape in pursuit of a shallow desire to be "well liked." His family is left to the frustration of embodying his unfulfilled dreams.

Pinter, Harold: *The Caretaker.* Grove Press, 1961. Mick tries to regain contact with his brain-damaged brother who engages a tramp as a caretaker for his house.

————: *The Dumb Waiter.* Grove Press, 1961. Two assassins wait in a hotel room for their victim, where they discover that they are expected to fill restaurant orders sent to them on a dumb waiter.

Osborne, John: *Look Back in Anger.* S. G. Phillips, 1957. Jimmy Porter, struggling for recognition, battles the established forces of class power in modern Britain. Hostile and driven, he represents a new generation on the move.

Sartre, Jean-Paul: *No Exit.* Random House, 1955. An existential hell surrounds three characters who realize their ultimate fantasies, only to be unceasingly bombarded by the sensations that eluded them in life. (This edition includes three other plays by Sartre.)

Shaffer, Anthony: *Sleuth.* Dodd, Mead, 1971. A British murder mystery that twists on the sinister machinations of two outwardly proper gentlemen, each increasingly capable of outdoing each other's nefarious deeds.

Shaffer, Peter: *Equus.* Avon Books, 1975. A quiet teenager has mutilated six horses. Dr. Martin Dysart exposes his own insecurities while helping Alan to free himself from boyhood torments of religious and sexual oppression.

Shange, Ntozake: *For Colored Girls Who Have Considered Suicide When the Rainbow is Enuf.* Macmillan, 1977. Bantam Books. A choreographed prose-poem that poignantly confronts the pain and beauty of being black and poor, women and proud against the blight of the urban landscape.

Shaw, George Bernard/Alan Jay Lerner: *Pygmalion/My Fair Lady*. New American Library, 1975. Shaw's classic tale of the transformation of a cockney girl into a well-spoken woman is bound with the hit musical based on his play.

Simon, Neil: *Barefoot in the Park*. Random House, 1964. Set against a backdrop of New York City's frantic pace, Simon has written a joyful comedy about young marriage and the timeless problems of achieving independence.

Stoppard, Tom: *Rosencrantz & Guildenstern Are Dead*. Grove Press, 1967. A brilliant replaying of Hamlet, from the perspective of two minor characters.

Swados, Elizabeth: *Runaways*. Bantam Books, 1979. A modern play capturing young people's intense energies, loneliness and rage in surviving the world today.

Sweetkind, Morris, ed.: *Ten Great One-Act Plays*. Bantam Books, 1968. A modern collection of European and American favorites that introduces the works of great playwrights from Chekhov to Shaw.

Watson, E. Bradlee, and Benfield Pressey, eds.: *Contemporary Drama, Eleven Plays*. Charles Scribner's Sons, 1956. An excellent collection which includes *Pygmalion; Green Pastures; Happy Journey to Trenton and Camden; Ways and Means; Hello Out There;* Anouilh's *Antigone; The Glass Menagerie; The Madwoman of Chaillot; Another Part of the Forest; Death of a Salesman;* and *Venus Observed*.

————: *Contemporary Drama, Fifteen Plays*. Charles Scribner's Sons, 1959. Also an excellent anthology. Includes *Hedda Gabler; The Importance of Being Earnest; Uncle Vanya; A Dream Play; Man and Superman; Riders to the Sea; Henry IV; Ah, Wilderness!; Blood Wedding; Murder in the Cathedral; Purple Dust; The Skin of our Teeth; Come Back, Little Sheba; The Crucible;* and *Look Homeward, Angel*.

Wilde, Oscar: *The Importance of Being Earnest*. Avon Books, 1965. A comedy of errors, the title a play on words. This drawing-room farce uses the plot device of mistaken identity to poke fun at Victorian manners and morals.

Wilder, Thornton: *Our Town*. Harper & Row, 1960. Avon Books. The New Hampshire village of Grover's Corners is the setting for this classic study of American youth growing from puppy love to marriage, facing family, parenthood, and death.

Williams, Tennessee: *Cat on a Hot Tin Roof*. New American Library and New Directions, 1975. The tensions and pretensions of a wealthy southern family and the strained relations between Maggie and her alcoholic husband.

————: *The Glass Menagerie*. New Directions, 1966. Torn by her mother's hope for the perfect southern marriage, yet aware that she is long past the age of desirability, crippled Laura tries to accept her place in life. The sweet attentions of a gentleman caller give Laura an increased sense of personal value, but cause a painful confrontation with Amanda's lost dreams.

Zindel, Paul: *The Effect of Gamma Rays on Man-in-the-Moon Marigolds*. Harper & Row, 1971. Bantam Books. In violent confrontations between a mother and her two daughters, Zindel explores the age-old theme of a parental generation attempting to fulfill lost dreams through its children.

————: *Let Me Hear You Whisper*. Harper & Row, 1974. A dolphin in a science laboratory pleads with a scrubwoman to save him from certain death as an experimental specimen.

13

Nonfiction: Something for Everyone

> Every addition to true knowledge is
> an addition to human power.
> —*Horace Mann*

This is a period of exploding knowledge. It is estimated that 90 percent of all the scientists who have ever lived are alive and working today. Because no culture has ever been so introspective we have great masses of information about our basic social institutions, our history, and ourselves. Knowledge is accumulating so fast that new theories and laws are overturned by newer discoveries before the person on the street is aware that they exist. It is estimated that a scientific principle has a life expectancy of ten years before it is superseded or drastically modified by newer information.

Individuals growing up today are faced with a lifelong task of running to catch up. What they learn as fact in school or college will probably not take them more than a few years into their adult lives. What they need in such a world is intellectual curiosity and the techniques with which to satisfy it. They need to become "learning" persons, not "learned" persons.

Most of the resources for learning are available in the incredible storehouse of books. Not only is human knowledge available in scholarly, ponderous texts, but often also in profusely illustrated books, written espe-

cially for adolescents. Our reservoir of factual books
for teenagers in America is unprecedented and un-
rivaled. Too few parents and teachers are aware that
such fabulous materials exist.

Each year the author reviews about 1,000 new books
for the adolescent reader, almost two-thirds of them
nonfiction: expository accounts of work in science,
the social sciences, the arts, technology and business;
books on hobbies and leisure activities, personal and
social problems, and almost every subject. Often the
appeal seems so limited that you wonder why the
publisher brought out the book. For example, about a
year ago a book came out devoted exclusively to hawks.
I didn't see why any young person would want to read
a whole book about hawks. But I heard of an adolescent in western Iowa who had become fascinated by
these predators: he had found nestlings, reared them
to maturity, and taught them to hunt. He was ecstatic
about the book, which could confirm his observations
and fill in the gaps in his knowledge.

The problem is to get the right book to the right
child. Almost always there is a useful book on any
interest an American teenager has. The books are not
so technical that they overwhelm the young reader.
They are not abridged college textbooks, but are written in clear expository prose. A kind of unwritten
principle among educators is: "Whatever can be explained and understood can be explained and understood more simply." In today's nonfiction books for
teenagers broad outlines are sketched accurately, and
the young reader can refine and add to his knowledge
through subsequent study.

PERSONAL EXPERIENCE

One palatable kind of nonfiction book tells some
personal experiences that human beings have lived
through—sometimes great feats of endurance which
push people to the limits of their capacities. In *Alive,*

Piers Paul Read tells what happened to the survivors, some of them seriously injured, of an air crash in the mountains of South America. Some of them resorted to cannibalism before they were rescued.

A book that fulfills every adolescent reader's dream is *Dove* by Robin Graham. At 16, he dropped out of school and set out to sail alone around the world. His diary is enthralling, along with many of the photographs he took. Books like these take their place alongside older accounts of sailing, mountain climbing, spelunking, and diving.

Another kind of personal experience is that of someone who has been in prison, or in a mental institution, or on a police force. David Harris, who was imprisoned as a draft resister for two years, tells the day-by-day life, the depersonalization, the horror of the prison system in *I Shoulda Been Home Yesterday*. Mark Vonnegut, after graduating from college and attempting to establish a commune in western Canada, found himself increasingly unable to cope with reality. In *The Eden Express*, he writes of his experience with schizophrenia and his treatment with massive doses of vitamins. Peter Maas's *Serpico* tells the life of an unusual officer in the New York City police department.

There are vivid accounts of people (often teenagers) facing incurable diseases. *Death Be Not Proud*, a father's loving memoir of his teenage son's courage in the face of a terminal brain tumor, has become a classic book of its type. Doris Lund in *Eric*, and Rose Levit in *Ellen* portray the anguish and spirit of a son of 17 and a daughter of 15 who have terminal cancer. A great favorite is *Brian's Song* by William Blinn, about the slow death of pro football star Brian Piccolo.

Sports experiences have always had an avid readership among teenagers. George Plimpton has written one intriguing book after another about the sports world, including *One for the Record*, the story of Hank Aaron's determination to break the home-run record held by Babe Ruth. Pat Jordan's *A False Spring* describes his one season on the farm teams of a major-league club. He had been a spectacular high-school pitcher and was bid on by many clubs. But after a slow move up through the farms he suddenly lost his ability to pitch and knew that he was done.

ARCHAEOLOGY AND ANTHROPOLOGY

In the last few years many books have presented the work of archaeologists and anthropologists to adolescents. It has been pointed out that the farther we move from our origins, the more we know about them. The two sciences devoted to the study of human beings and the development of their culture began rather recently; interest in the remnants of past civilizations did not develop until a century ago, while the study of the origins of man is an outgrowth of Darwin's theory of evolution, presented in 1859.

C. W. Ceram's *Gods, Graves, and Scholars* deals in narrative form with scientists and their discoveries in Greece, Egypt, Babylonia, and Mexico. *Earth Magic* by Francis Hitching goes farther back into time, putting together many bits of information about megalithic peoples, those who lived more than 5000 years ago. Far from being "primitive," they left no written language, but had a culture that was rich and sophisticated in its production of artifacts and was knowledgeable about the movement of the stars. Laurence Swinburne tells of the discovery of the tomb and treasure of Tutankhamen in *Behind the Sealed Door,* richly illustrated with modern photographs of the treasures as well as pictures taken at the time of the discovery. Von Hagen's books about the Incas, Mayas, and Aztecs are some of the best accounts we have of the civilizations in the New World before the European discovery. Twenty-five years ago this kind of book for the adolescent reader was almost nonexistent; now four or five exciting narratives of discoveries about man's great past are published each year.

SOCIAL SCIENCES

These books cover every aspect of humanity's long struggle to find ways of living together in groups.

Of the books that deal with individual countries, regions, and states, a popular one is John McPhee's *Coming into the Country,* a journalist's discovery of the vastness of Alaska: a sort of travelogue, history, and economic and ecological survey.

Teenagers are interested in books about the workings of government institutions. Gerald W. Johnson has written a series of them, including *The Cabinet* and *The Congress,* which give the history and development of an institution and clear information about its current status and operation.

Ernest Fincher's *The Presidency* is a readable presentation which discusses the lure of the office, the choosing of a president, and his relationship with Congress. *A Guide to the Supreme Court* by Dorothy A. Marquardt deals with the purpose and authority of the court, with a brief history of the eras of the chief justices from John Jay to Warren Burger. She ends by discussing the landmark decisions of the court that have changed the course of American life.

The story of the birth of the American Constitution is told by Catherine D. Bowen in *Miracle at Philadelphia,* which gives a fascinating, accurate picture of the Constitutional Convention as it framed the government of the United States. A number of books delve into the hidden or unsavory side of government and society. The very titles of Jules Archer's books imply their content: *Superspies: The Secret Side of Government;* and *Police State. Witch Hunt* by Michael Dorman deals with investigations by congressional committees, with chapters on Martin Dies, Joseph McCarthy, and Whittaker Chambers and Alger Hiss, as well as on blacklisting of the 1950s.

Among books dealing with special aspects of social history, Alice Fleming has written a history of gambling in *Something for Nothing* and Richard Deming discusses the female criminal in *Women: The New Criminals,* developing the thesis that until recently there has been a division between the types of crimes committed by women and by men. Walter Webb's *The Great Plains* and Floyd B. Streeter's *Prairie Trails and Cow Towns* are studies of the American West.

Edwin Hoag's *How Business Works* looks at American enterprise, giving facts and figures about the range of the business world and the size of its work force. There are thumbnail sketches of individual businesses and how they started, and a discussion of business and society. Laurence Pringle's short *Our Hungry Earth: The World Food Crisis* focuses on a lasting world problem.

SCIENCE

Beautifully illustrated, clearly written books for teenagers give accurate information about most aspects of scientific development. The works are attractively bound and often outstanding examples of the printer's art. The adolescent who wants technical and scientific information, often far in advance of his science classes in school, can find it readily in bookstores and libraries.

Since the advent of spaceflight there has been increased interest in astronomy. Timothy Ferris deals with the expanding universe in *The Red Limit*. He explains what is meant by the "red shift," and presents theories about the creation of the universe, concepts of time, and the ultimate fate of our solar system. Isaac Asimov's *Alpha Centauri* is not only about the nearest star to us, but a whole introduction to astronomy. Roy A. Gallant's *Beyond Earth* is a junior version of Carl Sagan's *Intelligent Life in the Universe:* both are about the hunt for signs of intelligent nonterrestrial life.

Books on the biological and physical sciences range from the gigantic tortoise of the Galapagos Islands (*Land of the Giant Tortoise* by Millicent E. Selsam) to Margaret D. Hyde's *Your Brain: Master Computer,* which describes the operation of the human mind.

The mystery of the compound DNA is clearly and carefully explained in James D. Watson's account of its structure, *The Double Helix*.

Current interest in psychology on the part of the young centers on the unconventional. Melvin Berger's *The Supernatural: From ESP to UFO's* takes up psychokineses, witchcraft, and faith healing. In *Mind-Reach*, Russell Targ and Harold Puthoff, two scientists, tell of experiments with people who seemingly have psychic abilities. Terry Lesh, a Ph.D. in counseling psychology, has written *Meditation for Young People,* in which he avoids particular cults and religious issues and explores research on meditation, how to begin a program of meditation, and the relation of meditation to the perennial search for meaning.

COMMUNICATIONS

The systems that have been slowly and painfully developed to help shape the world of nature to man's ends and understanding are often so familiar to us that we don't think about them. But each has its own fascinating story. Harry E. Neal's *Communication: From Stone Age to Space Age* traces communications systems from cave drawings and sign language to printing and television. For communication without language, try Edward T. Hall's *The Silent Language,* about our meaningful looks, distances, and gestures. And because of the perennial fascination with names, particularly one's own, the reader will have great fun with Elsdon C. Smith's *American Surnames*.

The Story of the Dictionary by Robert Kraske is a simple presentation of the history of dictionaries in English. It begins with the glosses of medieval monks and has chapters on the work of Samuel Johnson, Noah Webster, and James Murray. Howard Greenfeld's *Books from Writer to Reader* lays out the process by which a writer's idea becomes a book in the hands of a reader. James Norman's *Ancestral Voices,* a book of both archaeology and linguistics, tells of the pains-

taking process of unlocking the ancient printed scripts
of peoples in the Near East, Egypt, Greece, and Meso-
america. Another interesting study of communications
systems is J. H. Prince's *Languages of the Animal
World,* which surveys the studies of how animals produce and hear sounds and how they signal one another.

FINE ARTS

Fine-arts books can be expected to feature beautiful printing and rich illustrations. There are many introductory books about painting. Thomas Craven's
large *The Rainbow Book of Art* is often used in high-
school libraries to give an overview of great painting,
and Janson and Cauman's *Basic History of Art* is also
a favorite. *The Visual Experience* by Bates Lowry is
for a somewhat more sophisticated reader. Extensive
text accompanies the illustrations and discusses what
you look at and for in a work of art.

Other books deal with only one artist or school of
artists: one beautiful example is Barbara B. Lassiter's
American Wilderness, which discusses the Hudson
River school of painters (Cole, Church, Cropsey, Bier-
stadt, etc.).

The Voice of Music by Robina B. Willson is a good
overview, providing a historical survey of the development of music, systems of notation, and various instruments such as carillons, clocks, and music boxes—not
to mention the human voice. A complementary book is
Elie Siegmeister's *Invitation to Music,* designed to increase your understanding and appreciation of the
forms of music. Lillian Erlich's *What Jazz Is All About*
not only gives accounts of the growth of jazz and biographical sketches of the great jazz artists but attempts
to explain what directions contemporary jazz is taking
and why.

An inside account of ballet is Joan McConnell's
Ballet as Body Language, which gives a brief history
of the dance, details the classic positions, and tells of
the endless practice and preparation for performance.

Coauthor and sister Teena McConnell is a model for illustrations and is a source for an inside look at a ballerina's life. *American Modern Dancers* by Olga Maynard is one of the best books about a unique American form.

For many teenagers, movies are the most influential contemporary art form. Interest in films may be amplified by reading the original novel or the novelized version of a popular movie. Screenplays containing the script, camera directions, production history, and stills are increasingly available for classic and modern films. Many schools and clubs provide relatively inexpensive, easy-to-use filmmaking equipment, and as teenagers begin to make their own movies they will become more interested in technique, famous directors, and personalities in the history of film. Besides the how-to books listed in chapter 2, they will find extensive information in *Behind the Screen* by Kenneth MacGowan. Richard M. Barsam's highly readable *In the Dark* takes up history, production, and criticism of movies.

THE ENVIRONMENT

During the last decade ecology, the science dealing with the relationship of organisms to their environment, has become a most important subject. Many books have been written about smog and pollution and their threat to human life.

Rachel Carson's *Silent Spring* (1962) was attacked as alarmist, laughed at by scientists, and generally ignored. Now opinion has swung in her direction; today's books also tend to be pessimistic about what human beings are doing to the natural environment. Robert McClung's *Hunted Mammals of the Sea* tells of the depletion of whales, dolphins, sea cows (manatees), polar bears, and walruses. He describes each animal's habits, its scientific classification, and the attempts being made to protect the species.

A logistical problem has evolved from this great mass of published nonfiction: how can the adolescent who wants information on a specialized subject find just the right book? Teachers and parents should become aware of the teenager's interests and curiosities, rather than turn aside valid questions. Encourage the questioning young person to seek the help of a librarian, and if still unsatisfied, he or she should try the paperback or hardback bookstore in your area.

Bibliography

PERSONAL EXPERIENCE

Allen, Woody: *Without Feathers*. Random House, 1975. Warner Books. Wildly inventive and comedic, Allen often appears to be in conflict with his environment.

Bach, Richard: *Nothing by Chance: A Gypsy Pilot's Adventures in Modern America*. Avon Books, 1973. A group of young men discover a new freedom by recapturing the barnstorming experiences of the 1920s.

Bishop, Jim: *The Day Christ Died*. Harper & Row, 1957. An imaginary moment-by-moment account of the day of the crucifixion.

———: *The Day Lincoln Was Shot*. Harper & Row, 1964. Using historical details, the author recreates Lincoln's assassination.

Brown, Claude: *The Children of Ham*. Stein & Day, 1976. Bantam Books. Ten deserted children band together to form a makeshift family in New York City's condemned housing. Each one tells his or her story in a series of vivid, poignant sketches.

———: *Manchild in the Promised Land*. Macmillan, 1965. New American Library. A true story of survival in the ghetto that is Harlem, New York City.

Castaneda, Carlos: *The Teachings of Don Juan*. University of California Press, 1968. Pocket Books. A young man learns about himself and mysticism by conversing with Don Juan, allegedly a Yaqui sorcerer.

Daley, Robert: *Treasure*. Random House, 1977. Ballantine Books. A sunken galleon carrying $600 million in treasure lies at the bottom of the ocean off Key West, Florida.

Durrell, Gerald: *Birds, Beasts, and Relatives*. Penguin Books, 1977. Stories of life in the bizarre Durrell family and menagerie at home on the island of Corfu.

Gill, Brendan: *Lindbergh Alone*. Harcourt Brace Jovanovich, 1977. Details the incidents on the historical solo flight across the Atlantic Ocean on May 21, 1927.

Graham, Robin Lee, and Derek L. T. Gill: *Dove*. Harper & Row, 1972. Bantam Books. Setting out in his sloop *Dove* to encircle the globe, a 16-year-old boy finds adventure and romance.

Griffin, John H.: *Black Like Me*. Houghton Mifflin, 2d ed., 1977. New American Library. After taking medication which darkens his skin, John Griffin learned first hand what it was like to be a black person in the deep South during the 1950s.

Harris, David: *I Shoulda Been Home Yesterday*. Delacorte Press, 1976. David Harris recounts his experience in prison as a result of resisting the draft during the Vietnam War.

Hayes, Billy: *Midnight Express*. E. P. Dutton, 1977. Popular Library. Drug smuggling is serious business, especially in Turkey. Billy Hayes's experience was shattering.

Herriot, James: *All Things Bright and Beautiful*. St. Martin's Press, 1974. Bantam Books. A young veterinarian begins his practice on large and small animals in rural England. Wise, witty, and warm. Not overly sentimental.

Heyerdahl, Thor: *Kon-Tiki*. Rand McNally, 1950. Pocket Books. A Danish anthropologist constructs a balsa raft and sails it with a crew of five from South America to the South Pacific islands.

Jenkins, Peter: *A Walk Across America*. William Morrow, 1979. Upon finishing college, the author sets out to see America up close, so he walks from one ocean to the other.

Johnson, Frederick: *The Tumbleweeds: Somersaulting up and out of the City Streets*. Ghetto kids learn acrobatics and develop into a performing troupe.

Jones, Ron: *The Acorn People*. Abingdon Press, 1976. Bantam Books. A tragicomic, intensely hopeful book, this is the true story of five handicapped boys at summer camp who learn to swim, cook, and climb mountains—defying everyone's notion of what handicapped children ought to be able to do.

Jordan, Pat: *A False Spring.* Dodd Mead, 1975. Pat Jordan recounts his spectacular success as a high-school pitcher, his recruitment by the Braves, his move into the farm leagues, and the sudden loss of his ability to pitch.

Lord, Walter: *A Night to Remember.* Holt, Rinehart and Winston, 1955. Bantam Books. A detailed, precise account of the sinking of the *Titanic* in 1912.

MacCracken, Mary: *Lovey: A Very Special Child.* J. B. Lippincott, 1976. New American Library. A profoundly disturbed child was trapped in the prison of her emotions until a gifted teacher helped her to break out.

McPhee, John: *Coming Into the Country.* Farrar, Straus & Giroux, 1977. Bantam Books. A blending of vivid character sketches, observed landscapes and descriptive narratives, the book's three principal sections deal with a trip through a total wilderness, experiences in urban Alaska and life in the remote "bush."

Margolies, Marjorie, and Ruth Gruber: *They Came to Stay.* Coward, McCann & Geohegan, 1976. A single woman, she had many problems in adopting two daughters, one Korean and one Vietnamese.

Morris, Jeannie: *Brian Piccolo, A Short Season.* Dell, 1972. Piccolo, an attractive, 26-year-old professional football player, comes to terms with his impending death from cancer.

Napier, John: *Bigfoot.* E. P. Dutton, 1973. Berkley. Is there really an Abominable Snowman living somewhere in the mountains of the High Sierra?

North, Sterling: *Rascal.* E. P. Dutton, 1963. Avon Books. The author tells of a pet raccoon he owned during his boyhood in rural Wisconsin around 1918.

Onoda, Hiroo: *No Surrender.* Kodansha International, 1975. Dell. For 30 years he continued to fight World War II. He could not believe that Japan had surrendered.

Patrick, Ted, and Tom Dulack: *Let Our Children Go!* Ballantine Books, 1977. An expert deprogrammer tells what it is like to deprogram young people who have been brainwashed by cults.

Plimpton, George: *One for the Record: The Inside Story of Hank Aaron's Chase for the Home Run Record.* Harper & Row, 1974.

Pirsig, Robert M.: *Zen and the Art of Motorcycle Maintenance.* William Morrow, 1974. Bantam Books. A spiritual journey with some practical applications.

Read, Piers Paul: *Alive.* J. B. Lippincott, 1974. Avon Books. A compassionate account of 16 young rugby players who survived a plane crash in the Andes.

Reed, John: *Ten Days That Shook the World.* Random House, 1960. An American journalist's on-the-scene account of the Russian Revolution of 1917.

Russell, Terry and Renny: *On the Loose.* Sierra Club Books, 1967. Ballantine Books. Photographs and hand-lettered text evoke the pleasure and fun of the wilderness adventures and explorations of two teenage brothers.

Scott, Sheila: *Barefoot in the Sky.* Macmillan, 1974. The adventurous life of a female racing pilot.

Taylor, David: *Zoo Vet: Adventures of a Wild Animal Doctor.* J. B. Lippincott, 1977. The author tells about treating a giraffe with swollen toes, a tiger with an injured spine, an elephant with a toothache, and many other creatures.

Terkel, Studs: *Working.* Pantheon Books, 1974. Avon Books. They tell it like it is. Many workers were interviewed by Terkel to get their true feelings about their jobs, their lives, their world.

Thomas, Piri: *Seven Long Times.* New American Library, 1975. An honest account of time spent in jail. No punches pulled.

Zassenhaus, Hiltgunt: *Walls: Resisting the Third Reich—One Woman's Story.* Beacon Press, 1974. Dr. Zassenhaus was a German citizen who opposed the Nazi regime. The story of her close calls and continuing heroism at the risk of her life is heartening and thrilling.

ARCHAEOLOGY AND ANTHROPOLOGY

Ardrey, Robert: *African Genesis.* Atheneum, 1961. A study of mankind's evolution on the African continent. Ardrey asserts that man developed from carnivorous predatory killer apes and that his age-old affinity for war and weapons is the result of inherited instinct.

Bibby, Geoffrey: *The Testimony of the Spade*. Alfred A. Knopf, 1956. New American Library. Results of archaeological and anthropological research and digs.

Brennan, Louis A.: *Beginner's Guide to Archaeology*. Dell, 1974. A step-by-step introduction to the science and the hobby.

Carter, Howard, and A. C. Mace: *The Discovery of the Tomb of Tutankhamen*. Peter Smith, 1923. Dover. The excitement of the discovery, in 1922, of a Pharaoh's tomb that had been undisturbed for over 3000 years.

Ceram, C. W.: *Gods, Graves, and Scholars*. Alfred A. Knopf, 1967. Bantam Books. An account of the explorations of scholars who delved into our remote past and found lost civilizations.

Cottrell, Leonard: *Anvil of Civilization*. New American Library, 1957. Deals with the earliest known remnants of civilizations.

Cousteau, Jacques-Yves, and Frederic Dumas: *The Silent World*. Harper & Row, 1953. Underwater exploration with an aqualung in search of ancient shipwrecks.

Desmond, Adrian J.: *The Hot-Blooded Dinosaurs*. Dial Press, 1976. Warner Books. He holds that some dinosaurs were warm-blooded like birds, rather than cold-blooded like lizards and other reptiles.

Farb, Peter: *Man's Rise to Civilization: The Cultural Ascent of the Indians of North America*. E. P. Dutton, 1978. Bantam Books. This classic study of the Indians of North America has been completely revised to include new findings since its original publication a decade earlier.

Halsell, Grace: *Los Viejos: Secrets of Long Life from the Sacred Valley*. Bantam Books, 1978. For a year the author lived with the Viejos, allegedly the longest-living people in the western hemisphere. She claims that these gentle people have found a joy and a peace that few find in more advanced societies.

Heyerdahl, Thor: *Aku-Aku*. Ballantine Books, 1974. A study of the civilizations of the Easter Islands. Attempts to find the origins of the great stone heads facing the sea.

Hitching, Francis: *Earth Magic.* William Morrow, 1977. Pocket Books. Discusses the mystery of the megaliths left by earlier civilizations.

Jastrow, Robert: *Red Giants and White Dwarfs.* Harper & Row, 1970. New American Library. What is surmised about the evolution of stars, planets, and life itself.

Leakey, Louis: *Adam's Ancestors: The Evolution of Man and his Culture.* Harper & Row, 1953. Discoveries about man's origins result from the fossils found in the Olduvai Gorge in Africa.

Macaulay, David: *Pyramid.* Houghton Mifflin, 1975. Fascinating drawings detail the probable construction techniques used in the Egyptian pyramids.

Selsam, Millicent E.: *Land of the Giant Tortoise: The Story of the Galapagos Islands.* Four Winds Press, 1977. Scholastic Book Service.

Vandenberg, Philip: *The Curse of the Pharaohs.* J. B. Lippincott, 1975. Pocket Books. Recent excavators and explorers have met untimely deaths.

Von Hagen, Victor W.: *Realm of the Incas.* New American Library, 1961. Describes the culture of the Incas of ancient Peru.

SOCIAL SCIENCES

Archer, Jules: *Police State: Could It Happen Here?* Harper & Row, 1977. A reporter's account of life in police states from Hitler's Germany to Castro's Cuba.

———: *Superspies: The Secret Side of Government.* Delacorte Press, 1977. Superspies in the American government and their effect on the lives of ordinary citizens.

Bennett, Lerone, Jr.: *Before the Mayflower.* Johnson, 1969. Penguin. Chronicles Black American history from 1619 to 1968.

Berger, Melvin: *The Supernatural: From ESP to UFO's.* John Day, 1977. A record of all kinds of strange and unexplained phenomena.

Billingsley, Andrew: *Black Families in White America.*

Prentice-Hall, 1968. Analyzes the history, structure, and problems of black families in a white-controlled society.

Bowen, Catherine D.: *Miracle at Philadelphia*. Little, Brown, 1966. The story of the Constitutional Convention which framed the government of the United States.

Brown, Dee: *Bury My Heart at Wounded Knee*. Holt, Rinehart and Winston, 1971. Bantam Books. The history of the American West, told from an Indian point of view.

Clarke, Arthur C.: *Profiles of the Future*. Harper & Row, 1973. Popular Library. Provocative glimpses into our technological future.

Coles, Robert: *Children of Crisis*. Atlantic Monthly Press, 1967–1973, 3 vols. Dell. Case studies of 20 Southerners, both white and black, recorded by a psychiatrist interested in people who are under tensions and in cultural crises.

Cook, Fred J.: *American Political Bosses and Machines*. Franklin Watts, 1973. A history of bossism, recording the blessings and faults of machine politics.

Coye, Molly Joel, and Jon Livingston, eds.: *China: Yesterday and Today*. Bantam Books, rev. ed., 1979. Updated readings giving a complete story of China—ancient and modern.

Deming, Richard: *Women: The New Criminals*. Nelson Hall, 1977. An exploration of today's rise in crime committed by females.

Ebenstein, William: *Today's Isms*. Prentice-Hall, 7th ed., 1973. Explains communism, capitalism, fascism, socialism, and other isms we meet today.

Fincher, Ernest B.: *The Presidency*. Abelard-Schuman, 1977. The changing nature of the office, its history, its future.

Fleming, Alice: *Something for Nothing. A History of Gambling*. Delacorte Press, 1978. Gambling: its ancient history, its current status, its inherent dangers.

Gaer, Joseph: *What the Great Religions Believe*. New American Library, 1963. Defines religion and gives a short explanation of the basic tenets of the major religions of the world.

Green, Mark J.: *Who Runs Congress?* (intro. by Ralph

Nader). Bantam Books, 3d ed., 1979. The new edition of the classic bestseller gives an up-to-the-minute look at how Congress really operates—how senators and representatives interact with each other, their constituents, the executive branch, and lobbyists.

Greenfeld, Howard: *Gypsies*. Crown, 1977. Covers the superstitions, history, and customs of a fascinating people.

Hapgood, David: *The Screwing of the Average Man*. Bantam Books, 1975. A witty, detailed, hard-hitting account of the many ways in which middle-income citizens are fleeced—by bankers, lawyers, doctors, car dealers, mechanics, college administrators, and most of all, the federal government.

Harris, Middleton, et al.: *The Black Book*. Random House, 1973. A scrapbook of over 300 years of black life in America. Profusely illustrated.

Hyde, Margaret O.: *Juvenile Justice and Injustice*. Franklin Watts, 1977. Explains the problems and gives possible solutions.

Jackson, Tom: *Guerilla Tactics in the Job Market*. Bantam Books, 1978. Based on the premise that it is not necessarily the most qualified persons who get the best job offers, but rather those who are most effective in the job search.

Johnson, Gerald W.: *The Cabinet*. Wiliam Morrow, 1966. The role of the president's cabinet in the government: how it developed, how it affects decisions, and its major historical accomplishments.

——: *The Congress*. William Morrow, 1963. Here is the whole process of Congress: how a bill is introduced, how committees work, the struggle for power, and the dangers of investigations.

Klass, Philip J.: *UFOs Explained*. Random House, 1976. Discusses some sightings and the various causes, some terrestrial, some not.

Kusche, Lawrence David: *The Bermuda Triangle Mystery —Solved*. Harper & Row, 1975. Warner Books. Presents both the legend and the facts available. Goes over many disappearances in some detail.

Langone, John: *Death is a Noun*. Little, Brown, 1972. Goes over its forms and meanings.

Lesh, Terry: *Meditation for Young People*. Lothrop, 1977.

A guide to meditation which cites available psychological and physiological evidence regarding its effects.

Lifton, Robert J., and Eric Olson: *Living and Dying.* Bantam Books, 1975. Discusses the meaning of living and dying as reflected in our culture's attitude toward both.

Lord, Walter: *The Good Years.* Harper & Row, 1960. Bantam Books. Social and political highlights are the focus for this documentation of American life from 1900 to 1914. This brisk narrative treats such events as the Wright Brothers' experiments, the San Francisco earthquake, and the sinking of the *Titanic.*

Maccoby, Michael: *The Gamesman: The New Corporate Leaders.* Simon and Schuster, 1977. The story of winning and losing the career game, the new strategies of today's leading corporate players, and a key to understanding the corporation of the seventies.

McHargue, Georgess: *Little Victories, Big Defeats.* Delacorte Press, 1974. Great writers discuss the horrors and pointlessness of wars.

Marguardt, Dorothy A.: *A Guide to the Supreme Court.* Bobbs-Merrill, 1977. The history of the development of the Supreme Court: how it operates in modern life, a record of all the chief justices, and some far-reaching decisions that the court has reached.

Marriot, Alice, and Carol K. Rachlin: *American Epic.* New American Library, 1970. The story of the American Indian.

Meltzer, Milton: *Never to Forget.* Harper & Row, 1976. Dell. A study of the "final solution" which led to the extermination of over 6 million Jews during World War II, and its aftermath.

Moody, Raymond A., Jr.: *Life After Life.* Mockingbird Books, 1976. Bantam Books. Absorbing testimony given by persons who have been declared clinically dead.

Moquin, Wayne, and Charles Van Doren, eds.: *The American Way of Crime.* Praeger, 1976. The scoop, from earliest gangs to Cosa Nostra.

Murphy, E. Jefferson: *Understanding Africa.* Thomas Y. Crowell, rev. ed., 1978. An outstanding overview of the African continent: geography, anthropology, and ancient cultures; the coming of the Arab and European slave traders, explorers, missionaries, and colonists; the rise of African nationalism; and the problems facing Africa today.

Nabokov, Peter, ed.: *Native American Testimony*. Thomas Y. Crowell, 1978. A history of Native American and white relations as seen through Indian eyes in a series of powerful and moving documents spanning four centuries of interchange.

Pringle, Lawrence: *Our Hungry Earth: The World Food Crisis*. Macmillan, 1976. Discusses the world food crisis in terms of food supplies, agricultural advances, and natural resources.

Reich, Charles: *The Greening of America*. Random House, 1970. Bantam Books. Analyzes the relationship between individual consciousness and social structures throughout American history.

Sanderlin, George: *A Hoop to the Barrel*. Coward, McCann & Geohegan, 1974. The making of the American Constitution.

Shuttleworth, John: *The Mother Earth News Handbook of Home Business Ideas and Plans*. Bantam Books, 1976. Thirty-six articles describing home business and self-employment ventures that anyone can start today on even a limited budget.

Steiner, Stan: *The New Indians*. Harper & Row, 1968. Dell. A report of the Red Power movement against the white man's culture and the debasement of tribal ways.

Stevens, Leonard A.: *Trespass*. Coward, McCann & Geohegan, 1977. The Fourth Amendment: individual privacy versus the power of the police.

Streeter, Floyd B.: *Prairie Trails and Cow Towns*. Devin-Adair, 1963. The "classic" treatment of the early trails and towns of the West.

Toffler, Alvin: *The Eco-Spasm Report: Why Our Economy is Running Out of Control*. Bantam Books, 1975. Concentrates on our current and future economic problems. Lays bare America's obsolete system of economics, showing how our current policies can only result in disaster.

————: *Future Shock*. Random House, 1970. Bantam Books. This book is about change and how we adapt to it. It is about those who seem to thrive on change,

who crest its waves joyfully, as well as the many who
resist it or seek flight from it.

Webb, Walter P.: *The Great Plains*. Grossett & Dunlap
(paperback), 1957. An authoritative treatment of the
history of the plains and their profound impact on
America's development.

Wilson, Forrest: *City Planning*. Van Nostrand Reinhold,
1975. Understanding the ways that humans settle, how
we organize our living space.

SCIENCE

Asimov, Isaac: *Asimov on Astronomy*. Doubleday, 1974.
Practical introduction to astronomy for the lay person.

————: *The Collapsing Universe*. Walker, 1977. Pocket
Books. The implications of those all-devouring black
holes in space.

————: *The Nearest Star*. Lothrop, 1976. An introduction
to astronomy.

————: *The Nuetrino*. Avon Books, 1975. Atomic structure and conservation principles of physics serve as
a springboard to discussion of the neutrino, a mass-
less, uncharged particle.

Barnett, Lincoln: *The Universe and Dr. Einstein*. Bantam
Books, 1974. Using language and illustrations the
layman can understand, this presents a clear, thoroughly readable report on Einstein's theories, the
discoveries and chains of thought that led to them.

Carroll, David: *Wonders of the World*. Bantam Books,
1977. Scores of photographs in brilliant living color
illustrate some of the many wonders that have em-
bellished the world—from the awe-inspiring tundras,
tidal waves, blue whales, and polar lights to mankind's most remarkable feats.

Clarke, Arthur C.: *View from Serendip*. Ballantine Books,
1978. Contains "The Next Twenty Years" and other
essays.

Cooper, Henry S., Jr.: *A House in Space*. Holt, Rinehart
and Winston, 1976. Bantam Books. The first book to
present, in fascinating detail, what happened in man's
first home in space—a marvelously vivid reconstruction of Skylab's workday regime.

Cousteau, Jacques-Yves, and Philippe Diole: *Life and Death in a Coral Sea.* Doubleday, 1971. A & W. Life in the oceans as seen by the research divers on Cousteau's team.

Engdahl, Sylvia L., and Rick Roberson: *The Sub-Nuclear Zoo.* Atheneum, 1977. New findings in particle physics.

Engelbrektson, Sune: *Stars, Planets, and Galaxies.* Bantam Books, 1975. Ranging from early man's fascination with the sky to planetary probes, this guide discusses wandering stars, galaxies, nebulas, and solar and sidereal time.

Ferris, Timothy: *The Red Limit: The Search for the Edge of the Universe.* William Morrow, 1977. Bantam Books. A look at the major discoveries in astronomy, physics, and geometry which led to the revolution in cosmology, as well as a discussion of "the foundations of contemporary cosmology: gravitational red shift, the big-bang theory, cosmic background radiation, quasars, black holes."

Gallant, Roy A.: *Beyond Earth: The Search for Extraterrestrial Life.* Four Winds Press, 1977. Scholastic Book Service. Speculation about the possibilities of life outside earth. Includes accounts of experiments to communicate with extraterrestrial beings.

Glasser, Ronald J.: *The Body is the Hero.* Random House, 1976. Narrative account of how the body protects itself against disease.

Golden, Frederic: *Colonies in Space: The Next Giant Step.* Harcourt Brace Jovanovich, 1977. How man will survive in space and give himself more room to expand by using colonies in deep space.

Hays, James D.: *Our Changing Climate.* Atheneum, 1977. What governs climate, how it changes, what may happen in the future.

Hellman, Hal: *Transportation in the World of the Future.* M. Evans, 1976. Predictions about new and better means of transportation for the technologically more advanced world of the future.

Hyde, Margaret O.: *Your Brain: Master Computer.* McGraw-Hill, 1964. The brain and how it works.

Lewis, Paul, and David Rubenstein: *The Human Body.* Bantam Books, 1972. A lucid account of how the various tissues and organs interact functionally in the living human organism.

Lorenz, Konrad: *On Aggression*. Harcourt Brace Jovanovich, 1966. Bantam Books. A scholar looks at aggressiveness in animals and provides interesting conclusions about the human animal.

O'Neill, Gerard K.: *The High Frontier: Human Colonies in Space*. William Morrow, 1977. Bantam Books. Viewing space colonies as a cure for the earth's environmental degeneration and overpopulation. O'Neill discusses the possibilities of outer space life-styles.

Papanek, Victor, and James Hennessey: *How Things Don't Work*. Pantheon Books, 1977. Shows design flaws in common objects and discusses ways to make your own objects.

Patent, Dorothy Hinshaw: *Evolution Goes on Every Day*. Holiday House, 1977. Recounts unpredictable changes in animals and plants that are occurring right now.

Postle, Denis: *Fabric of the Universe*. Crown, 1976. Discusses nuclear physics as a clue to who we are in the grand scheme.

Puthoff, Harold, and Russell Targ: *Mind-Reach*. Delacorte Press, 1977. Research in the realm of parapsychology with case studies.

Pyke, Magnus: *Butter Side Up! The Delights of Science*. Sterling, 1977. Teaches, in an entertaining way, many basic concepts of science and dispels many stereotypic misunderstandings.

Rogers, Michael: *Biohazard*. Alfred A. Knopf, 1977. The pros and cons of DNA experimentation are discussed.

Rosen, Stephen: *Future Facts*. Simon and Schuster, 1976. Discusses quite probable things which will be commonplace in the near future, such as flying trains and 3-D TV.

Sagan, Carl: *The Dragons of Eden*. Random House, 1977. Ballantine Books. Speculations on the evolution of human intelligence, written with sprightly humor and great perception.

Sayre, Anne: *Rosalind Franklin and DNA*. W. W. Norton, 1975. Gives Ms. Franklin due credit for her achievements in the discovery of the structure of DNA.

Silverberg, Robert: *Clocks for the Ages*. Macmillan, 1971. Explains how scientists date the past.

Silverstein, Alvin & Virginia B.: *Sleep and Dreams.* J. B. Lippincott, 1974. Shows the patterns and rhythms of sleeping and dreaming, discusses REMs, and delves into current research on sleep and dreams.

Taylor, L. B., Jr.: *Gifts From Space.* John Day, 1977. There have been many spin-off benefits from the space program: miniaturization of electronic components, new fabrics, and Teflon, to name a few.

Watson, James D.: *The Double Helix.* Atheneum, 1968. New American Library. Steps in discovering the structure of DNA, by the young scientist who was awarded half of the Nobel prize for his research.

The Way Things Work. Simon and Schuster, 1967, 1971, 2 vols. Clear, detailed line drawings show how many mechanical objects work for us.

Weinberg, Steven: *The First Three Minutes: A Modern View of the Origin of the Universe.* Basic Books, 1976. Bantam Books. The first authoritative presentation of "the standard model" theory of the origin of the universe—of what is believed to have happened during those first three minutes.

MATHEMATICS

Asimov, Isaac: *Asimov on Numbers.* Doubleday, 1977. Pocket Books. Covers the uses of numbers, various meanings of symbols, zero, pi, googols, etc.

Bell, Eric T.: *Men of Mathematics.* Simon and Schuster, 1937. Short biographies of famous mathematicians, from Zeno to Poincare.

Cook, Peter D.: *The Ages of Mathematics: The Modern Age.* Doubleday, 1977. Deals with the latest mathematical theories and the people behind them.

Deming, Richard: *Metric Now.* Dell, 1976. We are going metric. This covers the hows and whys.

Devi, Shakuntala: *Figuring: The Joy of Numbers.* Harper & Row, 1978. The endless fascination of numbers is dramatized with puzzles, shortcuts, and mathematical tricks and oddities—from how to add long columns in your head to how to determine the day of the week for any date since 1582.

Diggins, Julia E.: *String, Straightedge and Shadow.* Viking Press, 1976. The story of geometry.

Gamow, George: *One, Two, Three . . . Infinity*. Bantam Books, 1971. The mathematical concepts of modern science clearly presented, including space, time, and relativity, the fourth dimension, and quantum mechanics.

Gardner, Martin: *Mathematical Carnival*. Alfred A. Knopf, 1975. A tantalizing roundup of mathematical puzzles and brainteasers.

Schlossberg, Edwin, and John Brockman: *The Pocket Calculator Game Book*. William Morrow, 1975. Bantam Books. Games to play using your pocket calculator. One or more players can participate.

Spencer, Donald D.: *Computers in Action*. Hayden Book, 2d ed., 1978. *Computers in Society*, 1974. These two easy-to-read books deal with the development and structure of computers; they even include directions for making your own.

COMMUNICATIONS

Barnouw, Erik: *Tube of Plenty*. Oxford University Press, 1975. An exposition of the evolution and development of American television.

Farb, Peter: *Word Play: What Happens When People Talk*. Alfred A. Knopf, 1973. Bantam Books. Shows how language can be analyzed according to theories of play and games, why dictionaries distort, what body language means, why some scholars claim that our minds are shaped by the language of our speech community.

Fast, Julius: *Body Language*. M. Evans, 1970. Pocket Books. What it means when a person makes certain movements, like crossing the legs or folding the arms.

Goldsen, Rose K.: *The Show and Tell Machine*. Dial Press, 1977. How your television works (on the inside) and how it works on you, also on the inside.

Greenfeld, Howard: *Books from Writer to Reader*. Crown, 1976. The making of a book is detailed from idea to finished book in the hands of a reader.

Hall, Edward T.: *The Silent Language*. Doubleday, 1973. How men communicate without words, by looks, distances, postures.

Kraske, Robert: *The Story of the Dictionary.* Harcourt Brace and Jovanovich, 1975. The history of the dictionary.

Laffin, John: *Codes and Ciphers: Secret Writing Through the Ages.* Abelard-Schuman, 1964. All kinds of codes and ciphers that have been used from earliest times are discussed, with many examples given that readers can use.

Lambert, Eloise, and Mario Pei: *Our Names: Where They Came from and What They Mean.* Lothrop, Lee & Shepard, 1960. The origin and meanings of hundreds of common names.

MacGowan, Kenneth: *Behind the Screen.* Dell, 1967. Describes the complex process of film-making.

McLuhan, Marshall: *Understanding Media.* McGraw-Hill, 1964. New American Library. Media massages man, media gives man the message and extends our reach.

Murray, Michael: *The Videotape Book.* Taplinger, 1975. Bantam Books. Personal creativity and group interaction are the focus of this fully illustrated guide to half-inch videotape production.

Neal, Harry E.: *Communication: From Stone Age to Space Age.* Julian Messner, 1974. History of man's communication efforts from cave drawing and sign language to television.

Prince, J. H.: *Languages of the Animal World.* Nelson-Hall, 1976. Animals from mammals to insects and crustaceans have developed systems of communication through sound, movement, and color.

Norman, James: *Ancestral Voices.* Scholastic Book Services, 1975. Decoding the language of the ancients.

Smith, Elsdon C.: *American Surnames.* Chilton Book, 1969. Lucid discussion of the common names in the United States with a listing of the 2000 most common surnames in order of frequency.

Strunk, William S., Jr., and E. B. White: *The Elements of Style.* Macmillan, 2d ed., 1972. Short and to the point, this is an excellent handbook of reminders and advice for the aspiring writer.

Wentworth, Harold, and Stuart B. Flexner: *Dictionary of American Slang.* Thomas Y. Crowell, 2d ed., 1975. Definitions of slang terms.

Winn, Marie: *The Plug-in Drug: Television, Children and the Family*. Viking Press, 1977. Bantam Books. Based on interviews with hundreds of families, teachers, and child specialists, the author presents a frightening picture of a society dominated by television.

FINE ARTS

Ames, Jerry, and Jim Siegelman: *The Book of Tap*. David McKay, 1977. Shows dancing styles, basic steps, and some variations.

Aylesworth, Thomas G.: *Movie Monsters*. J. B. Lippincott, 1975. Illustrated guide to horror movie heroes.

Balanchine, George, and Francis Mason: *101 Stories of the Great Ballets*. Doubleday, 1975. From *Giselle* to *Duo Concertante*, plot lines of the ballets most often performed.

Barsam, Richard M.: *In the Dark*. Viking Press, 1977. Critiques of movies, history of productions, and other movie buff lore.

Batterbury, Michael, and Arline R. Ruskin: *Primitive Art*. McGraw-Hill, 1972. Primitive art is not necessarily simplistic. This shows caves, temples, and pueblos.

Campbell, Ann: *Paintings*. Franklin Watts, 1970. How to look at great art and begin to understand what the artist wanted to communicate.

Chase, Alice E.: *Looking at Art*. Thomas Y. Crowell, 1966. With many illustrations, the author discusses the nature of art.

Collier, James L.: *The Great Jazz Artists*. Scholastic Book Services. Includes such jazz greats as Louis Armstrong and Charlie Parker.

Craven, Thomas: *The Rainbow Book of Art*. Collin-World, 1956. A highly successful collection of great masterpieces.

Downer, Marion: *Discovering Design*. Lothrop, Lee & Shepard, 1947. Great art and craft work is organized and discussed in a historical pattern.

Erlich, Lillian: *What Jazz Is All About*. Julian Messner, 1975. A history of jazz with sketches of some great jazz artists.

Escher, M. C.: *Graphic Work of M. C. Escher*. Hawthorn Books, rev. ed., 1967. Ballantine Books. His

paradoxical patterns and designs draw the viewer right
into the work.

Feininger, Andreas: *Basic Color Photography*. Prentice-
Hall, 1972. A realistic handbook, full of technical
advice and hints.

Finch, Christopher: *The Art of Walt Disney*. Harry N.
Abrams, 1973. New American Library. Drawings and
designs from Mickey Mouse to the Magic Kingdom.

Green, Douglas B.: *Country Roots*. Hawthorn Books,
1976. The history and origins of country music.

Gutman, Bill: *Duke*. Random House, 1977. An adventure into the musical life of Duke Ellington.

Harris, Ann S., and Linda Nochlin: *Women Artists: 1550–
1950*. Alfred A. Knopf, 1977. A historical survey of
little-known women artists and their work.

Heilbut, Tony: *Gospel Sound: Good News and Bad Times*.
Simon and Schuster, 1971. The singers, their music,
and the life which allows them to flourish.

Huygen, Wil: *Gnomes*. Harry N. Abrams, 1977. Bantam
Books. Fascinating fantasy. Pictures and explanations
of gnomish life and times. Fully illustrated in color
by Rien Poortvliet.

Janson, H. W., and Sam Cauman: *A Basic History of Art*.
Prentice-Hall, 1974. An illustrated survey from prehistoric times to the present.

Lassiter, Barbara B.: *American Wilderness: The Hudson
River School of Painting*. Doubleday, 1978. An illustrated survey of 19th-century landscape painters.

Lowry, Bates: *The Visual Experience: An Introduction to
Art*. Harry N. Abrams, 1961. An introduction to art
appreciation.

McConnell, Joan and Teena: *Ballet as Body Language*.
Harper & Row, 1977. The onstage glamour of ballet
is clearly presented, as is the offstage work, sweat,
and pain.

McLanathan, Richard: *Art in America*. Harcourt Brace
Jovanovich, 1973. Milestones in American art history.

Maynard, Olga: *American Modern Dancers: The Pioneers*.
Little, Brown, 1965. An introduction to modern dance
through biographical studies of early experimenters.

Price, Jonathan: *Video-Visions*. New American Library,
1977. How to use video with the arts and in the community. A hands-on approach.

Rachlin, Harvey: *The Songwriter's Handbook*. Funk & Wagnalls, 1977. From A to Z, everything you need to know to write a song.

Rolling Stone Press: *Rolling Stone Illustrated History of Rock and Roll*. Random House, 1976. Covers everyone from the early days of Elvis Presley through the Beatles and the Stones up to and including Elton John. Many illustrations.

Siegmeister, Elie: *Invitation to Music*. Harvey House, 1961. Shows how to understand and appreciate various forms and types of music.

Smallman, Kirk: *Creative Film-Making*. Macmillan, 1969. Bantam Books. A complete, lucid guide to film production for beginners.

Steranko, James: *The Steranko History of the Comics*. Crown, 1971, 2 vols. Everyone reads them; this shows the subculture's classics and its influence on other areas.

Terry, Walter: *Ballet Companion*. Dodd, Mead, 1968. Background information, pictures, material on dance and dancing.

Willson, Robina B.: *The Voice of Music*. Atheneum, 1977. The wide range of classic, pop and mechanical music, and the instruments used in music making.

THE ENVIRONMENT

Archer, Jules: *Hunger on Planet Earth*. Thomas Y. Crowell, 1977. The world is threatened with widespread starvation.

Aylesworth, Thomas G.: *This Vital Air: This Vital Water*. Rand McNally, 1973. Pollution of air and water not only by organic substances but by sound.

Bartlett, Jen and Des: *The Flight of the Snow Geese*. Stein & Day, 1975. Follows them from Siberia to Texas.

Callenbach, Ernest: *Ecotopia*. Banyan Tree, 1975. Bantam Books. The year is 1999. Ecotopia is a fledgling nation formed when America's Northwest seceded from a crisis-ridden United States. Reporter William Weston enters Ecotopia as the first official observer, and this book is his "notebook," describing a society which has taken charge of its biological destiny. A political fantasy.

Carson, Rachel: *Silent Spring*. Houghton Mifflin, 1962. Fawcett Books. A moving argument against the use of pesticides; the book that started it all.

Commoner, Barry: *The Closing Circle*. Alfred A. Knopf, 1971. Bantam Books. Discusses the nature, cause, and possible solution of the impending environmental disaster that man has created with his own technology.

Fuller, R. Buckminster: *Operating Manual for Spaceship Earth*. Simon and Schuster, 1970. Pocket Books. Controversial architect Fuller explains his theories for survival in this crucial time.

Graham, Frank, Jr.: *Since Silent Spring*. Houghton Mifflin, 1970. Fawcett Books. The author, field editor of *Audubon* magazine, reviews Rachel Carson's 1962 book on pesticides, discusses what has and has not been done since, and gives startling facts about today's situation and possible remedies.

Halacy, Daniel S.: *The Coming Age of Solar Energy*. Harper & Row, rev. ed., 1973. Avon Books. Solar energy may provide us with a partial answer to our energy crisis.

————: *The Energy Trap*. Scholastic Book Services, 1975. How can we escape the fate our greedy machines and cars may foist on us?

Hellman, Hal: *Energy in the World of the Future*. M. Evans, 1973. We have dwindling supplies and badly need new sources of cheap energy.

Kavaler, Lucy: *Noise: The New Menace*. John Day, 1975. Noise pollution is as real and as harmful as air pollution.

McClung, Robert: *Hunted Mammals of the Sea*. William Morrow, 1978. Deals with efforts to save some rare species from extinction.

————: *Lost Wild Worlds*. William Morrow, 1976. The extinct and vanishing wildlife of the eastern hemisphere.

Mannix, Daniel P.: *Troubled Waters*. E. P. Dutton, 1969. Dirty rivers and dirty streams are killing our wildlife.

Milne, Louis J. and Margery: *Water and Life*. Atheneum,

1964. The story of our need for clean, unpolluted water.

Mitchell, John G., and Constance Stallings, ed.: *Eco-tactics*. Simon and Schuster, 1970. The Sierra Club handbook for environmental activists.

Moore, Ruth: *Man in the Environment*. Alfred A. Knopf, 1975. Human beings' role in the world of living things.

Olson, McKinley C.: *Unacceptable Risk: The Nuclear Power Controversy*. Bantam Books, 1979 (revised edition). From the evidence presented in this book, nuclear power is a threat that has reached crisis proportions.

Papanek, Victor: *Design for the Real World: Human Ecology and Social Change*. Pantheon Books, 1971. Bantam Books. A constructive blueprint for survival, charging the industrial design establishment with criminal negligence of almost everybody.

Plowden, David: *The Hand of Man on America*. Chatham Press, 1973. Photographic revelations of what men have done to the landscape.

Pringle, Laurence: *Recycling Resources*. Macmillan, 1974. Ideas on putting "garbage" to productive use.

Shuttleworth, John: *The Mother Earth News Almanac: A Guide Through the Seasons*. Bantam Books, 1973. This constructive anthology offers the widest range of practical experience articles ever published—from harvesting and camping tips to recycling Christmas trees, to arranging for free air travel and building homes and communes.

14

Literature by and About Women

I tell you, there are a great line of women stretching out behind you into the past, and you have to seek them out and find them in yourself and be conscious of them.

— *Doris Lessing*

If men and women are to understand each other, to enter into each other's nature with mutual sympathy, and to become capable of genuine comradeship, the foundation must be laid in youth.

— *Havelock Ellis*

Women's literature, like ethnic and minority literature, is being isolated and examined. Female writers are discovered and rediscovered as new voices with a perspective that adds to our understanding of human experience. Female writers of literary history are being reevaluated in the light of sex-fair criticism. Female characters in literature written by males and females are being analyzed in terms of our increased sensitivity to the socialization process and new concepts of social roles. And books dealing directly with the women's movement add to an understanding of it and of the nature of female sexuality.

Studying literary history fosters an understanding of the battles women fought to publish their works, and brings to light previously ignored authors and works. It uncovers the tenets of feminism in works formerly considered handbooks of conventional behavior and in works rejected for serious literary study because, at the time, they seemed trivial by male standards of literary criticism.

As teachers and librarians attempt to balance book collections by including more female writers, they discover few traditionally esteemed women authors in 17th- and 18th-century England. Journals and diaries of the women who did achieve publication help explain the pattern and are well worth adding to libraries. At that time in England most men deemed writing an unsuitable activity for women. Fanny Burney (1752–1840), for example, was forced to write secretly because her father punished her when he discovered a piece of her writing. Burney, Austen, and others published under pen names with the help of supportive brothers, fathers, or friends to manage the business details with their editors. Male pseudonyms of the 19th century included Currer and Acton Bell (Charlotte and Anne Brontë), George Eliot (Marian Evans)—and the less familiar Ennis Graham (Mary Molesworth), Allan Raine (Anne Puddicombe), and Claude Lake (Mathilda Blind). Women used these disguises because they realized that as females they had a slim chance of publishing their works and getting a good reception from critics. Men considered women mentally and physically incapable of writing well because they believed that creative energy conflicted with women's biological role of bearing children. And of course, those whose works were acclaimed and who were later discovered to be female were said to be abnormal.

In spite of the odds, a number of women writers were financially successful. Aphra Behn (1640–89) was the first Englishwoman to earn a living by writing, primarily drama, but also poetry and novels. Mary Shelley's mother, Mary Wollstonecraft (1759–97), was the first Englishwoman to earn a living from journalism. Their works are usable for small-group readings in any situation that warrants the reading of classics by older adolescents.

Aphra Behn's *Oroonoko, or The Royal Slave* is short, has a style at least as readable as *Gulliver's*

Travels, and offers a plot with considerable action, the tale of a West Indian prince and his sweetheart who are captured by slave traders. Themes include the nature of civilized man, the nature of the savage, the double standard of sexual behavior, and man's inhumanity to man. The author's life (she was a spy in Holland for Charles II and had lived in the West Indies) helps counterbalance the Jane Austen stereotype of the English female who spends her whole life within a few miles of home and writes about the social interactions of a select group.

Mary Wollstonecraft's *Maria, or the Wrongs of Woman,* unfinished when she died, was published with the alternative endings suggested by her notes. The endings offer excellent material for thought about lifestyle options open to women. She dramatized women's oppression in this story of a middle-class woman's flight from her abusive husband, capture, and later escape from an asylum where he had placed her. Born into a society that considered women inferior and made them legal wards of their fathers and husbands, Wollstonecraft spoke out against these wrongs in *A Vindication of the Rights of Women,* a less readable but more influential theoretical tract.

One of the best novels of manners for high-school students is Fanny Burney's *Evelina.* Longer than *Oronooko* or *Maria,* it offers a charming story of a young orphaned girl's entrance into society and her reunion with her natural father. Satires of fops, social climbers, and courting manners of the day, plus some very humorous scenes, keep readers moving through the intricate plot. An outstanding feminist aspect of *Evelina* is the presentation of androgynous characteristics embodied in Evelina and Lord Orville (the man Evelina marries) and epitomized in Selwyn, who had the mind and assertiveness of a man but the manners of a woman. These aspects are subtle, and may require carefully guided reading to keep *Evelina* from being dismissed as a silly, sweet book for girls.

The most attractive classic is Charlotte Brontë's *Jane Eyre.* Girls' enthusiastic response to it is obvious.

Boys can be won to the book by asking them to react to the characters of John Reed, Rochester, and St. John as models of masculine behavior and to assess Jane as a potential mother, girlfriend, and/or wife. All students will be interested in identifying the characteristics that relate Jane to mid-20th-century liberated females. They will enjoy considering the terms under which Jane married Rochester and their similarity to current marriage agreements as partnerships. Readers can question the symbolic significance of Rochester's temporary blindness: when women declare their liberation, is it necessary for men's status to decline? Thus adult readers should approach the book in a new light before recommending it to students. As Elaine Showalter writes in *A Literature of Their Own*, "the significance of Brontë's use of structure, language, and female symbolism has been misread and underrated by male-oriented twentieth-century criticism, and is now only beginning to be fully understood and appreciated." A complete discussion of *Jane Eyre* and other works by English females can be found in Showalter's book.

These four English novelists are only an introduction to later novels by women such as Ellen Glasgow, Edith Wharton, Katherine Anne Porter, Willa Cather, Bess Aldrich, and Kate Chopin.

Educators may be tempted to omit works from the curriculum that have no female characters, include derogatory remarks about women, or present them in restricted roles. But teaching students to understand why women have been depicted in such a way can yield more positive results. Teachers need to place these works in their historical and geographic setting and to consider the traditional male view of women's capacities and roles. For example, students should know that many early novels evolved as guidebooks for social behavior and were written by men who wanted to protect women from the "evils" of the outside world by keeping them safely at home, with their time absorbed in bearing and rearing children, dealing with "trivial" social affairs, and leaving the important decisions of the world to men. When women transgressed the boundaries of that existence, they were punished; hence the wealth of victimized females in *Madame Bovary, Sister Carrie, The Scarlet Letter, Anna Karenina,* and *Tess of the d'Urbervilles,* all written by men with sensitivity toward women's experiences.

The theater has been even slower to admit female writers. Most collections of major dramatists since Aeschylus omit female writers, although Aphra Behn and Fanny Burney were popular English playwrights of the 17th and 18th centuries.

Not until the 20th century did women write and produce plays addressing themselves to women's problems. Two who are sometimes acknowledged in collections are Lillian Hellman and Clare Boothe Luce. Hellman's *The Little Foxes, Watch on the Rhine,* and *The Children's Hour* are major contributions to American drama. Luce's *The Women* created a stir because of its biting attitude toward females.

Black women in America have written over 125 plays, beginning with Angelina Grimké's *Rachel* in 1916. Lorraine Hansberry's *A Raisin in the Sun* (1959) was the first play by a black female to be produced on Broadway. Adrienne Kennedy and Micki Grant have won awards for best off-Broadway play of the year. Other playwrights to add to library or classroom collections are Natalia Ginzberg, Megan Terry, Maureen Duffy, and Alice Gerstenberg.

The status of female characters in plays by male dramatists can reveal the status of women in their culture. Examples range from Antigone and Electra in ancient Greece through the female characters in Shakespeare's plays to Nora in Ibsen's *A Doll's House* and Hedda in *Hedda Gabler.* Restoration drama presents a satiric view. Eugene O'Neill's *Anna Christie* and Tennessee Williams's *The Glass Menagerie* and *A Streetcar Named Desire* offer interesting female characters caught in a patriarchal society.

A similar reevaluation can be made of female poets. Flipping through a standard anthology of British and American poetry reveals a few names: Christina Rossetti, Emily Dickinson, Amy Lowell, Edna St. Vincent

Millay, Elizabeth Bishop, Marianne Moore. Elizabeth Barrett Browning, once considered the queen of Victorian poets, fell from popularity but is now experiencing a revival. Her *Sonnets from the Portuguese* are acclaimed, but she wrote another major work that deserves attention: *Aurora Leigh*, the only long verse novel written by a female. Its themes are so relevant to today's women's movement that it is difficult to believe it was written in 1856. Aurora refuses an offer of marriage by her cousin Romney because he scorns her poetry as frivolous and declares he needs her as a helpmate for his important work in social improvement. Not until Aurora experiences life as a professional author and not until Romney is blinded and comes to appreciate the beauty and power of Aurora's poetry are they able to meet on a nearly equal basis—a pattern in many ways similar to that in *Jane Eyre*.

Today's women poets offer readers a view of women's evolving self-perceptions and struggles with their role in society. Chief among them are Sylvia Plath and Adrienne Rich; many others appear in anthologies devoted to women poets. A major theme is the struggle of women's artistic creative desire with the distracting force—the Angel in the House, as Virginia Woolf so aptly names her—the indoctrinated female who finds it impossible to devote her entire attention and energy to writing, but must be sensitive to the needs and wishes of others before her own.

Works should be added to library shelves or classroom collections according to proportion of the sexes as well as qualitative evaluation. For biographies and autobiographies, a quick assessment can be made by pulling forward the works about women. Gaps can then be filled with books by/about women like Golda Meir, Elizabeth Stein, Ida Tarbell, Mary Shelley, Mahalia Jackson, Margaret Sanger, Mary Cassatt, Margaret Chase Smith, Margaret Mead, Dr. Florence Sabin, and Rachel Carson. Fictionalized biographies of little-known women, like Pauline Gedge's *Child of the Morning*, the story of Hatshepsut, Egypt's only female ruler, should be sought.

Evaluation of literature written for, by, and/or about adolescents presents a different challenge. There is no problem in finding female authors, since much of the best adolescent literature has been written by women such as Irene Hunt, Madeline L'Engle, Hope Campbell, Gertrude Samuels, Elizabeth Speare, Jeannette Eyerly, and Lynn Hall. Indeed many female authors have written for adolescents because the market is more encouraging than for adult fiction. Some female authors still use pseudonyms or initials to conceal their sex in order to gain wider readership. S. E. Hinton and C. H. Frick both feel their works would not have been as readily accepted by boys had their female identities been evident on their early works. One of the newest adolescent novelists, Harriet Luger, used her full name when she published *Chasing Trouble,* which has a female protagonist; but used H. C. Luger when she released *The Elephant Tree,* which has a male protagonist.

The problem in adolescent novels lies in the kinds of female images presented. If teachers wish to offer sex-fair, nonstereotyped characters, and to guide students to works with more complex male and female characters, they must be aware of the slowly changing female images in the history of adolescent literature.

Studies by Mary Beaven and Ruth Stein, centering on the female adolescent from the 1930s through the 1960s, have concluded that adolescent novels of the 1930s presented nonintrospective, fairly active females in rather sentimental, tepid plots. Girls of the 1940s engaged successfully in careers, frequently serving in wartime manufacturing plants and USO organizations. High-school girls were from the middle class and were not concerned with financial or political problems. Maureen Daly's *Seventeenth Summer* became the model for the girls' books of the 1940s and 1950s, the best including *Paintbox Summer* by Betty Cavanna and *To Tell Your Love* by Mary Stolz. Many writers ignored *Seventeenth Summer*'s realistically ambiguous ending, and settled for happily-ever-after patterns which declared that a girl's worth is in her relationship to a male. The heroine in the 1950s was from the upper middle class, was intelligent but plain, and succeeded in attracting a handsome athletic hero who invited her to the high-school prom.

The 1960s saw a major shift in female protagonists, who came from a wide variety of ethnic and socioeconomic backgrounds and began to acknowledge their problems, openly discussing sex, politics, religion, and their status as females. Nora Stirling explored sexual mores and the pressures on adolescent girls to engage in full sexual relationships in *You Would if You Loved Me,* and Jeannette Eyerly dealt realistically with the impact of adoption in *A Girl Like Me.* The protagonists no longer had to live happily ever after: many books tended to end grimly or pessimistically with the girl's death or with her expressing the feeling that there were no positive solutions to her overwhelming problems, as in Everly's *Bonnie Jo, Go Home,* in which a young woman experiences an abortion.

Fiction of the 1970s continues to present girls with serious problems. Two books by Patricia Windsor are typical: *The Summer Before* follows Alex Appleton's struggles to regain emotional stability following her boyfriend's accidental death; *Diving for Roses* shows a young woman carrying the double burden of her isolation and her mother's alcoholism. The change from the 1960s is that females tend to find more constructive approaches to dealing with their problems. Geri in Sandra Scoppettone's *The Late, Great Me* finds help for her drinking problem through a teacher who leads her to Alcoholics Anonymous. Girls may be helped by another character, or occasionally may assertively solve their own problems. Anna in Elizabeth Christman's *A Nice Italian Girl* decides to keep her baby. She was to have given it to a childless couple who ordered a nice Italian baby through a vicious adoption ring.

Protagonists continue to come from a variety of ethnic and socioeconomic backgrounds, such as Marvina in *Listen for the Fig Tree* by Sharon B. Mathis and Dee Dee, Nita, and Connie in Claude Brown's *The Children of Ham*—all of them black girls searOCR-ing

ing for personal identities in an unfriendly environment. Only the occasional girl comes to know herself and feel self-sufficient. Hila Colman's *After the Wedding* is the outstanding story of Katie Holbrook's discovery that she and her new husband are worlds apart in life-styles and interests. She decides that her path to self-fulfillment begins in separation and leads to a life of independence in a small-town setting.

The presentation of adolescent girls' sex life is changing too. Significant numbers of female protagonists reaffirm traditional concepts of emotional involvement as a vital part of the sexual relationship; however, more female protagonists than ever are experiencing sex without social condemnation or the physical punishment of pregnancy. Norma Klein's *It's OK if You Don't Love Me* deals with the emotional impact of a sexual relationship on the lives of an adolescent couple. Jody's perception of love reflects her degree of maturity and experience, not an adult's sophistication or idealism.

The rapidly changing world of women's athletics is being explored in adolescent literature. A few girls compete with males in contact sports. R. R. Knudson's *Zanballer* and *Zanbanger* follow Suzanne Hagen's determination to organize a female football team to play the boys' team and later to join the boys' basketball team in interscholastic play.

Adolescent girls' relationships to other females in their families follow a pattern. They relate poorly to their mothers, who are almost always presented negatively. Many mothers are immersed in their own world and ignore their offspring. Clara Cleary in Audrey Thomas's *Songs My Mother Taught Me* operates in a world of status symbols and neglects her daughters' emotional needs. Deirdre in *Diving for Roses* practically lives in her bedroom drinking alcohol, and Shelley's mother in *Run, Shelley, Run!* neglects her home and Shelley for drinking and sexual promiscuity. The girls seem not to dislike their mothers as people, but criticize the restrictions that the role of motherhood places on them. Shelley loves her mother and repeatedly attempts to return to her. And Geri in *The Late, Great Me* comments to her mother, who has gone back to an imaginary life of the 1950s: "There's nothing wrong with being a wife and mother but that's not *all* there is. Being a wife and mother has to do with other people. What are *you,* just for *you?* Huh?"

Adolescent protagonists have not changed as much as most feminists would like, but they are a radical departure from conventional females, such as those in the Dick and Jane readers, who stand passively watching boys engage in active play. In an attempt to break this stereotype, readers have demanded that females be given a variety of more positive characteristics. Naturally not every female possesses all these characteristics, nor does every male for that matter. But the following criteria are useful in evaluating adolescent literature.

1. *Intellectuality.* Does the female character enjoy using her mind to explore a variety of interests and to reason logically?

2. *Independence.* Is she seen as a self-sufficient person, capable of making her own decisions?

3. *Acceptance.* Is she accepted equally by males and females for her capabilities in a variety of fields—athletics and mechanics as well as motherhood and homemaking?

4. *Options.* Does she have a variety of choices open to her, personally and professionally?

5. *Positive literary treatment.* Does the author and do other characters in the book refer to her without derogatory sexual comments?

Books important to the current women's movement should be considered. A classic is Betty Friedan's *The Feminine Mystique,* which sparked a reawakening to the negative effects of sex-role conditioning on females. Elizabeth Janeway explores the mythical origins of sex roles in *Man's World, Woman's Place.* Concern for girls' knowledge of their bodies as a step toward personal freedom is the focus of the Boston Women's Health Collective's *Our Bodies, Ourselves: A Book by and for Women.* A self-help book written for adolescent females is Andrea Eagan's *Why Am I So Miserable If These Are the Best Years of My Life?: A Survival Guide for the Young Woman*. And Nancy Friday interviewed hundreds of women to explore how the mother/daughter relationship affects their lives in *My Mother/My Self*. Many other works speak to young women's interests in their status and problems as females.

Science fiction is a good genre for examining the status of women as authors and characters. Early science fiction had no female protagonists; women were in the background as relatives of the protagonists, were used as helpless victims to be rescued, or served as an ignorant audience for the hero's brilliant technical explanations. Occasionally females were considered threatening to males, but more often they were sex objects, both in the plots and on the covers of pulp magazines.

Some early science fiction authors such as H. G. Wells were interested in women's rights, but they did not explore the issue in their works, perhaps because they perceived science fiction as escape reading for males. Other authors such as Robert Heinlein have presented females in fairly active, responsible roles; but Heinlein nevertheless allows them to exhibit stereotyped behavior, such as the heroine of *Podkayne of Mars*, who chooses marriage and a family over space exploration and who uses feminine wiles to conceal her intellect.

In more recent works, such as Arthur Clarke's *Rendezvous with Rama*, women are an integral part of the space crew. Occasionally they occupy a position parallel to men and equal to them in importance. In an excellent adolescent work, *Rite of Passage*, Alexei Panshin presents Mia Havero and Jimmy Dentremont undergoing identical education, training, and survival trials before admittance to adult society.

The progress of female authors of science fiction parallels that of traditional literature, but is much more recent, although some literary critics claim that Mary Shelley originated the genre with *Frankenstein* (1818).

Two women who published under male pseudonyms were Francis Stevens (Gertrude Barrows) and James Tiptree, Jr. (Alice Sheldon). Others used initials, such as C. (Catherine) L. Moore. Catherine Moore, Leigh Brackett, and others wrote from the male point of view in order to be accepted by editors and readers of science fiction magazines. Gradually women writers have increased until, Pamela Sargent estimates, now 10 to 20 percent of science fiction writers are women.

Anne McCaffrey is the first woman to win national and international acclaim for science fiction. In 1968 her novella "Dragonrider" won the Hugo award, and in 1967 her novella "Weyr Search" won the Nebula award.

One of the greatest gifts women have brought to science fiction is more complex character development—a weakness in the older science fiction. Andre Norton's books for younger readers are notable for character and for vivid descriptions of alien society. The most progressive authors have transcended sex-role reversal and are exploring the implications of societies without a matriarchal or patriarchal base. Ursula K. Le Guin presents a society of shared sexuality in *The Left Hand of Darkness*. Because the Gethenians are neuter except during "kemmer," the mating season, and because each Gethenian can become either male or female during that time, there is no societal pattern of dominance/submission, but only acceptance as a human being. The society in Samuel R. Delany's *Triton* does not have fixed gender, and in fact is so differentiated that no generalizations can be made about individuals, except as they act at the moment.

Delany, Joe Haldeman, Alexei Panshin, Hal Clement, and other male writers are trying to break female stereotypes that have limited science fiction's potential readership. They set good examples for the kinds of changes educators must make in their thinking.

Sex-fair approaches to the language arts curriculum can be established by reconsidering and rearranging books now suggested or recommended to students, carefully evaluating new books for purchase, and taking positive steps to change one's personal orientation toward literature written by and/or about women.

Bibliography

Alcott, Louisa M.: *Little Women.* A dearly loved account of the March family with four girls who experience love, death, heartache, and dreams.

Angelou, Maya: *I Know Why the Caged Bird Sings.* Random House, 1970. Bantam Books. *Gather Together in My Name.* Random House, 1974. Bantam Books. *Singin' and Swingin' and Gettin' Merry Like Christmas.* Random House, 1976. Bantam Books. These three volumes of Ms. Angelou's biography take her from childhood in Stamps, Arkansas, to adolescence in San Francisco and young adulthood traveling through Europe with a theatrical troupe. She is multitalented, marvelous, and a joy to know.

Alther, Lisa: *Kinflicks.* Alfred A. Knopf, 1976. New American Library. Concerns a young woman's quest for liberation. Many flashbacks to Virginia Bliss's high-school days and later lead the reader through a series of humorous adventures leading up to her heightened awareness.

Arnow, Harriette S.: *The Dollmaker.* Macmillan, 1962. Avon Books. A gentle mountain woman manages to keep high spirits and a sure sense of her own worth despite being transplanted in urban Detroit.

Atwood, Margaret: *Surfacing.* Simon and Schuster, 1973. Popular Library. On a remote Quebec island the heroine and four friends search for her father. It turns into a physical contest with nature as well as an interior voyage in which the narrator eventually surfaces with a whole spirit.

Banner, Lois W.: *Women in Modern America.* Harcourt Brace Jovanovich, 1974. A brief history of women from 1890 to the present. Examines the history of various groups of women, including working-class, blacks, immigrants, farm, and middle-class women.

Behn, Aphra: *Oroonoko.* W. W. Norton, 1973. The sympathetic portrait of a black prince and his sweetheart who are sold as slaves to a considerate master, but who die seeking freedom.

Brown, Rita Mae: *Rubyfruit Jungle.* Daughters, 1973. Bantam Books. A happy-go-lucky young lesbian, Molly Bolt travels from rural poverty to the big city. Very funny, very real, and very true.

Brownmiller, Susan: *Against Our Will.* Simon and Schuster, 1975. Bantam Books. Heralded as one of the decade's most important social documents, this book is the definitive study of the history and meaning of rape. Ms. Brownmiller postulates a theory of rape based on power rather than eroticism—rape as a device by which men can satisfy their desire to control women.

Browning, Elizabeth (Barrett): *Aurora Leigh.* Academy Press, 1978. A long narrative poem following an independent woman who chooses to support herself by writing rather than accept a comfortable marriage to a wealthy man who devalues her poetry.

————: *Sonnets from the Portuguese.* Several editions.

Burney, Frances: *Evelina.* Oxford University Press, 1978. An 18th-century romance presented in a series of letters which describe Evelina's introduction to London society, her choice of a worthy mate, and the discovery of her true parentage.

Cavanna, Betty: *Paintbox Summer.* Westminster Press, 1949. Kate spends an exciting Cape Cod summer exploring sailing, art, and romance, and finally realizes that her own interests are in art school.

Chesler, Phyllis: *Women and Madness.* Avon Books, 1973. Psychologist Chesler examines attitudes and prejudices about women on the part of primarily male mental health practitioners and calls for a new, unconventional female psychology.

Chesler, Phyllis, and Emily Jane Goodman: *Women, Money, and Power.* William Morrow, 1976. Bantam Books. This timely, provocative book asks important questions about our society's attitudes toward money and power, and about how women are trapped by those attitudes.

Dillard, Annie: *Pilgrim at Tinker Creek.* Harper's Magazine Press, 1974. Bantam Books. Reflections on the power and sheer beauty of nature. Dillard lived alone in the woods, keeping a diary of her thoughts as she observed the daily changes in the natural life cycle.

Dreiser, Theodore: *Sister Carrie*. Several editions. An innocent country girl struggles to rise above the poverty and degradation found in city life.

Ephron, Nora: *Crazy Salad: Some Things About Women*. Alfred A. Knopf, 1975. Bantam Books. Cynical musings on current topics by a seventies journalist with a firm hand on the pulse of urban America.

Eyerly, Jeanette: *Bonnie Jo, Go Home*. J. B. Lippincott, 1972. Bantam Books. The grim experience of seeking abortion prematurely ages a high-school senior.

————: *A Girl Like Me*. J. B. Lippincott, 1966. Berkley. When Robin James's closest friend becomes pregnant, Robin, who herself was adopted, identifies with the prospective baby and searches for her own biological mother.

Flexner, Eleanor: *Century of Struggle: The Woman's Rights Movement in the United States*. Harvard University Press, 1975. A historical survey of the position of women from colonial times to the enactment of the suffrage amendment in 1920.

Friedan, Betty: *The Feminine Mystique*. W. W. Norton, 1963. Dell. The Bible of the women's liberation movement. It dared to insist that the time had come for society to reorient its views toward the sexes.

Giovanni, Nikki: *Gemini*. Bobbs-Merrill, 1971. Penguin Books. Ms. Giovanni calls this book "an extended autobiographical statement on my first twenty-five years of being a black poet."

Greer, Germaine: *The Female Eunuch*. McGraw-Hill, 1971. Bantam Books. This is an all-inclusive book on the subject of women—their cultural history, their psychological development, their relationship to men.

Hellman, Lillian: *An Unfinished Woman*. Little, Brown, 1969. Bantam Books. *Pentimento*. Little, Brown, 1973. The autobiographical volumes of one of America's leading playwrights and social commentators. From a privileged southern girlhood through political protest in the McCarthy era, Hellman has remained independent and outspoken. The poetry of her language brings decades of 20th-century cultural history into focus.

Holliday, Laurel: *Heart Songs*. Bluestocking Books, 1978. Excerpts from the intimate diaries of ten young girls, ages 11 to 18, from the 16th to the 20th century. All are strong, interesting persons who have an identity and something to say about their lives.

Houston, Jeanne Wakatsuki, and James D.: *Farewell to Manzanar*. Houghton Mifflin, 1973. Bantam Books. Forced to spend the war years in a Japanese internment camp, Jeanne Wakatsuki reflects on her lost adolescence, the inhumanity of the United States government's treatment, and her family's attempt to maintain its dignity and heritage.

Kahn, Kathy: *Hillbilly Women*. Doubleday, 1973. Avon Books. Nineteen self-portraits of hillbilly women; the daughters, wives, and widows of the coal-mine camps and mill towns of southern Appalachia.

Kennedy, Florynce: *Color Me Flo: My Hard Life and Good Times*. Prentice-Hall, 1976. Lawyer, civil rights activist, feminist, and social critic, Kennedy takes a hard look at her road to success as an outspoken black American woman.

Kingston, Maxine Hong: *Woman Warrior*. Alfred A. Knopf, 1976. Vintage Books. The myths of Chinese history trapped and tortured Maxine Hong as she searched for her personal female identity. Growing up in California, she learned to recognize, then exorcise the cultural ghosts that suppressed her development.

Knudson, R. R.: *Zanballer*. Delacorte Press, 1972. Dell. Suzanne Hagen becomes impatient with her physical education class and forms her own all-female football team which challenges the boys' team at Robert E. Lee High School.

Lerner, Gerda, ed.: *Black Women in White America*. Pantheon Books, 1972. Vintage Books. An interweaving of letters, journals, court transcripts, and other writings in which black women tell not only what it is like to be doubly oppressed—as blacks and as women—but also how they have managed to survive.

Lifshin, Lyn, ed.: *Tangled Vines*. Beacon Press, 1978. A collection of mother-daughter poems by Anne Sexton, Shirley Kaufman, Erica Jong, Marge Piercy, and others.

Lifton, Betty Jean: *Twice Born*. McGraw-Hill, 1975. Penguin Books. One woman's search for her true roots. Although she felt guilty about the seeming rejection of her loving adoptive parents, Lifton was driven by her need to open the file on her past. A compelling argument for adoptees' rights.

Lurie, Alison: *Love and Friendship*. Avon Books, 1975. A cynical look at the academic community as a security blanket for intellectually gifted but emotionally immature adults. A professor's wife subjugates her creativity for the sake of her husband's career, only to find that she is growing up without him.

Miller, Isabel: *Patience and Sarah*. Fawcett Books, 1976. A poignant love story captured by Miller in the gentle style of 19th-century America. Enigmas to society, Patience and Sarah fought against the classic women's roles and formed an enduring partnership during the era of westward expansion.

Moffat, Mary Jane, and Charlotte Painter, eds.: *Revelations: Diaries of Women*. Random House, 1975. Excerpts from the diaries of Louisa May Alcott, George Sand, Ruth Benedict, Kathe Kollwitz, Virginia Woolf, and many others.

Morgan, Robin, ed.: *Sisterhood is Powerful*. Random House, 1970. A pioneer collection of writings on the emerging feminist movement in the 1960s.

Munro, Alice: *Lives of Girls and Women*. New American Library, 1974. Del Jordan narrates vignettes of her rural Canadian girlhood. From the viewpoint of a woman who escaped the tedium of a small town in Ontario come poignant reflections on love, family, religion, and friendship.

Murray, Pauli: *Proud Shoes: The Story of an American Family*. Harper & Row, 1978. Dr. Murray—lawyer, civil rights activist, feminist, teacher, poet, and now one of the first women to be regularly ordained an Episcopal priest—tells the story of her maternal grandparents, Robert G. and Cornelia Fitzgerald, and of the blend of races and cultures—slave and free-born blacks, slave-owning whites, Cherokee Indians —which is her heritage.

Olsen, Tillie: *Tell Me a Riddle.* Delacorte Press, 1978. Dell. Four long short stories which express the lives of women, their needs, their strength, and their fears.

O'Neill, Eugene: *Anna Christie.* Vintage Books, 1973. A four-act play centering on the young daughter of a Swedish sea captain who falls in love with an Irish seaman and is nearly rejected by him and her father when she confesses to having been a prostitute.

Partnow, Elaine, ed.: *The Quotable Woman.* Corwin Books, 1977. Anchor Books. A fascinating collection of quotations gleaned from the writings and public utterances of women from 1800 to the present. Most of the women are American or English.

Piercy, Marge: *Small Changes.* Fawcett Books, 1978. The female characters, including Miriam and Beth, go through slow, painful changes in their lives. They move from isolation to community, from paralysis to action.

Ruddick, Sara, and Pamela Daniels, eds.: *Working It Out.* Pantheon Books, 1977. Twenty-three women writers, artists, scientists, and scholars talk about their lives and work.

Sarton, May: *Mrs. Stevens Hears the Mermaids Singing.* W. W. Norton, rev. ed., 1974. In her 70s, Mrs. Stevens, a successful poet and novelist, muses over her life and work and the women and men she has loved.

Segnitz, Barbara, ed.: *Psyche: The Feminine Poetic Consciousness.* Dell, 1973. Concentrates on ten women considered to be major poets, that is, serious and original: Emily Dickinson, Marianne Moore, Denise Levertov, Adrienne Rich, Sylvia Plath, and five others, equally worthy.

Shelley, Mary Wollstonecraft: *Frankenstein.* Macmillan, 1961.

Shulman, Alix Kates: *Burning Questions.* Alfred A. Knopf, 1978. Bantam Books. Moving from a small town to Greenwich Village, the heroine adopts all the causes of the sixties and early seventies, including marriage and children, Vietnam, civil rights, and women's liberation. A strong female character with brains and heart.

Sills, Beverly: *Bubbles: A Self-Portrait.* Bobbs-Merrill, 1976. Warner Books. Never one to shrink from a chance to be a star, Bubbles Silverman took a direct route from Brooklyn to the New York City Opera. Beverly Sills has humanized a classical medium, sharing her triumphs and personal sorrows with warmth and humor.

Singer, Frieda, ed.: *Daughters in High School.* Daughters, 1974. An anthology of poetry, short stories, and essays by high-school women from all over the United States.

Spark, Muriel: *The Prime of Miss Jean Brodie.* J. B. Lippincott, 1962. Dell. A schoolteacher uses wit, cunning, and a zany approach to life to free her students from the conventions of British society. Raising generations of independent spirits, she remains the enigma of their adolescent years.

Stirling, Nora: *You Would If You Loved Me.* M. Evans, 1969. Avon. Trudy Munroe struggles with increasing pressures to accept a sexual relationship, but she resists and emerges feeling she has active control over her life.

Stolz, Mary: *To Tell Your Love.* Harper & Row, 1950. A sensitive, withdrawn high-school senior observes her closest friend's early marital problems and her older sister's engagement, and painfully matures as she survives the end of her first romance.

Thomas, Audrey: *Songs My Mother Taught Me.* Bobbs-Merrill, 1973. Isobel takes a job the summer following her high-school graduation and begins the transition from innocence to experience.

Truman, Margaret: *Women of Courage.* William Morrow, 1976. Bantam Books. A collection of short biographies of courageous American women: 12 who challenged society with creative demands for growth and equal opportunity. Margaret Truman places her pioneering figures in the context of modern social history.

Valens, Evans G.: *A Long Way Up.* Harper & Row, 1966. *The Other Side of the Mountain.* Warner Books, 1975, 1978, 2 vols. Just before the 1958 Winter Olympics, skiing champion Jill Kinmont was paralyzed in a violent fall. Her personal strength has been the catalyst for a growing trend in equality for the handicapped.

Walker, Alice: *In Love and Trouble: Stories of Black Women*. Harcourt Brace Jovanovich, 1973. A collection of short stories that presents a diverse portrait of black women's lives.

Wolitzer, Hilma: *Ending*. William Morrow, 1974. As Jay slowly dies from bone cancer, Sandy must face her resentment, cope with single parenthood, prepare to be self-sufficient, and still remember the love that supports her independence.

Wollstonecraft, Mary: *Maria, or the Wrongs of Woman*. Norton Library, 1975. When Maria is committed to a mental institution by her husband because she disobeys him and leaves home, she shares books with Henry Darnford, another unjustly committed inmate, whom she comes to love and wishes to marry after their escape from the asylum.

Zaharias, Babe Didrikson: *This Life I've Led: An Autobiography*. A. S. Barnes, 1955. Dell. From a poor Texas town through victory in the 1932 Olympics and on to glory as a professional golfer, Zaharias assumed women's equality and paved the way for the current crop of athletic superstars.

15

Science Fiction and Fantasy

Imagination is more important than knowledge.
—*Albert Einstein*

Science fiction and fantasy may be the most exciting genres available to teenage (and adult) readers today. While fantasy has always been respected as a literary genre, science fiction (SF) has only recently achieved that status. In the thirties SF was considered by most literary authorities to be subliterature, appropriate only for comic books and pulp magazines. In the forties and fifties it advanced to a higher level of literary recognition, and in the seventies it was discovered by the critics, and its authors were acclaimed as some of the most creative and perceptive writers of the decade.

SF and fantasy hold a special allure for the teenager because they permit the reader to move into a universe of limitless possibility. Fantasy carries on directly from childhood reading of such classics as *The Wind in the Willows, The Little Prince,* and *Alice's Adventures in Wonderland,* while most teenagers first read SF as adolescents—the stage in development when abstract thinking can be grasped. Adolescents see themselves as the center of a limited universe. Tales of heroes and heroines overcoming incredible obstacles take on a personal meaning for teens, who find it easy to step into exciting roles that relate to their hopes and desires.

SF and fantasy present alternative worlds ruled by their own laws and principles and, in some way, transcending our limited view of reality. They are unique visions, emblematic of the unknown, which allow the reader to explore unanswerable but fascinating questions: What could be? What should be? What if?

HOW DO SCIENCE FICTION AND FANTASY COMPARE?

SF and fantasy are like two ends of a continuum. At the fantasy end are such books as J. R. R. Tolkien's *The Lord of the Rings* trilogy and at the SF end, Isaac Asimov's *The Fantastic Voyage*. But a book like Madeleine L'Engle's *A Wrinkle in Time* has affinities with both genres. While SF and fantasy are usually discussed together, they are distinct genres.

Fantasy literature is as old as humankind. It can be traced back to myths and legends of dead civilizations, long before the emergence of children's fairy tales. SF can be said to have begun with early utopian visions such as Plato's *Republic* and More's *Utopia*. A science fiction world describes functions according to natural laws, usually based on an advanced technological state. For example, Asimov's robots (*I, Robot* and *The Rest of the Robots*) have "positronic" brains made of a special metal alloy. We cannot produce a similar robot with present-day technology, but someday it may be possible.

SF is sometimes broken down into categories of "hard" and "soft" science. Hard SF uses scientific theories and technical terms as the basis or backdrop for the plot, while soft SF emphasizes sociological, political, or economical developments. However, much of SF straddles the fence. Arthur C. Clark's *2001: A Space Odyssey* is hard SF because of the emphasis on hardware and technical science: the spaceship, the spaceship's computer, the conquest of outer space. By contrast, William F. Nolan's soft SF novel *Logan's Run* depicts a seemingly utopian society which masks an overpopulation problem so great that no one over 21 is allowed to live.

Fantasy uses different trappings, ranging from talking animals to wizened witches. Magic and practitioners of magic abound in lands full of fantastic creatures. The improbable and unlikely become, through the author's skill, acceptable and believable. Fantasy does not have to stay within the rigid limits of possibility as does SF. The author puts forth a set of assumptions about the world he is creating, and once the reader agrees to accept them, the story can go anywhere. Although events might be scientifically explainable, they are presented as being magical or just the way things are.

SF characters are much like the ones we know, with similar foibles, frustrations, emotions, who live in different environmental and technological conditions. Fantasy characters may be more "magical." SF plots are sometimes overtaken by events or scientific discoveries that contradict their basic assumptions. Thus pre-1969 stories of landing on the moon are uninteresting, compared to the real thing. And as the year 1984 approaches, the interest of teenage readers in the vision of life in Orwell's *Nineteen Eighty-four* is diminishing rapidly. Fantasy, on the other hand, is immune to disproof.

Themes

Good science fiction and fantasy use many of the themes that appear in other genres, but use them with freshness of perception and treatment. In well-written SF and fantasy, as in good poetry, there are layers of symbolic meaning and different levels of interpretation.

Common themes of fantasy include the triumph of love over all; the struggle between good and evil; the successful meeting of a series of challenges; knights and other good men battling against odds for the right; the triumph of the little man against superior forces; the search for knowledge or beauty; the survival of the meek and good.

SF often treats similar themes in a more technological dress, and tends to be more oriented to social commentary and predictions. But the many SF adventures centering on the exploration and colonization of the universe (A. E. van Vogt's *The Voyage of the Space Beagle,* Arthur C. Clarke's *Earthlight,* Robert Heinlein's *The Red Planet,* Isaac Asimov's *The Stars Like Dust*) illustrate the theme of overcoming odds. Stories of alien encounters (John Wyndham's *The Day of the Triffids* and Clarke's *Childhood's End*) can be seen as ingenious replays of the theme of meeting with dragons. Anne McCaffrey's *The Dragonriders of Pern* and Larry Niven's *Ringworld* give new slants on love in the future. And the struggle of good versus evil results in all-out war in Joe Haldeman's *The Forever War* and Harry Harrison's *The Deathworld Trilogy.* Even the SF utopias and dystopias such as Samuel Butler's *Erewhon,* where machines are banned as a threat to man's supremacy, and Aldous Huxley's *Brave New World,* where eugenics guarantee a pleasant, uncreative life, are counterplays to the fairy tale's ". . . and they lived happily ever after." Ursula K. Le Guin's *The Left Hand of Darkness,* a remarkable story of an androgynous people living on the planet Winter, explores the old theme of survival. As in other types of fiction, fantasy and SF treatment of themes can range from simple to complex, casual to didactic, asexual to pornographic.

Literary Qualities

Both science fiction and fantasy emphasize setting, sometimes to the point that the setting can be considered the protagonist of the story. This obsession is understandable: the creation of a universe or world is the basic premise of these genres, and the writer's ability to convince us of its reality is essential. The telling details about the imaginary world and its inhabitants reflect the writer's breadth and quality of imagination. Some of the finer examples include Bradbury's vision (in his play *The Veldt*) of a nursery that projects the child's imaginary world on the wall of a room, permeating the room with the smells and temperature of an "unreal" place, and Herbert's almost waterless planet in which water becomes the most sacred possession (*Dune*).

Plot, secondary to setting in most SF and fantasy, centers on a conflict of forces in the external world that is localized as an inner struggle of the leading characters. In Tolkien's *The Lord of the Rings* trilogy, Frodo is caught in a battle between good and evil forces. His ability to resist the lure of evil, at great cost, teaches him the meaning of courage and heroism, and ultimately saves Middle-earth—at least for a time. While evil can never be annihilated, its weight in the balance of good and evil can be shifted.

SF and fantasy call for extended exposition, as readers make the transition from the world they know to the fictional world. (Realistic writers do not have the same problem.) The fictional world must be explained logically, even if the logic differs from what the reader is accustomed to. And there must be a mode of "entering" the fictional world. Someone from our world may make the transition with the reader (Alice in *Alice's Adventures in Wonderland,* or Paul in *Dune*); or tales from the "history" of the fictional world may be added to its current events to make the shift gradual and plausible (as in Tolkien's trilogy).

Why Read Science Fiction and Fantasy?

Most enthusiasts are drawn by the experience of moving into a different, often startlingly vivid world where exciting struggles take place. The writing may be speculative, drawing the reader in with the age-old question: "What if it were I?" The teenage reader tests a relatively limited experience against a new and mind-boggling backdrop.

SF and fantasy are often placed together on bookshelves, but the reader who finds the magicians and talking rabbits of *Watership Down, The Crystal Cave,* or *The Lord of the Rings* exciting fare may be uncomfortable or bored with the technical details of SF, while the SF devotee may be left cold by wizards and magical swords.

SF, long a male reading interest, has recently appealed to a wider female readership; contrariwise, except for books by Tolkien, fantasy still appeals most to females. (Adult preferences by sex are more balanced.) Research shows that 10 to 15 percent of students list SF and fantasy as a primary reading interest. Many of these read mainly for the excitement of the story line rather than for symbolic or deeper meanings.

Cult Phenomena

Science fiction and fantasy, unlike other genres, have produced a cult phenomenon. Something catches the public imagination and spawns all sorts of peripheral activities. "Star Trek," "Batman," "Spiderman," "Wonder Woman," and "The Hulk" have resulted in elaborate merchandising campaigns. Perhaps "Star Trek" is the most prestigious cult. After 59 episodes were aired on TV from 1965 to 1968, devotees of the show, known as Trekkies, have demanded and received a wealth of derivative consumer products, from novelizations of the television episodes and original novels based on the characters to blueprints and plastic models of the starship *Enterprise* and technical manuals, plus T-shirts, buttons, posters, and postcards. Trekkies hold conventions to hear lectures and meet other Trekkies. Such has been the enthusiasm of the fans that the government named its space shuttle after the *Enterprise* and, ten years after the show went off the air, Paramount made a movie with the same characters as the original show. Enthusiasm may have been engendered by the series' presenting the exploration of a frontier in an intelligent, humane manner. The mission of the spaceship was to gather information, not to conquer; the viewer was presented with a variety of topics in which right and wrong were decided without using strength to conquer the weak.

Fantasy has long been an accepted genre, but SF was sneered at by mainstream writers for many years. This fostered a sense of community among SF writers and readers. In Victorian times there were Browning and Wordsworth societies, but today the only genre that boasts clubs and fan magazines (fanzines) is SF. Fans organize many conventions around the country and the world, where they can meet like-minded readers as well as authors and artists. This has created a participatory atmosphere; some of the younger authors began as fans, and were encouraged by writers they met or heard speak at a convention.

Awards

Two major SF awards are made each year. Since 1953 the Hugo awards, determined by participants in the annual World Science Fiction Convention, have gone to the best novel, short story, magazine, motion picture, fan letter, and dramatic presentation. Awards tend to emphasize popularity among fans and speculative quality.

The Nebula awards have been given by the Science Fiction Writers of America for best novella, short story, and novel, since 1966, and tend to consider things important to writers, such as style, characterization, plot structure, and imaginative excellence.

SF and fantasy offer a wide spectrum of choice to the novice reader, who often starts by reading a single author's works or a lot of books on a given topic (such as robots). A good way to begin is by picking up a volume of the year's best. Daw Books publishes a best SF annual and a best fantasy annual. The Nebula award winners are collected annually and the Hugo award winners have also been collected.

Bibliography

SCIENCE FICTION

Anderson, Poul: *Tau Zero*. Doubleday, 1970. Berkley. An out-of-control spaceship is saved and its crew finds a home on a new planet, but not before the universe dies and is reborn.

Asimov, Isaac: *The Fantastic Voyage*. Houghton-Mifflin, 1966. Bantam Books. How a miniaturized submarine carrying a team of doctors travels through the bloodstream of a brilliant scientist to save his life.

————: *The Foundation Trilogy*. Avon Books, 1974. (Includes *Foundation; Foundation and Empire;* and *The Second Foundation*.) In this classic SF tale, the Foundations are created by Hari Seldon to preserve human culture during the dark ages after the collapse of the first galactic empire—the trilogy follows developments as the Foundations struggle to survive and fulfill the mission.

————: *I, Robot*. Doubleday, 1950. Fawcett Books. Nine positronic robot stories in which Asimov introduces the Three Laws of Robotics and robopsychologist Dr. Susan Calvin.

————, ed.: *The Hugo Winners*. Doubleday, 1962, 1971, 2 vols. Chronological presentation of the Hugo-winning stories, with Asimov's usual high-quality, readable introductions. An excellent beginning point for new readers wanting to meet some of the best SF writing and writers.

Benford, Gregory: *Jupiter Project*. Thomas Nelson, 1975. Living in a laboratory orbiting Jupiter, young Matt Bowles must prove himself or be returned to a hostile earth.

Bester, Alfred: *The Demolished Man*. Garland, 1975. Pocket Books. Committing murder in the 24th century is not simple when the police have telepathic powers, but ruthless Ben Reich tries anyway.

Blish, James: *Cities in Flight*. Avon Books, 1970. Four novels constitute a future history in which earth's cities, using the "spindizzy" drive, leave the planet to escape repression and take up nomadic existence in space.

————: *Star Trek*. Bantam Books, 1970–75, nos. 1–11. *The Star Trek Reader*. E. P. Dutton, 1976–1978, 4 vols. Compilations based on the characters and plot line developed for the popular TV series.

Boulle, Pierre: *Planet of the Apes*. Vanguard Press, 1963. New American Library. Two men from earth land on a planet governed by intelligent but cruel apes who have taken over as humans have become weaker.

Bova, Ben: *City of Darkness.* Charles Scribner's Sons, 1976. Ron Morgan explores life in the now isolated dome of New York City, where rival youth gangs strive for dominance and plot an invasion of the "outside."

————: *The Multiple Man.* Bobbs-Merrill, 1976. Ballantine Books. President James J. Halliday has a top-level security secret: several exact duplicates of himself have been mysteriously killed.

Brackett, Leigh: *The Long Tomorrow.* Doubleday, 1955. Ballantine Books. Len Colter lives in an antiscientific age after World War IV and must decide whether or not to join dissident scientists who want to renew technology in the hopes it will not again be misused.

Bradbury, Ray: *Fahrenheit 451.* Simon and Schuster, 1967. Ballantine Books. Montag, a fireman whose job is burning books, undergoes a conversion from book burner to preserver and joins the underground of "living books."

————: *The Martian Chronicles.* Doubleday, 1958. Bantam Books. A series of episodes relating the colonization of Mars by Earth beginning in the late 20th century.

Brunner, John: *Sheep Look Up.* Harper & Row, 1972. Ballantine Books. The ultimate ecological disaster story in which "subversive" ecologist Austin Train battles to alert the world to its impending doom.

————: *The Shockwave Rider.* Harper & Row, 1975. Ballantine Books. Everyone's life is ruled by computers until Nickie Haflinger, a computer whiz, plants the "worm" that gives people back their freedom.

Caidin, Martin: *Cyborg.* Arbor House, 1974. Warner Books. An air force test pilot becomes the first cyborg. This book was the basis for the TV show "The Six Million Dollar Man."

Campbell, Hope: *The Legend of Lost Earth.* Four Winds Press, 1977. On the soot-covered and gray-skied planet of Niflhel, legends persist of a green and beautiful earth somewhere in space.

Campbell, John W.: *The Best of John W. Campbell* (ed. Lester Del Rey). Ballantine Books, 1976. An even dozen stories by a pioneer writer and editor of SF.

Capek, Josef and Karel: *R.U.R.* Oxford University Press,

1961. Washington Square Press. This is the international classic play that coined the word "robot." (The
initials of the title stand for "Rossum's Universal
Robots.")

Capek, Karel: *The War with the Newts*. Gregg Press, 1975.
Berkley. A race of giant, intelligent newts is discovered and enlisted to do man's work underwater—
digging harbors and canals. Eventually, they learn
man's ways all too well, and turn on their masters.

Carr, Terry: *Creatures from Beyond*. Thomas Nelson,
1975. Nine short stories about strange and terrifying
aliens who find their way to earth.

Christopher, John: *The City of Gold and Lead*. Macmillan,
1967. *The Pool of Fire*, 1968. *The White Mountains*,
1967. Earth has been conquered by aliens from outer
space; technology has been destroyed, and the people
are controlled by brain implants. The trilogy is concerned with humans getting a second chance, but the
prospects aren't bright for creating a better world.

————: *No Blades of Grass*. Avon, 1975. A catastrophe
novel which explores the attempts of mankind to
survive and make good on a second chance.

Clarke, Arthur C.: *Childhood's End*. Harcourt Brace Jovanovich, 1963. Ballantine Books. Earth is subdued
by a superior species and tutored until mankind is
developed enough to enter the cosmic oversoul.

————: *Rendezvous with Rama*. Harcourt Brace Jovanovich, 1973. Ballantine Books. A team of scientists
are sent to explore a space capsule en route through
our galaxy from an unknown civilization to an unknown destination.

————: *2001: A Space Odyssey*. New American Library,
1972. After a signal/sentinel is discovered on the
moon, astronauts set out to trace the source of the signal, only to have their plans endangered by a computer
gone berserk.

Clement, Hal: *Mission of Gravity*. Gregg Press, 1978.
Ballantine Books. Mesklin planet has a gravity 700
times that of earth, and its inhabitants are only 15
inches long, but they manage to help recover a
crashed earth observer satellite.

Crichton, Michael: *The Andromeda Strain*. Alfred A.

Knopf, 1969. Dell. Earth's destruction by a super-virus is averted at the last moment by virologists in this well-plotted, suspenseful tale.

————: *The Terminal Man*. Alfred A. Knopf, 1972. Bantam Books. Harry Benson, psychopath, is selected for an experiment to modify behavior by psychosurgery, but things go wrong and Harry goes berserk.

Dann, Jack: *Starhiker*. Harper & Row, 1977. In a future world controlled by a race of benevolent despots called the Hrau, a spark of humanity lives on in an imaginative minstrel who wanders in search of truth and love.

Delany, Samuel R.: *Nova*. Doubleday, 1968. Bantam Books. In a modern myth set forth in the SF idiom, Captain von Ray dares to sail through the splintering core of a disintegrating sun.

Del Rey, Lester: *Moon of Mutiny*. Holt, Rinehart and Winston, 1961. Ballantine Books. Fred Halpern is expelled from the Space Academy for disobeying orders but is given another chance to become a spaceman by joining an expedition to the moon.

Dick, Philip K.: *The Best of Philip K. Dick* (ed. John Brunner). Ballantine Books, 1977. Weird, wonderful, wild stories of a world gone mad, by the master of SF madness.

Dickinson, Peter: *The Blue Hawk*. Atlantic Monthly Press, 1976. Ballantine Books. When Tron takes the Blue Hawk, destined to be sacrified to renew the old king, it sets in motion a superb story about freedom, loyalty, courage, and love.

Dickson, Gordon R.: *Dorsai!* Daw Books, 1976. The Dorsai are born to fight, and fight they do in this exciting novel of interstellar warfare.

————: *The Far Call*. Dial Press, 1978. Dell. The first group of immigrants are on their way from earth to Mars and neither those going nor those left behind will be the same again.

Dickson, Gordon R., and Harry Harrison: *The Lifeship*. Harper & Row, 1976. Pocket Books. A human spokesman tries to save himself and others from the death-in-space credo of the alien Albenareth, who is in command of their emergency lifeship.

Dozois, Gardner, ed.: *Another World: Adventures in Otherness*. Follett, 1977. An anthology of short stories which serves as an excellent introduction to SF.

Ellison, Harlan: *Deathbird Stories*. Harper & Row, 1975. Dell. Upsetting, controversial stories by a master of the short story.

Ellison, Harlan, ed.: *Dangerous Visions*. New American Library, 1975. *Again, Dangerous Visions*. Ultramarine, 1972. Two of the most significant collections of short stories ever published; superior stories by top writers freed of the conventional restraints SF had imposed.

Elwood, Roger, ed.: *Children of Infinity*. Franklin Watts, 1973. SF stories about young people for young readers.

Engdahl, Sylvia: *Enchantress from the Stars*. Atheneum, 1970. *The Far Side of Evil*. 1971. Two adventures of Elana, a member of the Anthropological Service whose mission is to aid developing civilizations without interfering with their natural evolution.

————: *This Star Shall Abide*. Atheneum, 1972. *Beyond the Tomorrow Mountains*. 1973. Two-part tale of the coming of age of young Noren, who begins as a rebel against the established order in his faraway world.

Farmer, Philip Jose: *To Your Scattered Bodies Go*. Berkley, 1973. What exists at the headwaters of the multimillion-mile-long river that the "Ethicals" want to keep Burton and Clemens from finding?

Finney, Jack: *Time and Again*. Simon and Schuster, 1970. Time travel takes Simon Morley back to the New York of the 1880s and readers feel they, too, are there.

Gerrold, David: *The Man Who Folded Himself*. Aeonian Press, 1976. A man inherits a time travel belt that creates duplicates of himself existing independently in other time streams. Complications and confusions follow.

————: *When Harlie Was One*. Ballantine Books, 1975. Harlie is a computer who thinks he's human; his psychologist agrees but wishes Harlie would grow up emotionally and prove productive before the project that created him is shut down.

Goulart, Ron: *What's Become of Screwloose?* Daw Books,

1973. Stories of mechanical devices gone wild and man's ability/inability to cope with the cyborgs of today and tomorrow.

Haldeman, Joe: *The Forever War*. St. Martin's Press, 1977. Ballantine Books. An SF variation of the "Catch-22" syndrome, in which once drafted into the army it becomes near impossible to get out.

Harrison, Harry: *The Deathworld Trilogy*. Berkley. Jason din Alt, gambler extraordinaire, gambles his life on three deadly planets.

Heinlein, Robert: *The Moon Is a Harsh Mistress*. G. P. Putnam's Sons, 1966. Berkley. Leaders of the moon colony declare themselves independent from earth with the aid of sentient computer Mike.

————: *Starship Troopers*. G. P. Putnam's Sons, 1960. Berkley. Unlike Haldeman's *Forever War*, this is a paean of praise for the men who fight to protect their homes and loved ones. Set in a time when citizenship is bestowed *only* through service in the armed forces.

————: *Stranger in a Strange Land*. G. P. Putnam's Sons, 1961. Berkley. Valentine Michael Smith, an earthman raised by Martians, returns to earth and upsets society by attempting to "grok" his new "water brother."

Henderson, Zenna: *Pilgrimage: The Book of the People*. Avon, 1970. *The People: No Different Flesh*, Avon, 1970. Survivors from a catastrophe in another solar system come to earth and learn that their psi powers make them unwelcome to some of earth's inhabitants.

Herbert, Frank: *Dune*. Chilton Book, 1965. Berkley, 1975. *Dune Messiah*. G. P. Putnam's Sons, 1976. *Children of Dune*. Berkley, 1976. Trilogy exploring the desert world of Dune, valued for its unique narcotic crop and inhabited by the hardy and the outcast.

Hersey, John: *My Petition for More Space*. Alfred A. Knopf, 1974. Sam Poynter is waiting in a line four-people wide and three-quarters of a mile long to see a government official about his request for more living space.

Hoover, H. M.: *Children of Morrow*. Four Winds Press, 1973. *Treasures of Morrow*, 1976. Adventure set in a future where two contrasting social orders have evolved among the survivors of widespread nuclear destruction.

Howard, Robert Ervin: *Conan the Conqueror*. Ace Books, 1977. Far from great literature, but Howard's Conan is the original sword and sorcery hero. Racist, sexist writing, but historically important.

Hoyle, Fred and Geoffrey: *The Inferno*. Harper & Row, 1973. As earth is threatened by an explosion at the galaxy's core, a Scottish astronomer returns to the highlands to survive and rebuild society.

Huxley, Aldous: *Brave New World*. Harper & Row, 1932. A futuristic study of the ideal society, Huxley's novel exposes the potential for human abuse in the quest for perfection. The story has many parallels in today's world of scientific expertise.

Jones, Diane: *Dogsbody*. Greenwillow, 1977. Sirius, the Dog Star, is falsely accused of losing the Zoi and as punishment is sentenced to roam the earth in search of it.

Keyes, Daniel: *Flowers for Algernon*. Harcourt Brace Jovanovich, 1966. Retarded, gentle, sensitive Charlie has a short living experience with superior intelligence in this story about the abuses of unchecked scientific experimentation.

Kuttner, Henry: *The Best of Henry Kuttner* (intro. Ray Bradbury). Ballantine Books, 1975. Kuttner wrote SF and fantasy; some of his best of both are here for readers to discover.

Kytle, Ray Jr.: *Fire and Ice*. David McKay, 1975. Two closely-bound families flee to the mountains for survival when a new ice age threatens.

Laumer, Keith: *Retief of the CDT*. Pocket Books, 1978. SF mixed with political intrigue and satire that many find funny.

Lawrence, Louise: *Star Lord*. Harper & Row, 1978. A beautiful stranger lands in the rugged Welsh mountain country and changes the lives of all who encounter him.

Le Guin, Ursula K.: *The Dispossessed*. Harper & Row, 1974. Avon Books. Neither the anarchy of Anarres nor the unfettered capitalism of Urras provide an atmosphere in which people can work creatively in freedom.

———: *The Left Hand of Darkness*. Ace Books, 1976.

Explores the relationship of Genry, an envoy from the galaxy's technologically advanced worlds, and Estraven, statesman of the Winter kingdom of Karhide.

————: *The Word for World is Forest*. Berkley, 1976. Claiming the planet Athshe, humans enslave the natives and ruthlessly log the forests until the Athsheans, who have learned to kill from humans, turn against their tormentors.

Lem, Stanislaw: *Mortal Engines*. Seabury Press, 1977. A short-story collection with robots as the protagonists.

Lewis, C. S.: *Space Trilogy*. Macmillan, 1975. (Includes *Out of the Silent Planet; Perelandra;* and *That Hideous Strength*.) In this trilogy (also know as *The Ransom Trilogy*), an English scholar leaves earth, the silent planet, and journeys to Mars and Venus where he gathers the strength and wisdom to battle the forces of evil on earth.

McCaffrey, Anne: *Dragondrums*. Atheneum, 1979. *Dragonsinger*. Atheneum, 1977. Bantam Books. *Dragonsong*. Atheneum, 1976. Bantam Books. A trilogy about Pern, featuring Menolly, the young woman who wants to be a harper. For younger readers than the trilogy below.

————: *Dragonflight*. Ballantine Books, 1975. *Dragonquest*. 1975. *White Dragon*. 1978. Series set on Pern, where man and dragon have formed a telepathic bond to fight off the periodic invasion of deadly space spores during Threadfall.

————: *The Ship Who Sang*. Ballantine Books, 1976. Helva, a human brain modified to control a starship as a person controls her body, retains all the human emotions and must adjust to her new life as a cyborg.

McHargue, Georgess, ed.: *Hot and Cold Running Cities*. Holt, Rinehart and Winston, 1974. A collection of SF stories on the theme of cities of the future.

McIntyre, Vonda N.: *Dreamsnake*. Houghton Mifflin, 1978. Dell. Snake is a healer, whose medicine consists of three snakes, the most important of which is the "dreamsnake." When hers is killed, she sets forth on a quest that provides high adventure and much insight into the human condition.

Merril, Judith: *The Best of Judith Merril*. Warner Books, 1976. A collection of the author's best short stories, including the classic "That Only a Mother."

Miller, Walter M., Jr.: *A Canticle for Leibowitz*. J. B. Lippincott, 1969. Bantam Books. A nuclear holocaust renders earth a barren world inhabited by people who have forgotten technology and returned to feudalism.

Moorcock, Michael: *Ice Schooner*. Harper & Row, 1977. In a future age when earth's cities are covered with ice, Konrad Arflane wins command of the schooner *Ice Spirit* and undertakes a voyage to the legendary city of New York.

Moore, C. L.: *The Best of C. L. Moore*. Ballantine Books, 1976. Short stories by an early SF author, including the superb "No Woman Born," a forerunner of cyborg tales.

Nebula Award Stories. Harper & Row. Annual reprinting of the nonnovel winners with additional contemporary stories reviewing the current state of the SF art.

Neufeld, John: *Sleep Two, Three, Four*. Avon Books, 1972. Six teenagers are on the run in a totalitarian police state of the future.

Niven, Larry: *Ringworld*. Ballantine Books, 1975. Four unlikely travelers explore an artificial world so enormous it encircles a star.

Niven, Larry, and Jerry Pournelle: *The Mote in God's Eye*. Simon and Schuster, 1974. Pocket Books. It is the 31st century and man has colonized most of the galaxy when he encounters his first alien civilization —and the "Moties" from the Coalsack Nebula almost get the best of it.

Nolan, William F., and George Clayton Johnson: *Logan's Run*. Bantam Books, 1976. Logan "runs" from the death sentence everyone receives on his 21st birthday, hoping to find the legendary Sanctuary and live out his natural lifespan.

Norton, Andre: *Breed to Come*. Viking Press, 1972. Ace Books. Mankind has fled earth and other species have evolved intelligence, notably the People, a race of cats seeking man's knowledge in the ruins of his civilization.

Nourse, Alan: *The Bladerunner*. David McKay, 1974. Ballantine Books. Billy Gump, an underground medical bladerunner, helps control an outbreak of meningitis which challenges the rigid bureaucracy of the Health Control system.

O'Brien, Robert: *Z for Zachariah*. Atheneum, 1975. Young Ann Burden and scientist John Loomis come into conflict as perhaps the only survivors of an atomic war.

Orbit. Harper & Row. An annual anthology of the best SF, noted for presenting new authors.

Orwell, George: *Nineteen Eighty-four*. Harcourt Brace Jovanovich, 1949. New American Library. A not-so-distant society reverses currently acceptable values and principles in this futuristic satire. The easy manipulation of men's minds by the forces of political power serves as a warning to all.

Panshin, Alexei: *Rite of Passage*. Gregg Press, 1976. Ace Books. To qualify for adult status in a world of the future, Mia must pass a test of survival on the wilds on an earthlike planet.

Pohl, Frederik: *Man Plus*. Random House, 1976. Bantam Books. Roger Torroway becomes a mechanical monster to survive without mechanical help on the surface of Mars. He finds his sanity threatened.

Robinson, Spider: *Callahan's Crosstime Saloon*. Ridley Enslow, 1978. Ace Books. The misfits of earth and elsewhere belly up to the bar at Callahan's and swap outrageous adventure stories.

Sargent, Pamela: *Women of Wonder*. Random House, 1975. *More Women of Wonder*. 1976. *New Women of Wonder*. 1978. An anthology of women SF writers writing about women for women.

Silverberg, Robert, ed.: *Science Fiction Hall of Fame*. Doubleday, 1970. Avon Books. Twenty-six classic short stories published before 1965.

Simak, Clifford D.: *Shakespeare's Planet*. Berkley, 1976. Carter Horton discovers an isolated planet with a mysterious past—had Shakespeare really been there? —and a feeling of things about to happen.

Sleator, William: *House of Stairs*. E. P. Dutton, 1974. Avon Books. Five teenagers find themselves in an experimental nightmare where they are being conditioned to become robots in a future society.

Spielberg, Steven: *Close Encounters of the Third Kind*.

Delacorte Press, 1977. Dell. Excellent novelization of the movie script about earth's firsthand contact with aliens from outer space.

Tilley, Patrick: *Fade-out*. William Morrow, 1975. Dell. Scientists throughout the world seek to unravel the mystery of five alien spacecraft that have landed on earth, disrupting radio transmission and threatening catastrophe.

Tiptree, James, Jr.: *Star Songs of an Old Primate*. Ballantine Books, 1978. Stunning collection of short stories by one of the best, including the incomparable "Houston, Houston, Do You Read?"

Townsend, John Rowe: *The Visitors*. J. B. Lippincott, 1977. Sixteen-year-old John is baffled by the inexplicable arrival and unconventional behavior of three visitors from the future.

Van Vogt, A. E.: *Slan*. Garland, 1975. Berkley. Despite being telepathic, physically and mentally superior, Slans are hated and hunted by bigots who despise anyone different.

Varley, John: *The Persistence of Vision*. Dial Press, 1978. Nine short stories by a writer every SF fan should know.

Verne, Jules: *Twenty Thousand Leagues Under the Sea*. Macmillan, 1962. Bantam Books. A classic (first published in 1870) by the author who is father to hard science SF writing.

Vonnegut, Kurt, Jr.: *Cat's Cradle*. Delacorte Press, 1971. Dell. The funniest, most satiric account of the end of the world.

Weinbaum, Stanley G.: *The Best of Stanley G. Weinbaum* (intro. Isaac Asimov). Ballantine Books, 1974. Intriguing stories by an early 1930s author who died before his contributions were fully appreciated.

Wells, H. G.: *The Time Machine*. Oxford University Press, 1977. Bantam Books. The first and still great adventure into time travel. (First published in 1895.)

Wilhelm, Kate: *Where Late the Sweet Birds Sang*. Harper & Row, 1976. Pocket Books. When humankind is faced with annihilation by the sterilizing effects of pollution and plague, cloning is the hope of continued existence—or is it?

Williams, Jay: *The People of the Ax*. Henry Z. Walck, 1974. Dell. Arne is taught to believe that the Crom are not truly human, yet he senses their humanity and sets out to make contact and peace between the two remaining civilizations of earth.

Wollheim, Donald A.: *The World's Best Science Fiction*. Daw Books, annual, 1972–   . Wollheim puts together his choices of the year's best—and no one does it better.

Yep, Laurence: *Sweetwater*. Harper & Row, 1973. Avon Books. The descendants of stranded starship crews live in the half-submerged city of Old Sion on the planet Harmony, where they must learn to accept the native people and their special talents.

FANTASY

Adams, Richard: *Watership Down*. Macmillan, 1975. Avon Books. A small band of rabbits flee the destruction of their warren and search for a new home.

Alexander, Lloyd: *The Book of Three*. Holt, Rinehart and Winston, 1964. Dell. *The Black Cauldron*. 1965. *The Castle of Llyr*. 1966. *Taran Wanderer*. 1967. *The High King*. 1968. Magical spells woven from Welsh legend and myth. Taran, the assistant pig keeper, ventures in search of his true identity in these five volumes of *The Chronicles of Prydain*.

Anderson, Chester: *The Butterfly Kid*. Gregg Press, 1977. Hoping to effect a nonviolent conquest of earth, aliens distribute blue pills that make people's fantasies real.

Anderson, Margaret: *In the Keep of Time*. Alfred A. Knopf, 1977. Scholastic Book Services. An ancient tower in Scotland proves a door into the 15th-century past and the 22nd-century future for four children.

Anderson, Poul: *The Broken Sword*. Ballantine Books, 1977. Valgard is a changeling, half elf, half troll, left to be raised by mortals, who engages in revenge when he discovers his heritage.

Anderson, Poul, and Gordon R. Dickson: *Star Prince Charlie*. G. P. Putnam's Sons, 1975. Berkley. Accompanied and prompted by his Hoka tutor, a young

Scottish scion, Charlie Stewart, travels to distant Talyina where he fulfills an ancient prophecy.

Anthony, Piers: *A Spell for Chameleon.* Ballantine Books, 1977. Bink must find his magic talent or be exiled and lose Sabrina.

Beagle, Peter: *The Last Unicorn.* Ballantine Books, 1976. A Unicorn senses that she is the last of her species to exist, and is told that if she is brave she can find others.

Bradbury, Ray: *Something Wicked This Way Comes.* Simon and Schuster, 1962. Bantam Books. It is late October when the Dark Carnival arrives in a sleepy little town, luring two small boys into a confrontation with the dark and dangerous.

Brooks, Terry: *The Sword of Shannara.* Random House, 1977. Ballantine Books. A Tolkienesque adventure about an attempt to secure a magical sword and save earth from the powers of darkness.

Burford, Lolah: *The Vision of Stephen.* Macmillan, 1972. The spirit of Stephen, the son of a warrior king in 7th-century England, escapes torture by traveling through time to Victorian England where he meets two children living at the site of his former home.

Cameron, Eleanor: *The Court of the Stone Children.* E. P. Dutton, 1973. Avon Books. In a San Francisco museum Nina meets the ghost of Dominique and sets out to disentangle the mystery of her father's execution on a false charge of plotting to kill Napoleon.

Carr, Terry, ed.: *The Year's Finest Fantasy.* Berkley, 1978. Stories by Stephen King, Woody Allen, and Harlan Ellison highlight this fine collection.

Chant, Joy: *Red Moon and Black Mountain: The End of the House of Hendreth.* E. P. Dutton, 1976. Ballantine Books. The three Powell children are catapulted from the English countryside to another world where each child participates in a different way in the final battle between good and evil.

Christopher, John: *The Prince in Waiting.* Macmillan, 1970. *Beyond the Burning Lands.* 1971. *The Sword of the Spirits.* 1972. England in 2000 has reverted to a feudal, antitechnological society and Luke Perry must battle to claim his princely heritage and lead his people into a civilized future.

Cooper, Louise: *The Book of Paradox*. Dell. Varka, wrongly punished for his beloved's death, must seek her in Limbo, using the Book of Paradox as his only guide.

Cooper, Susan: *Over Sea, Under Stone*. Harcourt Brace Jovanovich, 1966. *The Dark is Rising*. Atheneum, 1973. *Greenwitch*. 1974. *The Grey King*. 1975. *Silver on the Tree*. 1977. Will Stanton, last of the Old Ones —immortals dedicated to the fight against evil— journeys to fulfill his destiny.

Dickson, Gordon R.: *The Dragon and the George*. Ballantine Books, 1978. Jim goes into the time machine a man and comes out a dragon who needs the help of an absent-minded wizard to help rescue Angie.

Donaldson, Stephen R.: *The Chronicles of Thomas Covenant, the Unbeliever*. Holt, Rinehart and Winston, 1977. (Includes *Lord Foul's Bane; The Ill-Earth War; The Power That Preserves*). Thomas Covenant, whose task is to defeat Lord Foul, the Destroyer, refuses to believe that the Land and its people exist except in his imagination.

Donovan, John: *Family*. Harper & Row, 1976. Dell. Four apes from a research laboratory escape and find a utopia, only to become victims of man's ignorance and brutality.

Garner, Alan: *Red Shift*. Macmillan, 1973. The lives of three young men in different periods of British history converge; each influences the destiny of the others.

Grahame, Kenneth: *The Wind in the Willows*. Charles Scribner's Sons, 1933. Dell. Classic recounting of the adventures of Mole, Badger, Rat, and Toad.

Gregorian, Joyce Ballou: *The Broken Citadel*. Atheneum, 1975. *Castledown*, 1977. Following a prophecy, Prince Leron goes on a quest to free Princess Dastra from her glass prison, but finds himself caught in the spells of her mother, the Deathless Queen.

Jones, Adrienne: *The Mural Master*. Houghton Mifflin, 1974. A mural master's art crosses space and time, carrying four friends on a strange adventure to rescue the master's friend from a land of terrifying beasts and carnivorous trees.

Juster, Norton: *The Phantom Tollbooth*. Random House, 1961. Young Milo passes through a magical tollbooth

into an absurd land where the mathemagician rules
the world of numbers and King Dictionopolis rules
the realm of words.

Kendall, Carol: *The Gammage Cup.* Harcourt Brace Jovanovich, 1965. *The Whisper of Glocken.* 1965. Adventures in the land of the Minnipins where non-
conformists prevent a war and go on a quest.

Kurtz, Katherine: *Deryni Rising.* Ballantine Books, 1976.
Deryni Checkmate. The High Deryni. The *Chronicles
of the Deryni* describes the world of Gwynned, where
the Deryni, a quasi-mortal race of sorcerers, have
been anathema for centuries but have hopes of acceptance when young King Kelson is forced to battle
against evil powers and fanatical priests.

Lee, Tanith. *Volkhavaar.* Daw Books, 1977. Colorful, exciting story of two who made separate pacts with
cosmic forces to rule a world—and had to fight it out
between good and evil.

Le Guin, Ursula K.: *The Wizard of Earthsea.* Parnassus
Press, 1968. Bantam Books. *The Tombs of Atuan.*
Atheneum, 1971. Bantam Books. *The Farthest Shore,*
Atheneum, 1972. Bantam Books. This trilogy follows
the life of Sparrowhawk from boyhood, when his misuse of his gift for magic releases an evil force, to his
old age, where his hard-won wisdom must grapple with
the destroyers of magic.

Leiber, Fritz: *Swords Against Death.* Gregg Press, 1977.
Swords Against Wizardry. Gregg Press, 1977. Ace
Books. *Swords and Deviltry. Swords and Ice Magic.
Swords in the Mist. The Swords of Lankhmar.* In
these volumes of the *Fafhrd and the Gray Mouser*
saga, the master swordsman Fafhrd, a barbarian giant,
and the Gray Mouser, an apprentice wizard, roam
the world of Newhon.

L'Engle, Madeleine: *A Wrinkle in Time.* Farrar, Straus
and Giroux, 1962. Dell. *The Wind in the Door.* 1977.
Meg and her companions tesseract through time in
search of her missing scientist father.

Lewis, C. S.: *Chronicles of Narnia.* Macmillan, 1970.
(Includes *The Magician's Nephew; The Lion, the
Witch, and the Wardrobe; The Horse and His Boy;
Prince Caspian; The Voyage of the Dawn Treader;
The Silver Chair;* and *The Last Battle.*) Adventures

in the world of Narnia, where mythological creatures are ruled over by the wise lion Aslan.

McKillip, Patricia A.: *The Forgotten Beasts of Eld*. Atheneum, 1974. Avon Books. Sybil, who has spent her life in the woods with a variety of strange and magical animals, must learn to live in the world of men.

————: *The Riddle-Master of Hed*. Atheneum, 1976. Ballantine Books. *Heir of Sea and Fire*. Atheneum, 1977. (Third volume to be published.) Morgan, prince of Hed, and his betrothed, Raederle, are linked in the fate that awaits him when he discovers his identity and his fate.

McKinley, Robin: *Beauty*. Harper & Row, 1978. A lovely, mature novelization of the Brothers Grimm story of "Beauty and the Beast."

Moorcock, Michael: *The Swords Trilogy*. Berkely, 1977. Prince Corum, one of the few survivors of the Mabden invasion of earth, is caught in the battle between order and chaos ranging across the 15 planes of reality.

Murphy, Shirley: *The Grass Tower*. Atheneum, 1976. Telepathic since earliest childhood, Bethany tries to find out why she is being drawn into another place and another time.

Nathan, Robert: *Heaven and Hell and the Megas Factor*. Delacorte Press, 1975. Emissaries from heaven and hell, sent to investigate the turmoil on earth, meet and fall in love.

Norton, Andre: *Witch World*. Gregg Press, 1977. Ace Books. *Web of the Witch World*. *Three Against the Witch World*. Gregg Press, 1977. *Year of the Unicorn*. Gregg Press, 1977. Ace Books. *Warlock of the Witch World*. Gregg Press, 1977. *Sorceress of the Witch World*. Gregg Press, 1977. Ace Books. *Spell of the Witch World*. *The Crystal Gryphon*. Atheneum Books, 1972. Daw Books. *The Jargoon Pard*. Atheneum, 1974. Fawcett Books. These volumes compose the *Witch World* series, sword-and-sorcery tales with strong feminine appeal.

Parker, Richard: *A Time to Choose*. Harper & Row, 1974. Stephen and Mary find themselves moving between their own world and a parallel one where they live on a utopian agricultural commune. Soon they must chose where they wish to remain.

Schmitz, James H.: *The Witches of Karres*. Ace Books, 1977. Three "witch" children and a salty starship captain save the human race from a maniacal computer and lizard, would-be conquerors.

Simak, Clifford D.: *Enchanted Pilgrimage*. Berkley, 1975. A medieval scholar journeys across the Wasteland in the company of elves, gnomes, and goblins to sample the wisdom of the Old Ones.

Stewart, Mary: *The Crystal Cave*. William Morrow, 1970. Fawcett Books. A retelling of the Arthurian legend, focusing on Merlin.

————: *Touch Not the Cat*. William Morrow, 1976. Fawcett Books. After her father's mysterious death, Bryony Ashley dangerously attempts to uncover the identity of her phantom lover, the person who shares her telepathic powers.

Tolkien, J. R. R.: *The Hobbit*. Houghton Mifflin, 1938. Ballantine Books. First of the adventures set in Middle-earth. Bilbo Baggins accompanies Thorin Oakenshield and his 12 dwarfs on a quest to recover stolen treasure from Smaug, the dragon.

————: *The Lord of the Rings*. Houghton-Mifflin, 1974. Ballantine Books. (Includes *The Fellowship of the Ring; The Two Towers;* and *The Return of the King*.) Epic account of the ending of the third age of Middle-earth as the free peoples unite to defeat the Dark Lord by destroying the One Ring of power.

Vonnegut, Kurt, Jr.: *Slaughterhouse-Five*. Dell, 1971. Billy Pilgrim gets "unstuck in time" and finds himself alternately at the fire-bombing of Dresden during World War II and in the future of the planet of the alien Tralfamadorians.

Walton, Evangeline: *The Children of Llyr*. Ballantine Books, 1973. *The Song of Rhiannon. The Islands of the Mighty. Prince of Annwn*. 1974. Love, curses, and high adventure combine to make these books of the Welsh *Mabinogion* an outstanding work of fantasy.

Wangerin, Walter, Jr.: *The Book of the Dun Cow*. Harper & Row, 1978. In an epic fantasy rich in medieval atmosphere and gusty humor, Walter Wangerin presents a cast of heroic if imperfect animals battling for their lives and beliefs in a timeless war between good and evil.

Zelazny, Roger: *Nine Princes in Amber*. Avon Books, 1977. *The Guns of Avalon*. 1974. *Sign of the Unicorn*. 1976. *The Hand of Oberon*. 1977. A saga of the royal family of Amber and their efforts to control the powers and forces that threaten their world and all the worlds of Shadow. (A final volume of the *Amber* series is still to be published.)

Appendix

BIBLIOGRAPHIC TOOLS AND SOURCES

BAYA Reviews. Included in membership dues ($3/year) from Sue Schwartz, 6625 California St., #4, San Francisco, CA 94121. Bimonthly reviews are sent to members with a list of books to be orally reviewed at the next meeting and a synopsis of past business and program meeting in the minutes. Each issue reviews 50–75 titles aimed at the popular reading tastes of young adults by the school and public librarians in the group. Reviews printed in 3x5 clippable format.

Booklist. Published twice monthly, Sept.-July and once in August. $28/year (U.S., Canada, and PUAS countries) or $30 other countries. Order from Robert Nelson, Manager, Membership, Subscription, and Order Services, 50 E. Huron St., Chicago, IL 60611. Recommends material for small and medium-sized public libraries and school media centers, with a regular YA [young adult] reviewing column and other sections of special YA interest: paperback reprints, science fiction, westerns, nonprint materials, and a column of hi/lo materials for reluctant readers. Includes foreign language vendors and vocational/technical material review columns from time to time. Slanted to school audience, which constitutes a majority of subscribers.

English Journal. Published monthly, Sept.-May. Available to members of National Council of Teachers of English ($20 annual dues) from NCTE Subscription Service, 1111 Kenyon Rd., Urbana, IL 61801. Includes a frequent column on "Books for Young

Adults" and many articles on books teens like. Prints the annual "Honor Listing of YA Books" from G. Robert Carlsen.

Kliatt: *Young Adult Paperback Book Guide.* Published 8/year (Jan., Feb., Apr., May, June, Sept., Oct., Nov. with occasional newsletter updates). $20/year; Canada $22/year. Address: 425 Watertown St., Newton, MA 02158. Jan. 1979 is vol. 13, no. 1. Comprehensive reviews of 300 titles per issue, paperbacks: originals, reprints, reissues from editors Doris Hiatt and Claire Rosser and a group of reviewers from Massachusetts. The categories are fiction, science fiction, language arts, biography, education and guidance, philosophy and religion, social studies, history and geography, nature and ecology, the arts, recreation, and miscellaneous. Letters to the editor and occasional brief articles focus on intellectual freedom issues. Especially useful for paperback selection; although reviews a little late, they cover the field from a public library and school library viewpoint.

McNaughton Young Adult Reviews. From McNaughton Book Service, P.O. Drawer 926, Williamsport, PA 17705. Part of the McNaughton YA rental plan; monthly review sheets can be received by asking to be placed on the mailing list. Reviews 30–35 titles monthly in descriptive paragraph including intended reader audience, criticism and any YA feedback gathered. Reviews are up-to-date with publication schedules. A very useful source.

Nassau (New York) Library System: Recommended Titles for Young Adults. Monthly. $15/year. Order from: Nassau Library System, Roosevelt Field, Garden City, NY 11530. Each issue contains reviews of 100 new hardcover and original paperbacks, as well as listings of reissues and adult titles with assignment fulfillment potential. The reviews are one-paragraph, giving plot synopsis, characters, and potential teen appeal; they are written by the school and public librarians of the Nassau Library System. Printed in 3x5 clippable format. Especially useful for school needs and occasional titles not found elsewhere. Sometimes reviews are very late; other times they are in sync with publication releases.

News from Alan. Newsletter from the Assembly on Literature for Adolescents of NCTE. Sent bimonthly by Ken Donelson and Aileen Nilson, coeditors. $5/year. Send to ALAN, c/o Mary Sucher, Dondalk Senior High, 1901 Delvale Ave., Baltimore, MD 21222. Reviews 20 titles per issue in a middle clip-out section printed in 3x5 format. The reviews are signed and are usually on adolescent novels, both paper and hardcover. The newsletter also prints articles on adolescent literature, curriculum suggestions, and movie and TV tie-ins.

Prince George's County Memorial Library: Young Adult Services Reviews. Published 8/year for $10/year. Order from and make checks payable to: Prince George's County Memorial Library, Young Adult Services, 6532 Adelphi Rd., Hyattsville, MD 20782. Approximately 65 recommended and nonrecommended titles, both hardcover and original paperbacks, are briefly annotated along with citations from other review media. New popular paperbacks are included in a supplemental listing. Reviews are aimed at the public library YA section's popular reading appeal and tend toward the "safe," with a preponderance of adolescent novels and gothics.

School Library Journal. Edited by Lillian Gerhardt. Published by R. R. Bowker Co. Monthly, Sept.-May. $17/year. Subscription address: Bowker Subscription Dept., P.O. Box 67, Whitinsville, MA 01588. Reviews by librarians for librarians of new hardback books and a few original paperbacks. Young Adult titles are reviewed in two places—the "Junior High up" section of the juvenile book review section (meaning books from the juvenile departments of publishers) and in "Adult Books for Young Adults" (meaning books from the adult departments of publishing houses). Twice a year *SLJ* has roundups: "Best Books of the Spring" in the May issue and "Best Books of the Year" in the December issue. Current reviewers are school and public librarians from the Boston area. The column is edited by Rose Morachian.

Voice of Youth Advocates. Bimonthly. $10/year; $11 if billed from Dorothy M. Broderick and Mary Kay Chelton, 10 Landing Lane, Apt. 6M, New Brunswick,

NJ 08901. Started in 1978, this new magazine includes news, articles, and helpful hints of interest
to youth professionals, emphasizing librarianship, and
reviews of new books in the following categories:
mysteries, audiovisual, pamphlets, professional, fiction, nonfiction, science fiction. Reviews are signed
and critical and include books not seen elsewhere.
Aimed at public and school libraries, with some assignment materials included.

Wilson Library Bulletin. Published monthly except July and
Aug. $17/year (U.S. and Canada); $20 foreign. Order
from: H. H. Wilson Co., 950 University Ave., Bronx,
NY 10452. Monthly column, "The YA Perplex," by
Patty Campbell, formerly with the Los Angeles Public Library. Patty takes a jaundiced look at currently
published materials for young adults and their ever
fluid choice changes. Mixing these together, each
month focuses on materials grouped around a theme
or issue of adolescent life (sex, friendships, what to do
with the rest of their life). Thought-provoking and
interesting.

YACBRG: Book Reviews. Young Adult Cooperative Book
Review Group of Massachusetts. Published quarterly
after meetings (Oct., Dec., Feb., Apr.). $10/year.
Make check payable to YACBRG. Order from:
Margaret L. Patti, c/o Winchester Public Library, 80
Washington St., Winchester, MA 01890. Collection of
reviews given orally at YACBRG meetings, 250–300
words, by public and school librarians, including some
ad hoc comments generated by the discussion. Books
reviewed are primarily adult titles.

The following four sources publish annual lists of titles
recommended for young adult readers.

Best Books for Young Adults. Published yearly (following
the annual ALA Midwinter meeting). Single copies
free from YASD Office, ALA, 50 E. Huron St., Chicago, IL 60611. This annotated list presents books
published in the previous year which are recommended as good recreational reading for young adults.
It is compiled by a committe of the ALA Young
Adult Services Division in cooperation with a na-
tionwide group of participating school and public

libraries. It is also published in *Booklist*'s Apr. 15 issue.

Books for the Teen Age. Published every Feb. by the N.Y. Public Library. Single copies free at any N.Y. Public Library branch. Copies mailed for $3 each, prepaid. Order from: Office of Young Adult Services, Branch Libraries, 8 E. 40th St., New York, NY 10016. Annually revised list of old and new titles of special interest to teenagers. All titles were read and selected by librarians who work with teenagers in the N.Y. Public Library and are described briefly. Most books listed are hardcover, some are paperback only. Index to paperbacks listed is available from Books by Mail Service, 82–27 164th St., Jamaica, NY 11432.

Books for Young Adults Honor List. Published in Jan. issue of *English Journal,* or request from: Books for Young Adults, Cooperating School Systems Program, West 312 East Hall, Univ. of Iowa, Iowa City, IA 52242. Annual annotated booklist chosen primarily by juniors and seniors in Iowa City public and private schools, under the auspices of G. Robert Carlsen and the Cooperating School Systems Program.

Young Adult Reviewers of Southern California. Published annually; $3.50 (California residents add 6% sales tax). Order from California Library Association, 717 K St., Sacramento, CA 95814. Brief one-sentence reviews of 300 hardback and original paperback titles. Entries are selected and annotated by librarians from high-school and public library systems who are members of YAR. The 1978 issue (no. 13) includes a list of outstanding books, the regular fiction/nonfiction section, special interests (means self-actualizing in subject matter), and school assignments.

Many large public library and consolidated school districts review and print their buying lists, which they may share with you freely for the asking. Several are listed below as free, and are worthwhile perusing, although I suppose a heavy volume of requests would limit their giving it away.

Young Adult Services
Westchester Library System
280 N. Central Ave.
Hartsdale, NY 10530

Office of Adult and Young Adult Services
Free Library of Philadelphia
Logan Square
Philadelphia, PA 19103

Young Adult Services (YA-YAK Review Sheet)
Santa Clara County Library System
1095 N. 7th St.
San Jose, CA 95112

INDEX

Adolescence
early, 36–39
late, 40–43
middle, 39–40
Adolescent life, stories of, 40
Adolescent literature
criteria for evaluating, 242
definition of, 1
evaluation of, 239–40
Adolescent novel, 56–99
measuring success of, 57
about young men, bibliography, 76–81
about young women, bibliography, 68–76
Adolescent, preference in books, 34–36
Adult book, popular, 100–120
bibliography, 109–120
qualities lacking in, 102–103
read by teenagers, 3–5
Adult life, transition to, 41–43
American history, 92–94
Adventure stories, 36
American literature, 153–155
bibliography, 160–162
American poetry, 164–165, 166–171
bibliography, 177
Ancient world literature, 150–151
bibliography, 157
Animal stories, 36, 62–64
animal-human relations, 63
bibliography, 81–85
nonfiction accounts, 63–64
talking animals, 62
wild animals, 62–63
Anthropology, 206
bibliography, 215–217
Appendix, 279–284

Archaeology, 206
bibliography, 215–217
Arts, see Fine Arts
Astronomy, 208

Ballad, 167
Bible, The, 150, 151
Bibliographic tools and sources, 279–284
Biography, 178–190
bibliography, 184–190
collected, 182
critical, 182
defined, 178
descriptions of, 181–184
objective or factual, 182
Body, coming to terms with, 15–16
Book fairs, 8

Career and college information, bibliography, 29–32
Censorship, 121–132
Classics, 147–163
from American literature, 153–155
bibliography, 160–162
from Ancient world, 150–151
bibliography, 157
from English literature, 151–153
bibliography, 158–160
from European literature, 155–156
bibliography, 162–163
modern. See Modern classic; Modern literature, significant
Classroom literature, categories of, 129

Comic books, 45–48
  crime, 46
  family life, 46
  hero, 46
  horror, 47
  love, 47
  pornographic, 47–48
  slapstick, 46
Communications, 209–210
  bibliography, 226–228
Contemporary teenage life, stories of, 60–62

Definitive biography, 181–182
Developmental tasks, 13–19
Drama, 191–202
  bibliography, 197–202
  defined, 191

Ecology, see Environment
English literature, 151–153
  bibliography, 158–160
Environment, 211–212
  bibliography, 230–232
European literature, 155–156
  bibliography, 162–163

Fantasy, 39
  awards, 259
  bibliography, 271–277
  themes, 255
Female characters in plays
  adolescents, 239–241
  readers, preferences of, 34–35
Fictionalized biography, 181
Fine arts, 210–211
  bibliography, 228–230
Folk ballads, 51
Foreign cultures,
  bibliography, 89–92
  books about, 65–66
Formulistic writing, 52–55, 131
Freedom of choice, 128, 130

Gothic romances, 104
Greek mythology, 151

Greek tragedies, 150
Growing up around the world, 37–38

Historical backgrounds, books with, 66–67
Historical novels, 39, 103, 105–106
History, U.S., bibliography, 92–94
Hobbies, bibliography, 20–26
Holmes, Oliver Wendell, 133
Home and family life stories, 38
Human experiences, unusual, 41
Human relations, tasks of, 13–15

Identity, search for, 12, 60–62
Independence and separation from parents, 13–14
Idols, 133–134
"In-between" books, 100–101
Interpretive biography, 182

Juvenile novel. See also Adolescent novel
  definition of, 19–20
  first of distinction and quality, 57
Juvenile series, 48

Knowledge, sources of, 203–204

Language of books, 122–124
Librarian, responsibility toward reading, 19–20
Literature, four dimensions of meaning, 125
Literature by and about women, 233–252
  bibliography, 245–252

Mathematics, bibliography, 225–226

Modern classic. *See also* Modern literature, significant characters, 138
defined, 133
Modern literature, significant, 133–146
bibliography, 139–146
Modern verse, 168–169
Monument biography, 182
Movie and TV tie-ins, 49–50
Mystery, suspense and adventure, 64–65
bibliography, 85–89
Mystery stories, 36–37
Mystical romances, 39

Nonfiction, 203–232
accounts of adventure, 39

Objections to books, dealing with, 131–132

Paperback books, 51
Past (olden times), 38–39
Patterned stories, 51
Peer relationship, changed, 14
Personal advice, bibliography, 26–29
Personal experience, 204–206
bibliography, 212–215
Personal values. *See* Values
Poetry, 164–177
collections and individual poets, bibliography, 172–176
general collections, bibliography, 171–172
impact of, 165
narrative, bibliography, 176
native American, bibliography, 177
from other countries, bibliography, 177
Poetry, two of best collections of modern, 168–169
Political intrigue novels, 107
Pop books, 5

Pornography and literature, distinction between, 124–126
Profanity, impact of, 124
Prose, 164
Psychological western, 108

Reading development, stages of, 33–43
Reading experience, 1–11
Reading interest(s)
conditions for continued, 7–8
decline of, 6
peak years, 6
teens, outside the scope of, 42–43
Reading patterns, research on, 33–34
Reading rights, 121–132
Realism, tradition of, 126
Role model, finding a significant, 15
Romance and adventure, adult, 48–49

Satire, 55
Scene(s)
classroom enactment of, 192–193
defined, 192
Science, 208–209
bibliography, 222–225
Science fiction (SF), 42
bibliography, 259–271
categories, 254
female authors and, 243–244
Science fiction and fantasy, 253–277
awards, 259
compared, 254–255
cult phenomena, 258–259
literary qualities, 256–257
preference by sex, 258
themes, 255–256
Screenplays, 211

Seventeenth Summer, 57–59, 61, 66
Sex in books, 124–128
    age of reader, 127–128
    details of, 126–127
Sexuality, coming to terms with, 16–17
Slapstick, 38
Social sciences, 207–208
    bibliography, 217–222
Social significance, books of, 40–41
Sport stories, 37, 67–68
    bibliography, 97–99
Status, sense of, 17
Subliterature, 44–55
    appeal of, 50–55
    false assumptions of, 52–53
    potential harm of, 52
Supernatural, tales of, 37
Surrogate hero, 64
Survival of book, qualities for, 148

Tasks involving self, 15–17
Teachers, responsibility toward reading, 19–20

Teenage books, 2–3
Teenagers' right to read, 130–131
Teenager's world, 12–20
Today's practice, 129–132
Translated books, 65–66

Values
    integrated system of, 17–18
    search for, 40
Vocational choice, making, 18–19
Vocational tasks, 18–19

Western culture, most important book in, 150
Women, literature by and about, 233–245
    bibliography, 245–252
Work experience, 18
World stories, bibliography, 94–97

Young adult (YA) books, 203

ABOUT THE AUTHOR

G. ROBERT CARLSEN is Professor and Head of English (High School) at the University of Iowa. He is a former president of the National Council of Teachers of English, and the author of *Social Understanding Through Literature*, *Brown-Carlsen Listening Comprehension Test*, and approximately 50 published articles. Of *Books and the Teenage Reader*, he has written: "I like to think that it offers the basic techniques for 'making a reader' out of a human being."

The MS
READ-a-thon needs
young readers!

Boys and girls between 6 and 14 can join the MS READ-a-thon and help find a cure for Multiple Sclerosis by reading books. And they get two rewards — the enjoyment of reading, and the great feeling that comes from helping others.

Parents and educators: For complete information call your local MS chapter, or call toll-free (800) 243-6000. Or mail the coupon below.

Kids can help, too!

TEENAGERS FACE LIFE AND LOVE

Choose books filled with fun and adventure, discovery and disenchantment, failure and conquest, triumph and tragedy, life and love.

☐	13359	**THE LATE GREAT ME** Sandra Scoppettone	$1.95
☐	13691	**HOME BEFORE DARK** Sue Ellen Bridgers	$1.75
☐	12501	**PARDON ME, YOU'RE STEPPING ON MY EYEBALL!** Paul Zindel	$1.95
☐	11091	**A HOUSE FOR JONNIE O.** Blossom Elfman	$1.95
☐	12025	**ONE FAT SUMMER** Robert Lipsyte	$1.75
☐	13184	**I KNOW WHY THE CAGED BIRD SINGS** Maya Angelou	$2.25
☐	13013	**ROLL OF THUNDER, HEAR MY CRY** Mildred Taylor	$1.95
☐	12741	**MY DARLING, MY HAMBURGER** Paul Zindel	$1.95
☐	12420	**THE BELL JAR** Sylvia Plath	$2.50
☐	13095	**WHERE THE RED FERN GROWS** Wilson Rawls	$1.95
☐	11829	**CONFESSIONS OF A TEENAGE BABOON** Paul Zindel	$1.95
☐	11838	**OUT OF LOVE** Hilma Wolitzer	$1.50
☐	13352	**SOMETHING FOR JOEY** Richard E. Peck	$1.95
☐	13440	**SUMMER OF MY GERMAN SOLDIER** Bette Greene	$1.95
☐	13693	**WINNING** Robin Brancato	$1.95
☐	13628	**IT'S NOT THE END OF THE WORLD** Judy Blume	$1.95

Bantam Book Catalog

Here's your up-to-the-minute listing of over 1,400 titles by your favorite authors.

This illustrated, large format catalog gives a description of each title. For your convenience, it is divided into categories in fiction and non-fiction—gothics, science fiction, westerns, mysteries, cookbooks, mysticism and occult, biographies, history, family living, health, psychology, art.

So don't delay—take advantage of this special opportunity to increase your reading pleasure.

Just send us your name and address and 50¢ (to help defray postage and handling costs).